(1179)

BOOKS BY MARTIN RUSS

HAPPY HUNTING
GROUND

MARTIN RUSS

HAPPY HUNTING GROUND

ATHENEUM

NEW YORK

1968

AUTHOR'S NOTE: The names used in this book are fictional. Any reference to persons with these names is unintentional and coincidental.

FOR ED

PUBLISHER'S NOTE

Martin Russ's first book, *The Last Parallel,* a journal of his experiences as a Marine during the Korean War, was published in 1957 and acclaimed as one of the best accounts of modern warfare we had yet had.

In the summer of 1966, Mr. Russ, long a civilian, found himself responding to the news from Vietnam with reflexes conditioned by his years in the Corps. There was a war, and he felt compelled to be there, to observe and write about men in combat, and once again to test his own responses to danger and death.

The book that follows is compiled from journal entries and letters sent to his wife during the six months he spent in the field with American, Vietnamese and Australian troops as an accredited but unaffiliated correspondent.

HAPPY HUNTING
GROUND

July 9th, airline terminal, 38th & First Avenue

Seems crazy to be writing you when we said goodbye only thirty minutes ago.

I caught a cab right away and could hardly restrain myself from telling the driver about the journey. I remember one day in '51 just before I caught the train to Parris Island, telling a cabbie I had joined the Marines, and how thrilled I was when he beamed at me. It puffed me up pretty good. Those days're long gone, yet I wish in a way I had that old ego back.

10:30 p.m. Kennedy International

It's wonderful being carried along from one place to the next like this—the cab ride, the limousine, and now flights upcoming to exotic places—to be passive and free as I was in prep school and the service. A fellow didn't have to think for himself then, that was the thing. And whenever you asserted yourself it was within a sort of framework and you risked nothing on your own. You had South Kent School or the United States Marines behind you. I liked having that backing.

11:20 Waiting in the crowd beside Gate 7. Just saw a young Marine private. He's sound asleep in one of the chairs, all slumped over. He has that solid backing I was talking about; he can slump freely in public places without embarrassment.

11:30 Just boarded the plane. Seat 19A, by the window.

Material for my book is already starting to parade before me. The Marine is either sick or very drunk, or both. When they opened Gate 7 and he didn't move, a lady came over and tried to wake him but he didn't respond. Another joined her and then a third, all middle-aged. None of them had any luck; he just sat there, breathing normally but slumped over. It was sort of humorous for the first few minutes, everybody in the crowd chuckling and so on, but then it got sad, I don't exactly know why. A woman behind me muttered 'Imagine sending a boy like that off to war.' By the time I left, a fatherly business type was sitting beside him with a big arm around his shoulders and a nervous supervisor was hunting up a doctor. Everyone seemed curiously moved by the sight of the passed-out Marine.

6:00 a.m., July 10th, Los Angeles International

Arrived around 2 a.m. Looked for Frank Thompson, Nick Cominos, George Mahaffy in phone book. Unlisted. Made me gloomy because it means there'll be no last-minute conversation with a familiar voice. And I don't dare call you because I'd surely croak.

I got some sleep on this bench. It grew cool in the building, had to open bag and get out sweater & coat. Impersonal Instant Airport all night long, very beautiful visually in pastels and plastics and indirect lighting, but strictly a passing-through place for strangers. A perfect setting for one of those films I'm always avoiding.

Such an awful feeling of disconnectedness too because I

was unable to check in for the next flight, all counters deserted and dark. There's that backing I mentioned. If I'd been able to check in, to give some clerk my name and baggage, I wouldnt've felt so isolated and lonely in this echoing chilly place. I would've had a clear identity, that of a certified traveler.

July 10th, 10:17 a.m. I'm sitting in the Japan Air Lines lounge. Start boarding at half past.

I saw the actor George Shibata below. He played a Nisei lieutenant in *Pork Chop Hill*. I went up to him and told him I recognized him and I think he was pleased. He handed me his card. (*George Shibata, attorney at law* and it gave his address in Huntington Beach.) Our conversation was brief but, for me, an emotional experience because I figured it'd be my last conversation in America.

10:28 a.m. It frightens me somehow that in a few minutes I'll no longer be in America. I feel sadly patriotic and full of love for our country. It bothers me too that I'm leaving on a Japanese plane instead of one of the U.S. airlines, but this is aside from patriotism: it's just that the break is going to be awfully abrupt.

They're calling the flight now, all aboard please. Goodbye America and Lucy!

An hour later. Trouble writing because neighbor is nosey. Stewardess in kimono just passed out a rolled towel, very hot, to each passenger. You unroll it and press it against your face, wipe your neck, rub away all New York grime.

Very shaky emotionally. Overly grateful for the comfort and reassurance of the hot towel. I recall that back at the airport I saw a teary-eyed lady with babe in arms saying goodbye to husband and got choked up too. The worst moment, though, was walking across to the plane. Relatives and friends calling out and waving from an overlook terrace. I'm fine now, though, full of life and confidence even though I am alone.

Stewardess just brought a bottle of Asahi, evoking memories of Korea and Japan, and a paper boat of hors d'oeuvres almost too good-looking to eat, except that nothing is that good-looking.

Over the Pacific, somewhere between Midway and Japan. I like Japan Air Lines. The stewardesses are constantly stuffing you with delicacies designed to drive you out of your head.

We're so high up the ocean is like another part of the sky, or maybe we're flying upside down.

7:50 p.m. Tokyo time I'm tired but exhilarated. As you know, it takes a lot of doing to get me warmed up, but already I can feel certain sections of long-numb brain tissue starting to buzz and tingle. It's great to be back in print again, to be alive in this sense again.

Landing at Haneda was quite an experience. About fifteen minutes out, they started playing dreamy Japanese music over the intercom, and we descended into a yellow cold-looking fog. Then we broke out into open a thousand feet above countryside that was familiar and friendly. Once you've seen the paddyfields and miniature mountains of Japan they stay with you.

8:30 a.m. next morning I'm on the plane now, just before takeoff. Good seat by the window. Got all choked up again walking to the plane, friends and relatives calling Sayonara . . .

Last night I took a stroll down the Ginza. The street is a continuous explosion and shower of neon fireworks, but subtle and soft in color, nothing at all like Times Square. One skyscraper was smothered entirely in checkerboards of constantly shifting purples and greens.

I saw a couple of lady vendors demonstrating electrically-illuminated yo-yos on the sidewalk. They stood in dark doorways, playing them out over the crowd. I nearly bought one.

I kept passing these mysterious-looking subway entrances, and finally went down one. It was all white and antiseptic down there and oddly silent even though there were many people. I was planning to take a ride but when I realized I'd have to buy a ticket from someone who probably didn't speak English and that I could easily end up lost and stranded in some suburb at two in the morning, I got the hell out of there.

It was a real adventurous evening.

Just before going to sleep I watched a few minutes of television. You never know how ludicrous American TV drama is till you've seen *Peyton Place* with Japanese dubbing.

I looked out the window for awhile, listening to music over the radio, too keyed up to think of sleeping. All I could see was three intersecting walls and a slice of sky, but somehow it was madly Japanese and great.

Hot towel again just now. A new joy discovered: you hold it to your face till the heat goes, then unfold the next fold and find another layer of heat, and below that still another.

It's beginning to sound like a travel book.
(Japan is a Land of Contrasts)

July 12th, Hotel Oriental, 36 Le Loi Street, Saigon

. . . The wait in Hong Kong was easy. Actually it was Kowloon, not Hong Kong. I walked all around town. I wished you could've seen the incredible food and non-food food for sale not only in shops but on the sidewalk and gutters. I saw stacks of odd eggs covered with black fuzz, with the fuzz scraped away partially, leaving white strips, very arty-looking. I went inside a meat and fish market, a big barnlike place, very dark, and halfway down the first aisle I thought *Lucy'd never survive this*, because everything was bloody and gory, with all sorts of torn-flesh displays and torture smells about.

I watched a man in a dirty turban split open a big silver fish, exposing red innards and a golfball-sized object that shone like a pearl. I saw tubs of live eels, all transparent, glowing in a dark grotto at the back. I saw pans of dwarfy-looking frogs, all gronking and slimily flurping. I saw butchered dogs hanging from hooks.

Out on the street two things impressed me: the way the rich natural odors kept changing as you walked along, and everything being unfamiliar; no matter where you looked, it was new, even the fire hydrants.

At the last minute I got interviewed by an English girl at the airport, a sort of Chamber of Commerce interview ('How much money did you spend during your stay?') She asked what advice I'd give anyone coming to Hong Kong for the first time and the only thing I could think of was, 'Be prepared for terrific heat.' She said, 'It's not always so hot. Last winter I got perishing cold.' That was the only interesting thing she said.

(All in all I found China to be a Land of Contrasts)

Air Vietnam turned out to be a great come-down after Japan Air Lines. I noticed right away that the stewardesses (in *ao dai*) didn't knock themselves out to beguile you, the way they do on good ole JAL. I got the impression the passengers were an inconvenience to them. This somehow depressed me and made me feel lonely; and I'd been in pretty good shape all through Japan and Hong Kong.

There were a lot of Koreans aboard, all construction workers. The one beside me didn't speak any English but we fooled around a bit. I conveyed to him that I had been to his country. He conveyed to me that he hadn't been to mine.

The only other thing I want to tell you about is the clouds. They started out as little puffs far below, all on the same level with flat undersides. They were like bits of cotton on a vast plain of blue glass. They got bigger as we flew along and their number increased, and you could see them for miles, maybe a hundred miles away. Finally there were great mountains of them, and in the distance thunderheads were building up on the horizon, and as it began to grow dark they turned pink. It was a spectacular array, the kingdom of some frost-creature who eats clouds for nourishment.

It was dark when we landed at Tan Son Nhut airport, and depressing to find the passenger terminal almost entirely shut down for the night—no counters open, no information booth, no snack bar. I wandered around in the fantastic heat (when they opened the plane to let us off, the heat came flooding in and I wanted to turn around and go back) looking for a place to exchange some U.S. currency for piastres. Meanwhile the passengers disappeared and I found myself alone with a hundred American soldiers in this big barn of a place illuminated by a couple of bare bulbs. I got in line with some men waiting to have their military scrip exchanged for piastres, or the other way round. Being among them like that, hearing their dreary service palaver, brought it all back sharply, all the dismal hours waiting in chow lines and pay lines and all the other lines. I felt awfully glad I was a civilian, because I knew I could never stand that any more. When I got to the head of the line the guy behind the screen said he couldn't handle U.S. currency. Outside there were no taxis left anyway and it looked as if I'd have to hitch-hike into town. By now all I wanted to do was go home, to hell with the whole project. I had a terrible sense of impending doom. Finally I happened to see a stewardess from the flight and she got me a ride in a truck. The first thing I saw on the road was a Bireley's orange drink sign, in English—which was sort of unpicturesque, I thought.

In downtown Saigon many cab drivers attacked me but I waded through them with my bag. How could I take a cab when I didn't even know where I was going? Finally I accepted a lift on the back of a motorscooter, deciding to ride around until I saw a hotel. The ride was great fun but terrifying too because I kept nearly falling off, my bag preventing me from getting solidly seated. We plunged into ferocious converging traffic all veering honkily around a circle, and it was so bad I had to close my eyes. I got off in front of the Caravelle Hotel and an

American military policeman began chewing me out and demanding my papers. I grandly told him I was a civilian. He said it made no difference: Americans are not allowed to ride on the backs of motorscooters.

They didn't have any room at the Caravelle but I was able to buy some piastres there. I found this room within twenty minutes and got a good night's sleep.

Saigon is teeming and steaming and very uncharming. The traffic is awful. Tiny blue & white Renault cabs and pedicabs and scooters and bicycles everywhere, and U.S. Army trucks and jeeps. The sidewalks are so choked with people it's easier to walk in the gutter. I'll be glad when I'm on my way north.

I had scrambled eggs & toast this morning in an American-style coffee shop. Maybe tonight I'll get up nerve to eat in a Vietnamese place.

I got my Vietnamese papers right away and then checked in at the U.S. press office. Remember that Defense Department paper I had to sign, agreeing to show them my manuscript before publication? Well, the people here haven't gotten their copy yet. Things looked bad for awhile but the head colonel said he'd call Washington tonight and get it straightened out.

July 13th, 2 a.m.

I'm booked on a military flight to Danang, leaving around five tomorrow. I'll be glad to get out of this lousy place.

I lay down at five yesterday afternoon and just woke up a few minutes ago. The heat drains your energy, must

be. I tried to go out just now but the clerk downstairs got
horrified and forbade me. It seems there's a curfew.

Danang, July 14th

I'm all checked in here at the press center, an absurdly
comfortable place. They have movies every night and a
bar. The place is like a motel without carports; I mean
that's what it looks like. Someone told me it used to be a
cathouse for French soldiers. All the rooms are the same.
There's a toilet and a cold-water shower, and electric
lights and a big Indo-China overhead fan. Three or four
bunks to a room.

I went for a walk this morning. Danang I sort of like, I
think. At least it's quiet and there're not many people
around. I saw a few moldy French colonial mansions on
the waterfront.

I spent this afternoon on a hilltop overlooking the huge
airbase, visiting a Marine 'Skyhawk' missile outfit. I was
just killing time, and Sgt. Anderson suggested it as a
good place to get my bearings. You could see for miles:
the city of Danang, Monkey Mountain and Marble
Mountain, the broad plain of paddies, the South China
Sea stretching away to the horizon. I saw smoke from an
artillery barrage across the plain but it didn't move me
much; it'll take infantry action to do that. The only thing
that impressed me was the sergeant in charge, a typical
Old Salt. He told me that the mosquitoes of Quang Nam
province are so big 'they can stand flat-footed and rape a
turkey.'

On the drive back Sgt. Anderson did a lot of honking
because the road was choked with pedestrians and cyclists.

'The only thing these people respect is force,' he said. 'You've got to make a lot of noise, let 'em know you're here. Try smiling at one, being nice, he'll knife you in the back.'

July 15th

They served pork chops last night. I had forgotten that the diet of the American soldier is derived mainly from pigs.

I don't much like it here. I'm impatient to get out with the 'grunts,' as they call field Marines.

The movie last night was, believe it or not, *Flying Leathernecks* with John Wayne. It was a strange experience to sit there and watch this simple-minded melodrama about Marines and their esprit de corps and all the crap I used to believe in. It turned me on slightly, though, which I was glad of.

Sgt. Anderson says if I cool my heels another day or two there may be something special on. I haven't any idea what it is.

Cam Lo

No time or inclination and too hot to organize this. I'm sitting on the grass amid grave humps just outside the village of Cam Lo, about twenty miles inland, ten miles south of the Demilitarized Zone separating the two Vietnams. Danang is a hundred miles southeast of here.

I'm hotter than I've ever been, and flies are swarming all around, buzzing in and out of my ears and nostrils.

But I'm doing precisely what I hoped to do back in New York when I got the original notion, i.e., living in the field with a unit of Marines. The unit is —— Company, 1st Battalion, Third Marines. It seems so long ago that I got the notion, and yet it was only a short time really; and here I am. It's fantastic.

I'll catch up as fast as possible.

I flew from Danang to a little place called Dong Ha with some of the press-center Marines and watched them set up a headquarters near the airstrip. Word was that a big battle was shaping up. I hung around, not knowing quite what to do. I figured the press headquarters'd be the best place to learn which units were engaged, and I could go on from there. I waited a couple of hours, and then a tall well-built Marine with a scarred-up face came stomping in in full combat gear. I went out of my way to make his acquaintance because he looked interesting, like a true Marine 'character' of some sort, and because he had a copy of *Mountain Gorilla* in his hand. It turned out that he was just another press Marine, not a grunt at all. His name is L/Cpl. Steve Beauregard (Twin Falls, Idaho). He told me he was en route to one of the rifle companies to gather material for the local Marine paper called *Sea Tiger*. I asked if I could tag along and he said sure.

Beauregard and I did a lot of walking and waiting that afternoon. At one point we were waiting beside the airstrip for a convoy out to where the action was. A company of Marines, about two hundred men, were standing at ease in a nearby field. They had just arrived by air from Phu Bai and were waiting for the convoy too. They stood in ranks, the three platoons separated, the officers in front, and seeing them really gave me a kick. It was the first time in thirteen years I'd seen true field Marines. I couldn't hear their palaver because of the planes but they certainly looked wonderful—just like Marines of yore.

It turned out they were going to guard the airstrip, so the convoy was canceled. Beauregard and I went looking for another. We walked across a red-dust plateau under a heavy sun and found a helpful lieutenant who assigned one of his men to escort us to where a convoy was forming. This little fellow was the first field Marine I examined close up and spoke with. He was scrawny and his face all drawn and taut and sunburned and blistered. He had the raw bony look of an old man; he even walked like one. His name was Pvt. Willie Otis (Oaktown, Illinois). There was writing on his helmet-cover and I asked him about it. He removed his helmet and handed it to me, looking slightly embarrassed. It was a verse from some folk song about the valley of death and how even if you aren't sure the Lord is with you, you can rely on your fellow Marines. He glanced at me with his washed-out blue eyes, to see what my reaction was. He kept calling me Sir. There was something awfully appealing about him, trudging along beside us, his big rifle slung across his shoulder, his too-big helmet bobbing at every step. And yet he was like a little old man, even though he was eighteen or nineteen. You'd have liked him. He left us at the end of a line of empty trucks, and went trudging back down the dusty road.

We waited a long time until a column of Marines came up and boarded the trucks. They were a mortar platoon and had their gear with them—mortar tubes, baseplates, aiming stakes and ammo, plus their packs and canteens and personal weapons. Beauregard and I helped some of them with their heavy gear.

I contributed to the war effort! (Sorry bout that.)

By this time it was common knowledge that North Vietnamese units had slipped into South Vietnam and Marine battalions were being deployed to intercept them. Maybe you're reading about it in the news right now.

The convoy started rolling, heading west. Some villagers came out of their huts and waved at us going by. The terrain is generally flat, with knolls here and there. You can see dark mountains far to the west, almost in Laos. The road is paved, with French kilometer markers in the ditch. The sun was getting low and shining in our eyes, casting long shadows across the fields. We rolled along very fast. It was a madly exhilarating ride. I guess everyone loves riding in the back of an open truck, but riding with Marines toward battle is something special. I attracted some attention by the way I was dressed (in my Sweet-Orr ensemble, looking like a delivery man) and one fellow wanted to know what outfit I was with. Civilians, I told him shamefaced.

Beauregard and I were dropped off at the wrong place, a 155 mm. artillery battery, but another helpful lieutenant lent us a jeep and a driver, and at the last minute shouted for a volunteer to 'ride shotgun' for us. A rifleman ran over and jumped in the back and off we went. The driver was apparently nervous about the lonely unguarded stretch of road because he drove the two miles to Cam Lo like a madman. It was worse than the scooter ride in Saigon.

It was dusk when we arrived at the 1st Battalion command-post—a tent between two grave mounds. Beauregard introduced me to Lt. Col. Marion Bell.

'Nothing's happening right now,' he said.

I told him I'd like to hang around anyway if it was okay with him.

'Why did you pick this battalion?'

I told him it was a random thing, based on Beauregard's plans. I told him I wasn't a reporter or anything like that, that I wanted to hang around to watch the privates and corporals at work.

'How about sergeants?'

'Them too,' I allowed. He kidded me by asking if I wasn't going to observe the officers and I told him I'd try to, and a couple of captains nearby laughed. The truth is, I don't know how to cope with officers, being an old enlisted man at heart. A Marine officer is still rather a godlike figure to me.

'And you're not even going to interview me?'

'Maybe later.'

More laughter.

Beauregard knew a couple of guys in —— Company and we headed over that way. The —— command-post was only fifty feet from the colonel's tent (I can see him now from where I sit: he's hunkered down over a canteen cup of water, shaving). Beauregard introduced himself to

the company commander, Captain Julius Prouty (Rae-
ford, North Carolina):

'I don't know if you remember me, sir, but I wrote a
couple of stories about your company—'

'Sure, I remember you.'

The captain's radioman was sitting nearby and just as
Steve turned to introduce me, the radioman jumped up
and yelled *Hey!* He had the earpiece against his ear,
listening hard. Capt. Prouty said *Excuse me* to Steve and
me, and went over.

'Barker's made contact," said the radioman. 'You can
hear the shooting!' and he put the earpiece to the captain's ear.

It turned out that —— Company had a small patrol
across the river, led by a sergeant named Barker. The
captain quickly organized a 'reactionary force' of twenty
men with one mortar tube and two machine guns, and as it
was about to take off I suggested to Steve that we tag
along. He gulped and said okay, and got permission from
the captain. The captain looked me up and down.

'You got a weapon?'

'No.'

He strode over to a sergeant, took his .45 and thrust it
butt-first at me. 'Better take a friend with you.'

The column moved out, Steve and me in the middle. It
was dark now. I caught up with the man ahead to get his
name ('Cpl. DiAngelo, call me Nick') because it's easy to
lose contact on a dark night and I wanted to be able to
whisper it if that happened.

I was all puffed up with a feeling of drama. The years
just fell away, smooth as water, thirteen long years, and it
seemed as if nothing had changed since my last Korean
patrol. But I had changed, even if war hadn't. I was only

too conscious of the pistol. Capt. Prouty had suggested I carry it inside my shirt since he had no holster for me; but the .45 is the world's most treacherous gadget and I held it out where I could keep an eye on it. Naturally I began thinking about the 6th Commandment. I had to figure out right away where I stood, because it was easy to imagine becoming involved in a big hand-to-hand mess, and that kind of situation is tough on a believer. I finally figured out what to do: say a prayer asking to be spared the necessity of shooting someone to save my hide— because that's the only circumstance in which I'd do it. Clearly I couldn't help the Marines unless it became a matter of survival. But the contradictions are staring me now in the face. Let's work it out some other time.

We crossed a dirt road and got swallowed up into a cowpath with thick foliage overhead, and thatched huts on the left with gardens and animal pens. Then a sudden stairway of broad stone steps leading down to the river, and we sloshed across in knee-high and very refreshing water.

But I've decided to cut this short, because Barker's contact turned out to be 'minor,' resulting in three dead North Vietnamese and two wounded Marines. Barker's group got back on their own, and we didn't even see them.

We headed back by a different route, and you could tell the men were cautious and a little jumpy. Everyone is aware that North Viet units are flooding into Quang Tri province and this means there'll be many sudden confrontations. The column halted frequently while the point men scouted ahead. During one of these pauses I found myself lying at the entrance to the courtyard of a large house with some clay jars out front. I heard a baby whimpering inside. It was a powerful moment, with three dead men lying out there in the dark not three hundred yards away. The whimper rose up into a lusty bawl and I could hear the mother murmuring and then someone lit a candle inside. Lady, I said to myself, you'd bawl too if you knew what was lurking outside.

When we got back, Steve and I went to sleep against one of the grassy mounds. I was tired but by no means exhausted. During the two hours my body felt exactly as it had on my last patrol, except for one thing: I was frighteningly dim of vision. I know it couldn't've been *that* dark. I lost contact with Cpl. DiAngelo twice and had to whisper a panicky *Nick!* and he'd whisper *Right here.* I'm hoping that all the years of artificial light and bad reading-habits haven't dimmed me so badly that a few days of sun-drenched open terrain won't bring it back somewhat. But maybe that's unscientific.

Cpl. DiAngelo by the way has taken it upon himself to educate me to the ways of the new Corps. He seems likable enough, but he's a typical Marine bullshit artist—an authority on everything, incapable of saying *I don't know.* His monologues are often hilarious because he's unusually misinformed—and yet an authority.

('How much does your radio cost, Nick?'

'This radio here? This radio here costs eight hundred and thirty-four bucks.')

Two days later

I went out on a patrol that lasted twenty-four hours, and I'm afraid I didn't hold up too well physically. But I'll tell about that when I get to it chronologically.

We gathered beside the battalion generator at dusk, night before last. The patrol leader was Cpl. Lester A. Sullivan, Jr. (St. Louis, Missouri), a stocky youngster with red hair and freckles. He reminded me of a young Spencer Tracy. He looks at you with brown eyes that radiate sincerity and solemn zeal. He's quite melodramatic. He blinked at me significantly and said 'If you get hit, give a yell. We don't leave nobody out there. We'll stay and fight to the last fucking man if we have to.' He said his squad was the best fucking squad in the company, and one of the other guys nodded and said it was true. I was impressed and even moved, in a nostalgic sort of way, to see this fierce and corny pride so characteristic of young Marines. I liked Sullivan and his men a lot. There was nothing in the least cool about them; they were *hot to go*, as we used to say.

The two scouts finally showed up. They were Vietnamese civilians, sent over by Intelligence to help us find our way. They were not very impressive and the Marines hooted openly at them. One was an old man with a carbine and a helmet much too big for his head. He was toothless; at least he kept trying to swallow his nose, which is a good indication. The other was a kid of fifteen, unarmed, scared but trying to look brave. They were both barefoot and dressed in black shorts & shirt.

Capt. Prouty and his executive officer strolled over and smirked at them and this brought on more guffawing from the members of the patrol. I felt a brief wave of anger toward the Marines. Peasants of the local militia, like these men, take seventy percent of the casualties suffered by the Saigon forces, and their loyalty is one of the foundations on which the government will rise or fall. It bothered me too that the Marines were oblivious to their bravery in volunteering. The Vietcong aren't gentle with countrymen who help the Americans.

We left the perimeter and forded the river and entered a strip of forest along a narrow path. The silence was noticeable. I've been enveloped in noise ever since I got here—generators, airplane motors, water pumps, jet engines, convoys and so on. The battalion generator is so loud you can hear it all the way to the river.

At the outer edge of the woods I found myself faced with an obstacle: a short bridge made of five bamboo poles loosely tied together. I watched the man ahead go across, noticing how deeply the poles bent under him—and me a lot bigger. It was too dark now (and I was too blind) to see how deep the drop was. But even if it was shallow the last thing I wanted to do was fall in and establish myself as a big civilian noisemaker. It occurred to me too that we were probably the first Americans to cross this slippery monkey-bridge, and that I was possibly the heaviest man in the column, and therefore the poles might crack under me. By now the fellow on the other side was loudly whispering *Come on, will ya* and the one behind said *Let's go*, so I took a deep breath and plunged over in a rapid pussyfoot, and fell in a sweating heap on the other side.

After that we crossed an undulating series of open fields. Around midnight we stopped beside an island of tall trees. Surprisingly, there was some kind of building there. I learned next morning it was a pagoda with painted dragons. How interesting to come across something like this in the middle of nowhere.

We stopped because Cpl. Sullivan became convinced the scouts were leading us into an ambush. He set up an all-night ambush of his own, covering the path around the tree island. Nine of us lay behind a raised dike overlooking the path, and the rest—three riflemen and a machine-gun crew—deployed on some raised ground behind us, facing the other way. The scouts stayed with them.

After the ambush was set, Sullivan came over and whispered his suspicions in my ear. He said that after we left the river the scouts tried to bend us toward the northeast and he had to go forward and correct them three times. Just before we stopped they tried it once again and this convinced him an ambush was waiting, and that it was too dangerous to travel further. I was skeptical (but naturally kept it to myself) until he told me that Barker's patrol had also been guided by militia scouts, who had vanished when the action started.

Sullivan got on the radio and conveyed all this to Capt. Prouty and he agreed the patrol should freeze. Sullivan handed me a grenade in his melodramatic way and said I could sleep if I wanted. Sometime later I was awakened by another man and asked to stand radio watch (helping the war effort again). All I had to do was listen to the constant waterfall sound of static and wake Sullivan if a voice came through. None did. I watched Sullivan sleeping. He lay on his back, his right arm moving slowly out from his chest to the side and back again.

It seemed fantastic to me that I had been in New York only a week ago.

At dawn we broke out some C rations, ate them cold, and resumed patrolling. The rest of the day was hard on me physically. The sun is awesome. You get the feeling that if you stood out under it bareheaded it'd strike you dead in thirty minutes. It's so strong that when you're walking along a shaded path and see a clearing up ahead, you dread having to leave the shade even for a few moments. And the air itself is the hottest and heaviest I've ever known. Sitting still in the shade is bad enough but moving around in open fields is worse, especially when the whole countryside seems to smell of sudden death.

During the day, whenever we stopped for a rest, I'd sit down with one of the guys and—if he felt like it—we'd talk in low voices. I talked with Pfc. Philippe Lacombe (Baie St. Paul, Quebec). I asked him why he joined the U.S. Marines.

'To see the world.'

'You mean adventure and so on.'

'That's right.'

I asked him how much of the world he'd seen so far.

'Puerto Rico, Dominican Republic, Japan and Vietnam. And the U.S.'

Lacombe is nineteen. His eyes have folds at the corner, making them triangular and merry-looking; but he keeps a straight face. I asked him what he thought of the war.

'It stinks.'

'In what way?'

'I dunno, it just stinks.'

I learned that Lacombe, a machine-gunner, was a member of Sgt. Barker's patrol the night before and actually shot one of the North Viets. As casually as I could, I asked him to tell me about it. For some reason I assumed he'd be reluctant, but that was naïve of me.

'In a few minutes I'll be able to show you where it happened,' he said. 'It's checkpoint seven.'

Checkpoint seven made an impression on me. It was oddly reminiscent of some sylvan glade in Minnesota or Wisconsin. You could almost see the Holsteins and Guernseys grazing and red barns in the distance. There was nothing Asian about it, except the merciless heat.

While the others hid from the sun under bushes and trees, Lacombe showed me how he shot his man. Barker's point man (following the Vietnamese scouts) had seen three North Viets 'diddyboppin down the trail like they owned it,' as Lacombe put it, and had dropped to the ground beside the trail. Next thing he knew, a grenade exploded, wounding him in the eye and neck, and the fire-fight began. Barker was wounded in the hand and legs by another grenade. The Marines killed two of the enemy, one of whom was carrying a 60 mm. mortar tube. Then Pfc. Lacombe caught sight of the third man trying to crawl away.

'See that tree over there?' There was a lone tree thirty feet from where we stood. 'I saw him just before he got to it, and dinged him. He tried to stand up and run, but he fell back down in the bushes there.'

They couldn't find any body, which means he either crawled off or was dragged away.

'So we got two confirmed kills and one unconfirmed.'

I asked if it was necessary to bring in a body for it to be confirmed and he said a piece of bloody clothing is enough.

'You're kidding.'

'I wouldn't kid you.'

He led me further along the path to show me where the two North Viets had died. The spots were fifteen yards apart with a little mound of dirt marking each. Lacombe explained that the dirt was there to cover up the blood. It didn't occur to me to ask why it was desirable to do that. None of this bothered me too much. What got me were the grains of rice in the grass beyond one of the spots. Lacombe had said that one of the men was killed by shotgun. He had been carrying a sock full of rice and here it was sprayed all over the grass, conveying in a sickening way the awful sudden violence of the moment of death. It didn't shock me exactly; it scared and depressed me, and made me feel vaguely, primitively that someone ought to be punished for what they'd done, that you can't just blast a man's head off and get away with it.

For the rest of the day I wasn't much good for anything. The heat got worse as the day wore on. Most of the guys carried three canteens of water but I had only one. The corpsman kept passing out salt tablets and I ate my share. I'm not going to pretend it was the sprayed rice that sent me downhill, although that joggled me pretty good; it was the searing sun. Sullivan says the heat takes a few days getting used to.

During the breaks I no longer sat with the Marines; I felt too lousy to be sociable. But one guy came over and sat down with me. His name was Pfc. Gerald Collins, and when he mentioned he was from Pennsylvania, I naturally told him we had just spent eight months in Huntingdon. He got all excited. The poor kid is homesick. He mentioned he attended —— State Teacher's College for one year. 'You probably never heard of it.' I told him sure I had and that my father-in-law teaches at ——. Well, he nearly had a bird. After that he began singing the blues, not whining or anything, just expressing in a quiet boyish way his affection and longing for the hills around home and so on. The trouble with all this was that it made me homesick too. Sitting out there under that sun, Collins and I actually got choked up. It was quite a moment; I'm sure he was as surprised as I was.

He told me a harrowing tale about his dad, who had worked for years in the state government and was accused of dishonesty and fired. He was later exonerated and sued the state, winning the suit, but things were tough for a few years. Mrs. Collins had to go to work, and she was in poor health. Happy ending though: Mr. Collins finally got a good job and is now working at the federal printing office in Altoona.

Later in the patrol however Collins told me his mom had recently died of cancer and he got all miserable, staring at the ground, and I got to thinking about . . . and it all came flooding back. What a pair we were, a couple of real comedians.

I had one of my headaches when we got back but the corpsman gave me a couple of Darvon tablets that got rid of it.

Conversation overheard:

'Man, what wouldn't I give for a lectrict fan.'

'Where would you plug it in, ya silly bastard?'

The villagers of Cam Lo have set up stalls around the perimeter, offering bread and pineapples and lemons and breadfruit. Steve and I bought a lot of everything. You either pay in piastres or trade C rations. A breadfruit is about the size and shape of a human head, brownish yellow, the outside like a stubbly porcupine. You split it open with a machete, and inside it's a sticky stringy red mess that smells like strawberries and bananas. Everybody is gorging themselves because of the heat. Pineapple is particularly refreshing, I notice.

I've never been anywhere in the world where you can sit still in the shade and still sweat heavily. I find myself dreaming of iced Tab. Whoever invented Tab is a towering genius, greater than Bach or Shakespeare.

I just thought of something. If I ever get famous, maybe the Tab company'll quote me, like Old Crow quotes Daniel Webster and Rudyard Kipling and so on.

Later in the afternoon an Ontos sergeant named Langley came over and handed me a miraculous can of cold beer. I grabbed it and gulped it down, liking him tremendously. He sat down and talked with, or rather at, me for an hour in an Arkansas twang. Never has less been said more twangily. After awhile I turned off his station and lay there sprawled in my own sweat. I think he thought he was being interviewed. As I was nodding off he jumped up and brought me another cold beer, so of course I began listening to him and liking him tremendously again. An Ontos is a tracked vehicle with six 106 mm. recoilless guns, and that's all he talked about. I tried to change the subject.

'Langley, you've told me more about Ontos than I or any man care to know.'

'Mister Ross, you ain't heard nawthin yet. Settle back thar and I'll tell ya moar.'

Finally, after an hour and a half, I got up and said goodbye and walked away. Langley followed, still talking. I gave him the slip (when he stopped to say something to a buddy) by literally hiding behind a grave mound.

* * *

I met the guy who killed the North Viet with a shotgun. His name is S/Sgt. Andy Moore (Waycross, Georgia). He's married and the father of two children. He has been in Vietnam for three weeks, and has one week to go. His regular duty station is Guam, and he's here on temporary detached duty. I think it gives him a feeling of satisfaction to've killed a gook in his short spell here.

He fascinated me, as any executioner would. He also frightened me a little. Unlike Lacombe who seems to've done his shooting in an impersonal way, Moore apparently relished it. Moore is a dark, good-looking fellow. His hands are nervous, almost trembling; he's always tapping two sticks together or snapping his fingers or something. His eyes are unblinking and slightly glazed. If you saw him in civvies with his family, in a supermarket, say, you wouldn't think him anything but an ordinary young father, maybe a little intense and nervous but nothing extraordinary.

When I asked him in what part of the body he hit the man he smirked and fixed me with his unblinking eyes and said, 'Blew the fucker's head off. Turned it to jelly.' I asked him if the man was blown backwards or what. He shook his head, keeping his glazed eyes on me. 'Nope. Folded up like a wet dishrag.'

There's a small South Vietnamese army outpost down the road and its men occasionally stroll through the graveyard begging rations and cigarets. Sometimes they come in pairs, holding hands. (*Do not laugh or point at grown men holding hands on the street. They are not 'queer.' This is a Vietnamese custom.*) Steve splutters in disgust every time they pass by. Me, I just laugh and point. Steve says the reason the South Vietnamese have such a lousy army is because everybody's all the time goosing each other.

There's a lot of action going on all around us, particularly in the mountains to the northwest. The battalion is on stand-by, meaning we're ready to pull out at a moment's notice. You can feel the excitement in the air. There's a lot of bloodthirsty talk about how many gooks're going to die and so on; but that's understandable: your U.S. Marine is not exactly a social animal.

Absurd as it may sound, I went out on a patrol last night to get away from Sgt. Langley—a desperate measure.

The patrol leader was Cpl. George Sohner (Amesbury, Mass.). There were nine of us, including DiAngelo. We hadn't gone more than a mile when word was passed from the rear, *Two guys following us. Keep moving naturally.* The column peeled off from the top and an ambush was set in beside the road. As we were doing this a civilian came pelting down the road on a bicycle, nodding gaily as he whizzed by. It sort of spoiled the illusion of being in the valley of death and so on. Anyway it turned out that the two men following us were civilians with proper identification papers, bound for a village up the road.

Soon we were moving through the village ourselves. There were open shops and doorless huts with people sitting around candles and kerosene lamps. You could hear conversations up ahead but as we crept up they died out. You could see people sitting glumly, pretending to ignore us.

Passing through a village with Marines was a strange experience because in Korea there were none where we patrolled; there was nothing to distract you from the hunt itself. No-man's-land was barren and chewed up from the months of mortar & artillery fire. If you ran into any humanity it was sure to be Chinese soldiers, never Korean civilians. Here the civilians are often the soldiers, if you know what I mean.

Half a mile past the village we came to a long concrete bridge. The banks fell away sharply and it was a long drop to the water. The river reflected the light of distant flares. There were frogs croaking below, so loud that if one of us had fallen off the bridge (no side railings) the splash would've gone unheard. It was an exotic heavy Asiatic sound.

The bridge had been blown at the far end, cutting us off from the northern bank. It had probably happened that very day, otherwise a spotter plane would've reported it. Sohner backed us off fast; it was too good an ambush site. For the next hour we tried to find a shallow ford; but there wasn't any. The actual crossing, at ten o'clock, was a wild experience because the current was strong and chesthigh most of the way, which meant neck-high for Nick DiAngelo holding his PRC-25 radio over his head. It was a ballet exercise: you bounded in slow motion from one foot to the other, floating in between, and in the heat of the night it was almost fun. (Anything to get away from Langley.)

We found the road on the other side and followed it half a mile and then took a path to the left. There was a cluster of huts, and a dog started barking. Everyone froze in position and the dog kept barking, announcing our presence to any North Viet patrols nearby. Finally we moved on, crossing a fragile footbridge even scarier than the one on Sullivan's patrol. We halted not far beyond it and

Sohner deployed his men in ambush overlooking the path. The only conversation was Sohner asking me how long I had been in Vietnam. When I told him he and DiAngelo looked at each other. Soon I fell asleep.

The next thing I knew, all sorts of explosions were going on in my dreams. I must've been in a deep sleep. I finally started coming awake with a heavy drugged feeling. I was having trouble opening my eyes until I heard Sohner shout *Fire a pop-up, a pop-up!* and DiAngelo was firing his pistol. Sohner fired an M-79 round from his grenade launcher. In these few seconds I experienced the kind of panic you'd feel if the elevator you were riding in suddenly plummeted. My first thought was this, that the best chance for survival was to stick with Sohner and his Marines and do whatever they did.

A pop-up is a hand flare, a tube that sends out a kind of Roman candle. When Sohner's man finally fired it, what we saw was not a North Vietnamese patrol but a water-buffalo. Actually *I* saw nothing; either I'm as blind as a mole or my eyes were too fuzzy from sleep or dazzled by the flare. During the homeward trip I assumed we had been in a fire-fight and it wasn't until later, when I asked DiAngelo for his version of it, that I learned what had happened. Some farmer is going to be awfully sore; a water-buffalo costs about 6000 piastres.

It was late when we got back but Steve was awake and wanted to gab. We did. It turns out he came over in the same troopship I went to Korea in, the *William Weigel*. He also told me his dad has an office in Twin Falls and you can see his neon sign downtown at night, BEAUREGARD INSURANCE. I told him what a neon nut I am, and that I'll have to take a look the next time I'm up that way. He talked about his father awhile. It seems they are es-

tranged, if that's the word. Anyway Steve slugged him
the last time he was home and feels bad about it. Or so he
says. I've noticed he tends to romanticize himself, as a
character in a picaresque novel, and I suspect he enjoys
finding himself in the role of Rebellious Son. However he
has nightmares about it. Later he told me about some of
the parties he'd been to up and down the West Coast. The
first time he spoke of his 'girl' I asked where she lived and
he shot back 'Which one?' and I said 'Well, both.' Turns
out he has a hundred and eighty-seven girl friends. He
has also been in sixty-two fist-fights and won them all.
Besides that he has consumed enough liquor in the past
two years to kill four camels twice over. You'd like him,
though, even if he is vain. He reminds me of a big shaggy
dog that wants to be admired for its friskiness.

Conversation overheard:
'Just a homeboy, that's me. We're all either homeboys
or hoods. *Now* will ya look at what they done to me.'
'What they done to you, Quinn?'
'Why, they made a fuckin killer out of me.'
Quinn was being ironic; Marines are never serious.
Later I heard another conversation between Quinn and
the same guy. He was saying you'd have to be a fool to
jump on a live grenade. 'A grenade land here and you
know which way *this* boy's heading, don't you? *That*-
a-way.' The other guy thought it was commendable for a
man to sacrifice himself to save his buddies. Quinn was
cynical about it. 'Save *who?* Listen, a grenade land here,
everybody's gonna take off like a flock of quail. And
you're telling me this one guy's staying behind so he can
jump on it?'
Steve said to me just now, 'There are a lot of mean

sons-of-bitches in the Crotch.' He was talking about his
boss, a sergeant in the Public Information Office. It occurred to me that the Corps is one place where you can be
a mean bastard and get away with it. He also said there
are no phonies in the Corps 'like you meet all the time on
the outside.'

The leader of last night's patrol was Cpl. Isaac Curtis
(Chicago, Illinois), a tall hawky sort of guy, all brown
from the sun, with big gaps between his teeth. A very
jumpy, fast-talking fellow. He's eager to please, though,
and there's something desperate in his eyes. I think I
made him nervous because he thought I was some kind of
celebrity. While the members of the patrol were getting
ready, we sat against a mound and he told me he'd always
wanted to be an actor. He still has hopes of becoming one.
I asked him how long he'd been in and he said seven years.
I felt sorry for him when he told me that. He went on to
name several actors who are former Marines. It seems that
Hugh O'Brian was the youngest drill instructor they ever
had at Parris Island. Jonathan Winters was a gunnery
sergeant. Steve McQueen was a tanker, 'and a brig rat
too.' Lee Marvin was a rifleman in the Pacific, 'a real bad
dude.' Suddenly Curtis asked for my autograph. He took
off his helmet and asked me to write on the camouflage
cover. He had read my first book and liked it, so I put
down *To my fan, Curtis* and signed it.

He told the other guys I was a former Marine and a
Korea vet. Instant acceptance. More than acceptance,
really. I recall the attitude in my day, when you learned
an older guy had fought in the big war, or that he'd been
'at the Reservoir.' It was as if you were in the presence of
a member of some secret and very exclusive fraternity.

Somehow the last war always seems a lot tougher than this one.

I'm sorry to report that Curtis' garrulousness finally got on my nerves and I moved away; he followed and I moved away again. I'm afraid I hurt his feelings. During the daylight part of the patrol I caught him giving me mournful tentative looks, but when he saw me looking his way he'd break into a big snaggle-toothed grin.

An enemy radio station had been pinpointed, by triangulation, atop a knoll overlooking the battalion perimeter. Our mission was to investigate the knoll. It was deserted when we got there and we spent the night in a thicket of thorn bushes. We stayed there until nine this morning. On the way back to the perimeter a couple of melancholy things happened.

A North Viet patrol had been spotted north of the river and Col. Bell sent out a couple of squads with mortars and machine guns to chase them. Cpl. Curtis' men were moved into a blocking position near a schoolhouse with a red-tile roof. It was a one-room building with a hole in the roof and nothing inside but shattered tile on the floor. Curtis and I sat listening to the flies buzz while his men lay in the sun waiting for the enemy. We sat there a long time. Curtis opened a can of peaches and gave me a couple of slurps.

Someone shouted from across the field and we jumped up. Two peasants in black pajamas and conical hats were walking along in the shade of a tree-line, both carrying bundles, followed by a little brown dog.

'Hold 'em up,' yelled Curtis.

One of the men shouted at them but they kept going. He shouted again and they didn't stop. Finally another man ran over and blocked their path. He searched them, then prodded them toward the schoolhouse. Halfway across I saw they were women, one old, one young, probably mother & daughter. The dog trotted along at their heels.

'They got no identification, but wait till you see the money.'

They were brought inside and made to stand by the window while Curtis went through their bundles. I got depressed and felt a wave of hostility for Marines in general. I was thinking, *Doesn't this neighborhood sort of belong to these people? Aren't we the intruders?* I was in a shaky mood anyway, what with the heat and the danger and the oddly moving propaganda leaflets I'd seen all over the fields during our march that morning. They were dropped from the air, directed at the infiltrating North Viets. They were mainly visual, with little writing, if any. One showed a family waiting for its soldier son to come home. There was the old father smoking his long pipe, and the mother cooking rice, and the wife suckling the baby. Crude and sentimental as it was, it made me feel bad. The pain and suffering and death on the one hand (remembering the strewn rice) and the warmth of one's home on the other. And now these two scared women, with Cpl. Curtis ready to shoot them down if they made a wrong move, and the bewildered little dog circling the building.

Curtis counted the money while the stocky daughter stared sullenly out the window, ignoring the dog when it stopped and sniffed up at her from outside. The older woman was badly cross-eyed and kept gesturing at the money and pointing to her eyes, as if there was a connection (needed it for an operation?). There was 8850 piastres in all—a mountain of dough for a peasant lady to be carrying. Curtis and the others thought she was a Viet

Cong paymaster. She and her daughter were kept in custody.

It wasn't fair of me to get sore like I did. Marines have
too many tales to tell of mine-planting women and
'women' who turn into burpgun-toting guerrillas as readily as Clark Kent into Superman.

The patrol chasing unit of Marines showed up around
noon and that was the end of it; the North Viets had
vanished. The patrol-chasers, by the way, had been joined
by a squad of local militia and one of them had a Brown-
ing automatic rifle. I had an urge to handle it (I carried
one in Korea) but decided that'd be unseemly.

We headed back together, the militia and Marines, and
I was struck by the beauty of some of the vistas where the
path overlooked the river. I saw five water-buffalo wallowing in a muddy place where the river curves around a
stand of trees. A boy in shorts was sitting nearby, holding
his bamboo prod. A mile further along, four women in
conical hats were net-fishing in shallow water, their panta-
loons rolled up above their knees.

The only way to really see a country is to be at war in
it.

We came to a tree-shrouded hamlet. The militia was
walking on the right side of the cowpath, us on the left. I
was having a daydream about inventing a hot-weather
suit for combat in the tropics. You could switch it on
whenever the heat began to get you down. This strikes me
as funny now—the GI so laden with comfort-making
equipment that he's rendered incapable of movement—but I was serious then. The heat is my only problem; it slows me up and makes me want to do nothing,
which is a dangerous way to feel over here. It takes a lot of
energy to stay alert.

A boy appeared, driving some cattle toward us. Bringing up the rear was a calf having a tough time keeping up. Two boys on a bike came along from the other direction, and just then the calf stumbled and fell. The bike-driver had plenty of time to swerve around, but he deliberately rode across the struggling animal's middle, which I thought a rotten thing to do. The militia guys thought it a riot, though.

In the mountains a few miles northwest of Cam Lo

We pulled out yesterday afternoon—a big helilift. No action for 1st Battalion yet, but there's doings all around us.

Taking off in a helicopter for the first time is quite an experience. You leave your stomach on the ground. The side-hatch is so big you're afraid of falling out. As soon as we got up about five hundred feet we could see the ocean over to the east, and it looked awfully inviting.

We're dug in atop a hill with mountains on either side. Word is that the 324B Division of the North Viet army is all over the place, trying to break through. Several companies've made contact already. Rumor that Kilo Company, 4th Marines, fired so much ammo at attacking waves that they ran out of pistol ammo. Some of these battles are clearly audible, one just on the other side of the hill. Everyone in —— Company is just sitting in holes, canteens and ammo hanging from belts, packs within reach for a sudden move.

Before we pulled out, several helicopters arrived, and who hops out but Nguyen Cao Ky himself in his blue flight suit and lavender scarf. General Thieu was with him, and General Walt. I got a kick out of seeing Walt since he personally nixed my New York request to live with a squad. Ky held a press conference in a big tent. Someone said his wife was with him but I hadn't seen her. After the conference he came out and inspected a display of captured weapons on the grass, including mortars and anti-aircraft guns. They were roped off, along with two North Viet prisoners in shorts who had tags tied round their necks. They stood there in the sun trying to act nonchalant. One Marine climbed over the rope barrier and posed with them while his buddy snapped a picture.

There were several correspondents nearby and I had an urge to go over and gab. I was feeling lonely. I'd have liked to say goodbye to —— Company and re-join the good ole civilians; but I just stood there blending in with the Marines around me—blending in because I was outfitted in Marine gear from helmet to boots.

Ky and cohorts went into another tent, where they were briefed: a succession of Marine officers stood at a big map and explained who was doing what to whom, and how. Surprisingly I was able to work my way forward until I was behind the line of people behind the generals. Mrs. Ky was in that line. She was wearing a khaki flight suit and her hair was hidden under a peaked khaki cap with a long bill (Thelma Frizzbaum's Fashion Notes From All Over). Her husband, seated in front of her in a deck chair, sucked languidly on his cigaret through a long plastic holder. He wore dark glasses. The only interesting part was when they brought in the two prisoners and made them sit at Ky's feet. He asked them questions while Mrs. Ky took notes on a spiral-type pad. The only thing that offended me was the American television crews, who practically knocked everybody over getting into position for a shot.

That's all there was to it. You can see I didn't get much 'material' out of it. For the reporters and television guys, though, it was perfect, just the kind of pre-packaged story they want. All facts, no impressions. Record the facts, jam them into a package, tie a ribbon round it and put it over the wire. But it's the other stuff I want. With Ky's visit there was no other stuff.

Before Ky took off, DiAngelo tapped me on the shoulder and said —— Company was moving out. I ran back for my pack and joined the column. A lot of the guys were carrying pineapples they had traded excess C's for.

Still waiting. No action yet.

Let me tell you about Pfc. Richard Mathews (Gaylorsville, New Hampshire). He's a small wiry guy who never looks you in the eye, and never listens to what you're saying. His eyes seem focused on distant horizons. Steve remarked back at Cam Lo that he thought Mathews had been here too long ('He's punchy.') Mathews is something of a celebrity because he killed five Viet Cong last month. They were crossing a river in a round boat when he got them. He has a multicolored tattoo on his right forearm: DEATH BEFORE DISHONOR.

Late last night I asked him what he planned doing when he got out. He came alive, drilling me with his mean-looking eyes, and started to talk. It seems his girlfriend's dad is a contractor. He has encouraged Mathews to go into that line of business. He described to me the first house he plans to build. It's a dream palace, of course, just the kind of place a homesick Marine would dream up: bars, swimming pools and beds all over the place. I recall one feature: a second-story porch jutting out over a heated pool 'so you can go direct from the master bedroom into the water.'

Nick DiAngelo overheard us and came over to tell about a house he has actually built in Secaucus, New Jersey, and Mathews went back to his distant horizons.

By the way DiAngelo, the supreme blowhard, told me confidentially that Premier Ky had interviewed two North Viet prisoners back at Cam Lo and that one of them had spit in the Premier's face and that the Premier had ordered them both executed on the spot.

I think one reason Mathews made an impression on me is because he made me realize that most of these guys are going to end up as service-station attendants, factory workers, shoe salesmen and delivery-truck drivers whether they know it or not; and yet they all have their dream of glory. Richard Mathews wants to build houses, Nick DiAngelo wants to become an officer, Doc Flayhav wants to start a hospital in the jungle, Lester Sullivan wants to drive stock-cars, Isaac Curtis wants to be an actor, and Steve Beauregard wants to be a gigolo in Vegas.

You remember my theory about every individual finding his own place in society, as water finds its own level. In other words, generally speaking, the garbage collector is doing the work he's best suited for and is probably contented enough. I know you disagree. This first occurred to me in Oregon when I was peddling sewing-machines. I couldn't imagine anyone functioning comfortably in such a job; but after a few weeks I discovered Mr. Metraw was actually having the time of his life, despite the grumbling & growling, and it seemed to me finally that he was born to be a salesman. (His dream of glory had been to be a prizefighter.)

The theory seems fuzzy now. Maybe the truth is, most people settle for a lot less than they started out for because they have to. I dunno.

No action yet, although there were battles all around us last night—tracers arching across the sky, mortars going off, flare ships overhead. A flare ship is a plane that drops flares.

At dawn this morning I saw what looked like a golden dome on the horizon. By seven o'clock it was gleaming in sunlight. It was massive, big as a city, and I was wondering about flying saucers and such when I noticed a ship riding the horizon nearby. The dome turned out to be the beach twenty miles away. The ship was an aircraft carrier.

There are seven dead Marines in the adjoining valley, left behind when their unit had to pull out fast or be overrun. Word is that General Hodges dropped in by helicopter and gave the battalion commander hell (not Col. Bell) for leaving them behind. Marines have a tradition of bringing their dead back; you'd think they were Buddhists.

I could tell you anecdotes about the battle, but what's the use. I want to describe only what I see. So far I've seen nothing in the way of action. I hear that Hastings is news in the States, that it's possibly the biggest battle of the war. Imagine being on the spot and no action to report. I've seen air strikes and artillery barrages galore, but that's mechanical stuff.

As of this morning the 'kill count' is over 650 North Viets killed, and around 100 Marines.

Right now a spotter plane is circling overhead, blaring propaganda from a loudspeaker. The words are bouncing back & forth around the mountains. Last night they played Buddhist funeral music.

July 28th, Danang press center

. . . Where I left off.

Around noon we saddled up and headed for a new position two miles to the southeast. Trash fires were smoldering behind us and every few minutes an unopened can would explode, exactly like a rifle shot, and everyone would flinch.

An hour later word was passed back that there were two North Viet bodies on the left. The prospect of seeing them made me nervous. Do you realize I've never seen a corpse by daylight? In Korea they were all at night.

A minute later by a rather neat coincidence I saw a dead bird just off the trail and I jumped, or at least my heart did. Finally where the jungle was thinning out I got the smell solidly. The only thing I saw, though, was a dark shape in the shadows and what might have been a bare foot.

We moved onto a barren field. It was one of the most atmospheric places I've ever seen. Something violent had happened there in the past day or two: there was abandoned gear everywhere—ponchos and helmets and flak jackets—and many craters where mortars had exploded. There were blood trails, and an object that resembled a plucked chicken without its head or legs. No one knew what company that gear belonged to. Marines are taught that abandoning gear is a grievous sin; whatever happened in that field must've been disastrous.

*   *   *

I was just thinking about the bare foot and the object, wondering why I got so worked up over a calf being run over by a bike, when the sight of a slaughtered man, or maybe two, leaves me cold.

Around three we stopped for a long time while a patrol scouted out our new position. My part of the column stopped within an exotic glade—steep banks leading down to a brook, the glade canopied over in super-green foliage. Dragonflies and butterflies flitted back & forth. There were three of us down there—Doc Flayhav, Gunny Roedel and me. A bird overhead kept making a sound like a faraway machine gun (maybe he was some kind of parrot). The hum of insects in the grass was loud. I watched a dragonfly land on a leaf above the water and slowly flap its transparent wings. I put my hand in the water and a tiny brown crab materialized in the mud, scuttling sideways to a new hiding place. Later on I fooled around with a plant. The banks were covered with the stuff. It looks like a miniature fern, and if you touch one of the leaves it claps shut in a rather frightening way (if you happened to be three inches tall). After that I followed the brook a few steps to its junction with a placid stream, water-striders skating about, and filled my canteens. It's almost incredible the amount of water you need in this heat.

The Vietnam sky is awesome. Even on the finest day you see clusters of magnificent clouds over the mountains, finely chiseled with dark innards and pearly flanks. I never realized how big the sky was till I came here.

When I got back to where the others were, Gunny Roedel handed me the paperback he'd just finished. It was *I, the Jury*, by Mickey Spillane. I started reading it and was surprised how quickly and thoroughly it swallowed me—like a reality-suppressing drug.

As I was sitting there reading, Gunny Roedel asked me if I was the guy who wrote *The Last Parallel*. After awhile he got around to mentioning he'd been a platoon sergeant in Able Company, First Marines, at the time I was a corporal in it! That's not all; wait'll you hear the rest. I found out that the reason I couldn't remember him was that he was wounded soon after I arrived. 'I got hit in a raid,' he said.

'Not Little Rock.'

He nodded and smiled. It happens that I wrote an account of the raid on Little Rock, a Chinese outpost. Three Marines were wounded and one killed. Gunny Roedel was one of the wounded; he got hit in the head and right foot. He still has shrapnel in the foot. In that torrid glade beside the stream, we talked about how cold it had been that night thirteen years ago, and how much trouble the Korean coolies had carrying the stretchers up the icy slopes.

His name is Sgt. Wayne Roedel (Arkadelphia, Arkansas). He's pudgy without being fat, and has a strawberry-colored face with pale blue eyes. His lips and ears are parched and peeling from old sunburn. The only remarkable thing about him is a certain kindness of expression and a shy manner. Most gunnery sergeants are made out of asphalt, leather and battery acid. Roedel has been a Marine for nineteen years and is up for retirement, and I got the impression he's not only very tired and overripe for retirement, but also sick of the Corps and the life. I learned later he recently turned down a promotion to master sergeant because it would require eighteen more months of service.

'Wouldn't be fair to my wife,' he said. 'She's been

waiting a long time and I'm not going to ask her to wait a year and a half more.'

I asked if he had any kids and he said he has an adopted daughter in her teens and a daughter six. He has that same faraway stare that Collins and Mathews have, but there's no bitterness in it, just a kind of dreamy sadness that is almost embarrassing. He carries a foam-rubber pillow with him and every time we stopped for a break he'd sink down on it with a sigh. I noticed he has little responsibility. He lumbers around every so often to ask the men if they've taken their salt tablets—that kind of thing. Probably the captain knows he's had it, and has retired him unofficially.

Late that afternoon we dug in atop a hill. A landing zone was cleared and several helicopters touched down briefly, bringing water & rations. The wind from the rotors blew down several hootches (puptents). The helicopters had malevolent eyes painted on the nose, the same 'genie eyes' you see on Vietnamese fishing boats to ward off evil spirits. Or so the guidebook says. Helicopters look like big bad dragonflies anyway, and with those eyes added, they're really sinister.

Soon after dark that evening a machine gun opened up in the second-platoon area, followed by grenades and rifle fire and flares, and that was the only contact made by —— Company during Operation Hastings. If it was a contact. There were no casualties.

The last thing I want to tell about is an ambush that didn't come off, and Doc Flayhav. The ambush turned out to be a sort of nature-study and not much else. After we got set in I noticed some glowing spots in the earth all around me. I reached out and touched them and found they were bits of soft wood. I gathered a few. Pfc. Hall put out his hands and I let the shiny nuggets tumble into them. He was familiar with the phenomenon. He reached out and snapped off a handful of twigs and rubbed off the paperlike bark, exposing a glowing core. A handful of them were like flaming faggots, firefly version.

So much for nature.

Humphrey Flayhav (St. Ignace, Michigan) is —— senior corpsman. He and I shared the same hootch—not by choice, but because the captain put us together. Doc and I didn't hit it off too good. He's a tall, stiff, slow-moving, distant, outwardly humorless and too-sincere man with a horseface and a big jaw. At first he never swore or cursed or used rotten words. I figured he was some kind of fanatic. But on the second day he tripped over a communications wire and toppled like a tree (he's very clumsy) and said a couple of things.

For a long time I couldn't figure out why I disliked him. Finally I saw it was because he reminded me too much of myself, not only physically but the way he carries on. Another reason I disliked him is that he cares too much about justice and poverty. It wouldn't've been so bad if he'd be cool about it, but oh no. 'Doc, you care too much,' I said, baiting him. He and DiAngelo and Mathews were having a big discussion about the people of Vietnam (Doc naturally calls the place Veet Nam; I told him that means Sick Duck but he keeps on). DiAngelo and Mathews are two simple grunts who believe the ordinary Oriental is greedy, ignorant and treacherous and that the only way to deal with one is to hit him upside the head. Flayhav tried to educate them, in his plodding humorless way, but got nowhere. He also got madder and madder, which made me dislike him less. The climax was when DiAngelo told how one of the guys in this company last May threw a grenade at an old farmer working in a field, and Doc said if he'd been there hed've wrapped his entrenching tool around that Marine's neck.

'Doc, you care too much.'

He plans to study medicine in Bangkok and become a true doctor, then start a hospital in northeast Thailand—where he spent a year doing Peace Corps-type work for the Navy. He's been in the Navy nine years. He's engaged to a Thai girl, whose picture he showed me.

About the only thing I ever bothered to ask him was what he carried in his Unit One. Here's a list he made for me:

Large, medium and small battle dressings; non-pneumatic tourniquet; a plastic pharyngeal airway (air-pump) ; various sizes of roller gauze; a wire splint; triangular bandages; various sizes of gauze compresses; elastic bandages; adhesive tape; suture needles; a couple of hemostats (for closing blood vessels or arteries) ; a needle driver (it holds the needle while suturing) ; knife handle and disposable blades; skin forceps (to lift up flaps of skin) ; a silver probe; a small pair of surgical scissors; a spoonlike probe; alcohol to sterilize equipment; one-quarter-grain morphine syrettes; salt tablets; malaria tablets; aspirin; Darvon for severe headache and toothache; two kinds of bacterial ointment; a skin antiseptic; a collapsible cloth stretcher; safety pins; cotton; Band-Aids; copper-sulphate pads (for white-phosphorus burns) ; field medical tags; a flashlight with a red lens.

Around noon one day, when it was obvious the show was over and I had missed it, I said goodbye and caught a re-supply helicopter to Dong Ha and a cargo plane to Danang.

Remember my big plans for visiting some of these guys after they get discharged? when they'll be working at their mundane jobs, going home at night to dreary houses in dreary places like Elyria, Ohio, and I'd get them talking about their days of adventure & promise when they were Marines; the idea being that for many of them their service years are the most challenging and fulfilling they'll ever know. But I forgot one thing. Those years can also be the worst of their lives, and are maybe better forgotten. It had completely slipped my mind what a harsh unlovely way of life it is to be a Marine. I had built up a romantic picture over the years, forgetting the endless drudgery and boredom and humdrum loneliness of it, the lack of privacy, the physical ugliness of barracks and warehouses, parade fields and guard shacks, post exchanges and motor pools, troop transports and oily beaches. I guess there are men who thrive on this, but for most it's a matter of counting the days they have left. One of my opening gambits during Hastings was to ask a guy how 'short' he was, and usually he'd tell me to the day.

July 30th, press center

I just got back from an afternoon in a repair hangar at Danang airfield, where I learned about the ejection seat of a jet fighter-bomber. I've been thinking about going along on an air strike, and Step One is learning how to work the seat. But now I think I wasted the time. An air strike is really a mechanical event—the pilot almost an automaton—and the machines of war don't interest me.

Amazing how thoroughly this war is being documented. There are television cameras and tape recorders all over the place, and everyone seems to own a camera. On Hastings, several men in —— Company carried Polaroids in their packs. As far as I'm concerned, one word is worth a thousand pictures.

Speaking of Hastings, I forgot to include the list of C rations I made out there, just to give you an idea of what they eat.

Here it is:

Chicken and noodles; boned chicken; beef steak with juices; ham with water added; pork steak with juices; spiced beef with sauce; beans with frankfurter chunks in tomato sauce; meatballs with beans in tomato sauce; pork slices with juice; beef slices with potatoes and gravy; turkey loaf; chopped ham and eggs. Fruit cocktail, pears, apricots and peaches. Cheddar cheese spread. Peanut butter. Grape, apricot and pineapple jam. Date pudding, fruitcake, pound cake. Instant coffee. Instant non-dairy 'cream.' Sugar. Cocoa. Candy.

As I said, the pig predominates.

One last thing about Hastings. I had a chance to talk briefly with a chaplain just before I left. I was waiting at battalion headquarters for a helicopter, and the colonel introduced me to Father William O'Dwyer (Peru, Indiana). I asked him what the Marines' biggest problem was. 'The problem of killing,' he said. 'It preys on their mind.' He was talking about those Marines troubled enough to seek him out; I didn't have to ask if it bothered most of them. I asked if he was a 6th Commandment man. 'Of course,' he said. I asked if he thought there was any conflict between that and his work over here. He said he didn't think so. 'There are just wars, and in my opinion this is one of them.' (Thou shalt not kill, except in certain circumstances.) I asked him what he wrote to parents of dead Marines. 'I tell them their son died in defense of his loved ones and his country. I tell them he did not die in vain, but for the things he believed in.'

. . . I got a wild notion last night. How about me visiting the Viet Cong? I don't know how I'd go about it, but I know it's possible. Maybe I could get captured, I dunno.

I'll think about it some more.

August 4th

I'm writing this in the town of Tam Ky, a few miles down the coast from Danang in Quang Tin province. I'm with a battalion of Vietnamese Marines. I joined them yesterday in Dong Ha (a place I never expected to see again). They had just come off Hastings and were quartered there. It was lucky timing on my part, because this morning they were loaded aboard C-130s and flown down here to join two other Viet Marine battalions for a new operation, which starts tomorrow or the day after.

Each battalion has two U.S. Marine advisors attached to it. Capt. Bizelle and Lt. Suggins are the advisors to the —— Battalion. I'll tell about them later; I have a lot of catching up to do.

I've eaten four Vietnamese meals so far and feel fine. The advisors keep warning me to expect sudden attacks and Bizelle went to a lot of trouble in Dong Ha finding me a certain kind of pill that blocks you up in case of disaster.

I like the food and there's plenty of it. Mainly it's rice. My only complaint is that Major Tran Buu Trung, the battalion commander, eats no breakfast and therefore the advisors and the visiting writer eat none too. I don't understand how anyone can get along on nothing all morning (but I'm learning). Actually the major does have a sort of breakfast: this morning we all had a glass of hot tea, which is just the thing in this weather.

I slept in a Vietnamese house last night. Capt. Bizelle tells me the major always picks out the biggest and best and simply moves in, and his company commanders take the next best. Trung and his officers ask only shelter and water from the homeowners (decent of them) and Bizelle says the homeowners are only too honored, which is a bit hard to believe. In yesterday's house the family kept pretty much to itself in the bedroom and the dirt-floor kitchen; but after nightfall the big-eyed kids came creeping out and beguiled us till lights-out.

The major and his bodyguard and the two advisors and I slept in the front room as if we owned it.

* * *

Yesterday we went to Quang Tri, the province capital. The major wanted to buy a certain song sheet and we went from shop to shop. Lt. Suggins sang it for me in Vietnamese and then translated as we strolled along: a soldier and his sweetheart used to go to a certain berry patch, but now the soldier is dead and the girl is remembering him, singing alone in the berry patch. It impressed me to hear these two Americans talking casually to shopkeepers in their own language. Major Trung speaks some English, but not much. The advisors talk to him in a mixture which includes French.

At one point we came to a bar where a fight was going on. The major glanced inside and recognized two of his troopers swinging away, and plunged in and dragged them out by their ears. They were comically submissive and terrified. By this time the rest of us had backed discreetly down the street. Capt. Bizelle said the advisors always keep their (big) noses out of 'internal affairs.' He said that these barfights often get wildly violent. 'These little guys'd just as soon go at it with pistols and grenades, as fists.' It turned out that the two troopers were off-limits, having a big blowout before the operation.

After that we went looking for a place to eat. In a Vietnamese town, nothing looks much like a place to eat. Finally Bizelle saw a sign saying *Pho So 1* and laughed because, he told me, it means Number One Soup.

We sat around a table on the sidewalk. Everybody ordered iced *Bia La Rue*, which is beer. It's light and gives the impression you can drink a lot with no problem. I drank a quart (in this weather you're always dying of thirst) but then had to sit silently because I found myself buzzing.

I watched the *pho* being made, inside the open shop.

First the cook grabs a handful of gummy noodles and throws it in a bowl. Then he slices off thin slices of raw beef and throws that in. Then he sprinkles on all sorts of seasoning, adds some vegetables, and last of all ladles a splash of boiling water over the whole mess, which cooks the meat instantly. He hands you the bowl and that's your serving.

Major Trung showed me how to season my soup further from the various jars & bottles on the table. There was lemon juice and *nuoc mam* and a hot sauce. The hot sauce looked like nail-polish. By mistake I put in too much and everyone laughed. The major stirred it for me, diluting it with lemon juice, shaking his head in big forebodings of what was going to happen when I tasted it. But he didn't know he was dealing with the Tabasco Kid.

After the meal we drove to the edge of town and looked at a couple of shops and a bar the Viet Cong had demolished. I asked Bizelle why they'd been demolished.

'To discredit the Saigon government,' he said. 'Show the people the government can't protect them. They want the people to think *they're* the real government.' He also said that possibly the shopowners had decided to stop paying taxes to the Cong.

Capt. Jake Bizelle grew up in Eveleth, Minnesota, now lives in San Francisco. Married, no children. Thirty-five years old. A former enlisted man, he was a platoon sergeant in Korea. Later he trained government troops in the Philippines (during the Huk rebellion). He's big and burly and slightly hog-jowled, and reminds me of the stereotype French bruiser, with beret slung over one eye and cigaret dangling. There's a merry twinkle in his eyes, though, even when his face is in repose. (By the way, the Viet Marines wear green berets and tiger-stripe dungarees and the advisors dress that way too, so Bizelle does wear a beret.)

Because I'm a writer he assumes I'm well-educated, and in the short time I've known him he has shown himself to be sensitive about his lack of formal schooling. He loves his present assignment and calls it the best in the Corps. He talks about his wife a lot, and I know you'll like him for that, if nothing else. They grew up in Eveleth, their fathers were pals; but she was three years younger and he says he never paid any attention to her. Then he joined up and went to Korea.

'When I came back she was eighteen and' (eyebrows going up & down) 'I noticed her.'

She has had a number of cancer operations ('scared us both pretty bad') but he says she's in good shape now. She works in the big naval hospital in San Francisco, where a lot of wounded Marines are flown. She's a floor supervisor (sort of a lousy job for a lady whose husband is a Marine in Vietnam). His R & R is coming up in October and he plans to fly to Honolulu and meet her there. Her boss at the hospital is all set to let her take off at a moment's notice.

Lt. Terry Suggins comes from Pikeville, Kentucky. He's twenty-six. A graduate of the Naval Academy. A bachelor. Tall and slender, has short blond hair and large blue eyes. A long scar on his right cheek. He is boyish and enthusiastic. Vietnamese women knock him dead. During our stroll in Quang Tri he was nothing but eyes. School had just let out for the day and many sweet young things were going by on bicycles, in conical hats and white *ao dai*. Suggins was bug-eyed and bedazzled, and kept grabbing me by the arm ('Did you see that one!')

He agrees with Bizelle that being an advisor is the best job in the Corps. Suggins is interested in the Vietnamese themselves, which sets him apart from most Marines. Like Doc Flayhav he is one who cares.

August 5th

Early in the morning. Still in Tam Ky.

I am sitting on the porch where I slept last night. A rainstorm just ended and there are big puddles in the yard. During the storm everyone disappeared except the one-eared Pvt. Quat, the major's bodyguard. He stood in front of the house like a statue, his carbine slung. Quat is about the most sinister-looking person I've ever seen. His face is like a pitted bas-relief on an ancient temple, and his fingernails are as long as Madame Nhu's.

Let me tell you about my first full-course Vietnamese meal. The major's private cook put a panful of steaming rice on the table, while the major passed out chopsticks. Then he brought saucers of shrimp, pork, bamboo shoots and some spinach-like greens. Also a saucer of *nuoc mam*, which is fish sauce. Suggins says it's strong enough to make you drunk. Anyway the advisors showed me how to eat a Vietnamese meal. You pick up a clot of rice in your chopsticks, dip it in *nuoc mam* and pop it in your mouth. Every so often you go for one of the other saucers too; but mainly it's rice and *nuoc mam*. After the meal the cook brought us each a glass of hot tea.

Yesterday Terry Suggins took me down the road where a bunch of troopers were listening to a blind singer. The singer was young, maybe sixteen, and had a horrible scarred gargoyle face. He accompanied himself on guitar.

His face was tilted toward the sky, his features working intensely over the words, and the overall effect was one of passion and fury. It was wonderful to see a singer put so much into a song. His little brother stood in front of him all raggedy and blank-faced, holding out a tin cup.

Suggins had a date last night. Capt. Bizelle looked aghast when he said he was going out; it seems Suggins had a date the night before too, in Dong Ha.

'Do I have to be your parent too?'

'Don't worry, sir. I'll be back before midnight.'

'That isn't what I'm worried about.'

'Oh, it's all very innocent, captain.'

After he left, Bizelle said: 'I really admire the kid. He works hard and he mixes in well with the people.'

This house belongs to a soldier of the regular army who happens to be home on leave. He nodded hospitably to us yesterday as we tromped in. (What else could he do?) Right now his eldest daughter is swinging the baby in a basket suspended from the ceiling.

Down the path, not twenty yards away, four troopers are standing in the blazing sun awaiting punishment for going over the hill. Bizelle says they'll be beaten and forced to lug great backbreaking loads throughout the operation. Just now their company commander came along and screamed at them, pacing from one to the next, stopping to hit them with a small stick every so often. Bizelle says this isn't the formal beating, which will be administered by Major Trung himself. He also said he wished the U.S. Marines used corporal punishment: 'A kick in the ass is worth a hundred words.'

Terry Suggins told me last night after supper I was eating too much. 'One of the things the advisors have to learn first is to suppress their desires.' He pointed out how little the troopers have in the way of food, that they fill up mainly on rice. 'Out on an operation they're lucky if they have a scrap of meat to add to it.' He said that although the major 'sets a pretty good table, we try and eat less than we would like.'

Of course I was deeply embarrassed, and sore at myself. But this morning the whole thing struck me funny. When I looked into my shaving mirror I found a smudge of dried *nuoc mam* on the end of my beak and a grain of rice in my left nostril. (The way you eat around here is, you hold the little bowl right up to your mouth, the edge actually inside, and shovel the rice in with your chopsticks in a little circular motion. The Vietnamese, being a short-nosed people, do very nicely at it, whereas etc.)

The average Vietnamese male is 5′3″ tall and weighs 115 lbs.—or so it says in the guidebook. I notice how Bizelle and Suggins sort of tiptoe whenever they move around inside the house—not because the house is fragile but, I think, because they feel self-consciously enormous compared with the Vietnamese.

The Viet troopers are interesting to watch, they're so elegantly graceful. I notice too how readily they respond to the neighborhood kids. And they are gentle in playing with them, unlike the Americans. You often see a trooper pick up one casually and just hold him or her and continue gabbing with a buddy.

There are an amazing number of kids around, and they're very appealing. They all (even the maimed ones and harelips) have a natural charm that springs to life when you speak to them or touch them. Touching them isn't easy, because they're afraid of Americans. The babies would destroy you; they wear little peaked caps or cowboy hats, and the toddlers go around in tiny sandals.

I haven't been around long enough to have a clear opinion of the Vietnamese but I'll give you some vague impressions. The thing that impresses me most is their attitude toward us, the Americans. They seem amused, in an impudent sort of way, as if we were big children in their midst. Individually they seem haughty and independent, and surprisingly sophisticated. They're the Oriental opposite of the Japanese, who tend to fade politely into the mass. I recall how sharp the difference was between the Air Vietnam hostesses and the ones on Japan Air Lines. The Vietnamese girls gave the impression they were doing you a big favor.

I forgot to mention that several troopers' wives and babies flew with us from Dong Ha to Tam Ky. It was kind of pathetic because the women were disguised as Viet Marines, wearing tiger-stripe dungarees and green berets and trying to be inconspicuous in the ranks (holding babies in their arms). Everyone was nervous at Dong Ha because they didn't know if the U.S. Air Force people were going to allow them aboard, in which case there'd've been trouble for the advisors, whose job it is to arrange things like that. At first I thought they were girl soldiers (after all, the Viet Cong have them) until I saw the babies. A pigfaced airman sidled up to Suggins and said 'They travel with their own whores, huh?' and Suggins coldly explained the situation to him. There were two companies of U.S. Marines waiting nearby and their Viet counterparts seemed to fascinate them, with all their pots & pans and bags of rice and of course the women, some of whom were very good-looking.

The presence of the women and babies depressed me. The airstrip was hot and dustswept and the giant throbbing engines made everything buzz; it was such a wrong place for women and babies to be. You can't imagine how rough and unlovely the Dong Ha airstrip is.

The Vietnamese laugh a lot. Their sense of humor seems highly developed. I was present an hour ago when Major Trung chewed out one of his officers, and when the man left, the major said he was like an outboard motor in that he starts up with a loud roar and lots of power, but then splutters out and you have to keep restarting him. All this with lots of raspberry sounds spraying us, the major convulsing himself. I also noticed that the major's anger at the officer was fake: he turned it on as the man came in, screaming and squeezing words out of his face like an actor in a samurai picture; but when the man left he calmly told us his joke about the outboard motor.

10 p.m. same day

It's raining outside. The army soldier is sleeping behind me. I'm sitting at a table beneath the family altar, writing by kerosene lamp. Bizelle is asleep on the porch. Suggins is on the bench beside me, reading one of my Spillanes. Major Trung is across from us, writing a letter. He showed me a picture of his wife and son and four daughters. The Viet Marines have a permanent base in a town near Saigon and their families live there. When a man is killed, the family can stay on in the compound at government expense.

I went to the briefing this afternoon. The speeches were translated, but the only interesting thing I brought away is that we're landing in a longtime VC-controlled area where government troops have never been.

Bizelle told me that one of the first things an advisor learns is to go slow with his counterpart. The average advisor wants to *attack, attack, attack,* but the Viets are in no hurry, said Bizelle. 'Why should they be? The war's been going on for years and it'll go on for years more.'

He said the matter of 'face-saving' is important. The Viet officers may accept advice occasionally, but only in a roundabout way. He gave me an example.

'Major, allow me to compliment you on the placing of your mortars—a very excellent position.'

'Thank you.'

Bizelle goes away and comes back five minutes later.

'Major, I've been meaning to ask you: what do you think about that spot over there for the mortars? Allow me to point out that it's near the road, so you'll have less of a supply problem. Also, it's in a gully and well out of sight.' And the advisor goes on to cite all the advantages of the new position.

'Usually Trung'll say nothing,' Bizelle told me, 'but a few minutes later he may come up and say he has an idea for a new mortar position. I just smile and say his idea is very excellent.'

August 6th, late afternoon

I'm writing this outside a mud-bamboo-thatch hut in a tiny isolated hamlet. An old couple live here, their only furniture a bamboo shelf for sleeping. Captain Ho Van Vui, his cook and I are staying here tonight. The nearest American is several hundred yards away and I'm feeling rather adventurous, isolated like this.

The lady of the house wears black pajamas and a rag around her head. When she saw me this afternoon she made a formal speech and I heard the word *Maline* (I'm dressed like an advisor). Capt. Vui translated: 'She say Marine welcome. She say you lie on bed, rest.' I declined.

We took off this morning from a big field on the outskirts of Tam Ky. (I recall seeing Lt. Col. Khan slurping down a bowl of *pho* at the last minute. Many troopers had loaves of bread tucked away which they'd bought from roadside vendors.) We rode in Sea Knight helicopters, twenty men in each. The back of ours was open and you could see the others in formation far behind, like a pursuing horde of pterodactyls. The flight took twenty minutes and we flew over jungle terrain without villages or roads.

The landing was sensational. We dropped onto a wet paddy and scrambled down the ramp like we were hitting the beach at Tarawa or something. The noise from the helicopters was terrific but even so you could hear long voluptuous bursts of automatic fire nearby. We all splashed ahead like mad. The paddy-water was five inches deep and quite clear, the bottom cracked like muck after it's baked in the sun. The green rice shoots stuck up five inches above the water. I saw long bamboo poles off to the left, planted in the paddy to discourage helicopters from landing; fortunately only a third of the paddy had them. They were about seven feet high and pointed. I noticed what a brilliantly beautiful morning it was (the sky had been overcast in Tam Ky) with sharp-edged black and purple mountains in the background and everything in the foreground richly green and satisfying to the eye. There were wisps of mist still hanging on in the valleys.

Several of us found cover in a sort of island of huts in the middle of the paddy. The island had dikes around it and the huts were on a lower level than the paddy, and I found myself lying atop someone's roof worrying about breaking through. Down below me a big goose strutted by, glaring at the crouching troopers. One of them made a grab for it and another jumped up and ran after it, but stopped when he lost his cover—there was still a lot of fire going over our heads.

I saw two civilians in black pajamas (I guess all peasants dress this way, so I'll quit mentioning it), one resembling Stanley Kubrick of all people. They stood behind the dike gawking at the monstrous green helicopters.

I saw a woman creeping between two huts holding a baby with dried blood under its nose, both of them seemingly oblivious to the clangor around them. Capt. Wilson nodded toward her and shouted in my ear: 'Right there's the worst part of this fuckin' war. That kid's probably dead.' There had been an air strike and artillery barrage just before we landed.

After the shooting died down (Viet Marines attacking into the jungle, out of sight now) we raced across the last portion of paddy and clambered up onto dry ground blanketed with green grass and tall trees overlooking. There was some small-arms fire beyond the trees and grenades going off.

I saw three prisoners led past. They were barefoot, wearing black shorts, and were tied together, one behind the other. The one in the rear had a bloody rag around his head covering his eyes and he stumbled along in a panic. I followed them a short way and watched as Capt. Vui questioned them. The prisoner in front was openly surly, almost defiant. Capt. Vui shoved him in the chest and all three toppled backward onto the grass. The one I felt sorriest for was the one with the rag—he was awfully helpless-looking, ducking his blind head all around, not knowing what was going on and undoubtedly wondering when they were going to shoot him.

Then I noticed a young woman seated calmly on the grass a few feet away, her back resting against a grassy hump, her arms gracefully encircling her knees. She wasn't a prisoner. She was just a civilian caught in the middle of the landing, sitting tight until we moved on. She must've been terrified, but her face was as blank as a face can be. She never glanced at the prisoners or the troopers or me; she sat looking into the distance with chaos all around her.

After the interrogation, Capt. Vui came over and said: 'North Vietnam soldier. They come south four month.'

It's getting too dark to write.

August 7th

Very hard catching time to write, because we're moving a lot. Still chasing North Viets.

Where I left off.

We moved into the trees eventually, passing some hammocks strung between trees, their owners caught by surprise and long gone. We kept moving. I saw no casualties yesterday, but it turns out there were plenty. The trees and brush were too thick to see much of anything.

We came to a clearing with a stone monument, and here Capt. Vui tried to recruit a frightened peasant to lead us through some especially dense brush. The man's little daughter stood by clutching his baggy pants. He tried to send her home, but she was as scared as he was and wanted to stay. She stood there bawling, rubbing her eyes with a grubby fist. Capt. Vui was beginning to act ferocious, so the man turned and yelled harshly at her, and she was so shocked she ran off howling into the trees.

We stopped for lunch in a hamlet with straw all over the ground, and the troopers stretched out in the shade of tall palm trees. There was still some shooting up ahead, maybe half a mile away, and it amazed me that the battalion would halt for lunch at a time like this. I mentioned this to the advisors, Capt. Wilson and Capt. Westervelt, and they broke out in tight-lipped mutterings and kept giving me dire looks of frustration throughout the meal.

(Let me explain that I'm traveling with one of the other battalions now because at the last minute Major Trung's battalion was held up for use as reserves.)

Lots of interesting booty was brought in as we ate our cold rice balls: several Russian rifles and two Chinese AK-47 submachine guns, a portable generator that you sit on and pump like a bicycle, several rolls of communication wire.

Another prisoner was questioned by Vui and led off. I can't convey what a dramatic thing it is to see a prisoner; you know it's probably the most frightening moment of his life. He knows he'll be tortured eventually and maybe killed. It is morbidly fascinating to watch the alternating terror and self-control on his face.

I'm sorry if I sound like a snake.

By mid-afternoon the sky clouded over, cooling things down a bit, and it was then I saw some action with my own eyes. I was traveling with Lt. Nguyen Ngoc Xuan, who had been assigned the job of hunting down an enemy mortar crew that had been harassing us throughout the

day. The rounds would drop with a hoarse *flomp* that
shook the ground and trees, sometimes landing so close
you could hear shrapnel singing through the canopy overhead. We zig-zagged around fast for two hours. The
enemy would fire one or two rounds, then pull up stakes
and move to a new position. I may as well tell you, I
hadn't the vaguest notion of what was going on; all I
knew was that we were moving from place to place and
Xuan was glowing with adrenalin.

It all became clear when he halted his men, deployed
them in covered positions (the terrain was generally flat
now and open, the jungle behind us) and started to move
off with his 57 mm. recoilless gun crew. I just had time to
ask if I could go along.

'You understand back-blast?'

I said I did and he said I could come along. We ran a
short distance, everyone bending low behind a dike, and
stopped. The gun was set up on one man's shoulder while
another loaded the projectile into the rear and armed it
and tapped the gunner on his helmet to signal him everything was ready.

Ahead of us was a sea of waist-high grass and on the
other side a tree-line and an isolated hut. We were behind
a dike with bushes along the top. The gunner poked the
muzzle of his silver-colored weapon through the bush in
front of him. What they were firing at, I learned a few
moments later, was the enemy mortar crew; they were
trying to hide behind the isolated hut.

The gunner stood up behind the bush, another man
holding his legs to steady him, and took aim. Then a crazy
thing happened—almost unbelievable. We were all up on
our knees, ready to watch the show, when suddenly a black
figure rose up in front of us, in the middle of the sea of

grass and directly in the line of fire. It was, so help me, a woman with a baby.

She stood there, gazing right and left, unaware of our presence. It was a tough situation for the gunner because by signaling her he might reveal himself to the enemy. But of course he did signal, and you could see she was nearly frightened out of her wits when she saw the muzzle.

After she was safely aside he fired, and the hut went up in a flash of smoke and flame. The troopers grinned exultantly and beat each other over the shoulders and jumped up & down, all in silence. Then one of them grabbed me and pointed in the direction of the smoking ruins, and I saw a dark head bobbing in the tall grass beyond, like a deer escaping a hunter's ambush. No one fired at him; he was too far away.

Afterward we moved to a meadow and sat under the trees. I had a talk with Lt. Xuan. I was surprised at how well he spoke English. It turns out he went through Basic Officer's School at Quantico, Virginia. He wore tinted glasses and seemed very bright. I showered him with questions about the war, his future, his impressions of America, but I soon realized he was giving me polite optimistic answers, telling me what he thought I wanted to hear.

Afterward I went back to Capt. Ho Van Vui and was with him when he moved into the hut I mentioned before. (He told me Capt. Wilson had been wounded and evacuated. He doesn't know the nature of the wound.)

It gets dark awfully fast around here. One minute it's sunset and the next thing you know it's night, seems like. Anyway Vui and I ate our rice just after nightfall, sitting inside on a mat on the dirt floor, the cooking fires burning down to embers in a pit nearby. He interests me, but I'm afraid I'll never get to know him because he doesn't like to talk. He's tall for a Vietnamese and has features that are almost Spanish. There's a fierce look about him, and his way of moving and standing remind me of a bullfighter.

He virtually ignores me, which I don't mind. I get the feeling he sees me as a useless member of the group, a sort of parasite, which I am. The only conversation we had during the evening was him asking if I had seen the dead VC nearby (the Viet Marines call them 'VC' even though they're North Vietnamese.) I said no and he said he'd show me in the morning. We all bedded down an hour after supper, Vui inviting me to share the mat with him. There was an underground shelter inside the hut, a small cave with its entrance behind the fire pit. An old lady and a child climbed in there and bedded down by the light of a candle. The old man and his wife, whose house it was, were lying on the sleeping platform just over my head. I could've reached up and touched the man's white beard. His face shone clearly in the candlelight. He was gazing dreamily at nothing, looking not very joyous.

Vui snuffed out the candle and the darkness closed in.

A minute or two later he snapped on his flashlight and aimed it at an old faded photograph tacked high up on the wall. It was a picture of a smiling young man in a white shirt, his hair slicked down. Vui exchanged a few words with the old couple, then told me the boy in the picture was their son whom they had lost track of years ago.

'Probably VC,' he said, a smirk in his voice. He gave a little laugh. '*Dead* VC by now.' He snapped off the light. A moment later he snickered in the dark, 'No young men in villages.'

Twice during the night Vui's cook had nightmares and his moans of terror woke everyone up. And at 2:30 there was a sudden burst of fire nearby and Vui batted me on the arm to alert me. We sat there with drawn pistols until word was passed that two VC had been killed nearby.

Capt. Vui didn't forget to show me the corpse he mentioned last night. Actually he had his First Sergeant take me there. The First Sergeant is impressively dignified, has a drooping mustache, and you can see a lot of Mongol in him. He's a former Viet-Minh, Wilson said. Anyway I was nervous following him because I had never seen a corpse in broad daylight before. I kept searching ahead with my eyes, so I wouldn't come upon it abruptly and scream *Aiee!* or something.

It's lying inconspicuously in one corner of a shady little field, on its back, legs apart, head to one side—a comfortable napping position. The mouth is slightly open and you can see gold-rimmed teeth glinting inside. The eyes are open too, but not enough to bother you. There are no wounds visible, but the skin is burnished a delicate purple. There is straw sticking to the arms and legs and face, giving the impression somehow of a bottle of old wine in a basket of straw. First Sergeant took a puff on his cigaret and said, casually, 'Probably napalm.' I took a good long look, waiting for some reaction, but I was as cold as the corpse. Many troopers grinned at me and the body as they passed by, and that was the only thing that bothered me.

One of them grabbed me and pulled me over to another part of the field and pointed down a hole (one of many tunnel entrances around here) saying 'VC!' All I could make out was a jumble of grey cloth and something flat and black that may have been a pool of blood.

Just then there was a commotion in the adjoining field and we stepped through the tree-line to see what was happening. There was a field of cultivated plants of some kind, all in rows, and in the middle were several troopers in informal stages of dress (one shirtless, one in pants and undershirt, one with a toothbrush in his mouth like a lollipop) surrounding a North Vietnamese soldier and closing in. They were moving warily and it was plain why: the North Viet, hunkered down on his heels and cowering, was holding a potato-masher grenade. Both hands were between his thighs and the grenade hung from one of them. He stared at the troopers, his eyes pleading, wide with fright. He thought he was going to die. Then he shouted a couple of words. The troopers laughed, and First Sergeant translated for me: 'He say *Save me.*' One of the men barked at him, pointing to the grenade. The North Viet glanced down at it, looked horrified and dropped it. The man jumped in and snatched it up, the others rushed in gleefully and for some reason started taking off the guy's pants. When they were off, one held them up for me to see and cried out, 'North Vietnam!' Underneath he was wearing black shorts. The men poked and prodded him, teasing and taunting him. He sat there gazing into their faces, waiting for the knives to come out. He was very young. When he saw me, his face fell a mile. I smiled but he just stared in horror. The trooper who had shown me the pants now bent down and pulled aside the crotch of the prisoner's shorts, exposing his shriveled yellow prunes, and said 'North Vietnam!' which brought down the house.

When we got back to the hut, Capt. Vui told First Sergeant to show me the two North Viets killed at 2:30 this morning. I began to wonder if First Sergeant was going to escort me relentlessly to every corpse in the neighborhood.

These two are spectacular. If you saw a shot of them in

a war movie you'd say it was corny and contrived and overdone. They're lying in the deep purple shade between two huts. I came upon them abruptly, distracted by a water-buffalo wallowing in a mudhole, and it was a shock. One of them had been crawling out of (or backing into) a tunnel that goes under one of the huts. In dying he had twisted around on his back, head thrown back, chin skyward and, I regret to say, eyes wide open and bulging. He looks like a man having an orgasm. The other one is worse—lying on his side, a knife in the palm of one hand, his brains all cowflopped in a purple-white heap beside the top of his head. The eyes are shut, the face peaceful. They probably died trying to get at us inside the huts. The one in the field is undoubtedly a survivor of this team.

I hung around a moment, waiting for some sort of human reaction, but there was none. I tried thinking of youth cut off in its prime, of wives waiting and parents losing track—all that. But the trouble is, the corpses are nothing but objects.

Later in the morning

We moved, but not far.

I'm impressed with the way these guys keep themselves clean. Whenever we stop in a hamlet—like now—the troops find the well and start drawing up water in banana-leaf buckets, and after they fill their canteens they wash. If the stop is long enough they take off their shirts and soap up. (The Marines on Hastings ignored water for washing and by the time I left were smelling like sick goats.) I'm learning how much better you feel when you're clean. For one thing, the heat doesn't bother you as much. Your clothing doesn't stick to you like oily canvas.

Incidentally the troopers are 'modest' in the old-fashioned sense: they don't like to display their collective wang. They keep their undershorts on and wash Down There by reaching in with the soap, and rinse off by pouring a helmetful of water inside. Vietnamese shorts are gaudy and have no fly.

Did I mention that each advisor has a cook-porter of his own? Capt. Bizelle told me it was embarrassing at first, especially when they ran into American troops. The point is, according to Bizelle, that his counterpart would lose face if the Americans carried their own packs and heated up their own rations and put up their own hootch.

A trooper just brought me a grapefruit from a tree nearby. The skin is green and thick, and even though the red meat is fairly tasteless it's refreshing in this torrid heat.

Since Suggins' advice in Tam Ky, I've been eating sparingly—so much so that when I laid up my chopsticks last night after only one bowl, Capt. Vui stared at me and said, 'You no appetite? Maybe too many VC-stink?' After much twisting of the arm, I grudgingly agreed to a second bowl.

I get the impression the troopers are pleased to have me deep among them, rather than in the advisors' shadow. I haven't laid eyes on a fellow American for twenty-four hours.

You know I still suffer from early Parris Island brain-washing. Often it's hard for me to think of a yellow person as anything but a gook. After all, the Marines have fought only Orientals in the past twenty-five years—Japanese, North Korean, Chinese and now Vietnamese. To a Marine they are all one, the collective gook. My outlook is therefore a bit twisted. In the past three days I've been half-expecting these guys to start torturing one another, or break out in wild pagan dances, or something.

Almost sundown

We're back in the hut where we slept last night, and I've seen how poor my navigational abilities are. We've been slogging all over the countryside today and suddenly here we are again. And I was sure we were at least four miles from last night. Actually the terrain roundabouts is impossible to stay oriented in without a compass and map. You have a series of little fields on different levels, separated by tree-lines or bushes. You find yourself descending into a patch of jungle, leaving the fields behind, and all at once there's an apparently deserted hamlet off to your left, all shadowed in the foliage. You break out into the open again, and there's a broad system of paddies in a curving sweep off to the right and out of sight around a grassy hill. Towering in the background are the mountains, but you're so close against them that the peaks flow into one long skyline and dead reckoning is impossible. Did I mention that there are no roads in this area? For miles around, not a single road. The people here are truly isolated; it's easy for the Viet Cong to keep a hold on them.

There are two kids in the hut tonight. Lien is the girl, Bon the boy. They sit staring at me and won't come near. (I learned their names through First Sergeant.) I read in some square article that the Vietnamese like it if you fuss over their kids.

* * *

We made contact about two hours after starting out. It was sudden and close, so close my ears rang from weapons firing in my direction. My part of the column was in a small field of crabgrass, a tree-line on one side and a line of bushes on the other. The fire was coming from the other side of the bushes. There was a lot of frantic yelling, then some of the troopers threw grenades and, after they exploded, opened fire with rifles and carbines.

I saw a man die. This is the first time I ever saw that; I mean my eyes were on him when he went. He was one of the few who had overcome fear enough to fire back (most of the troopers were still glued to the grass). I saw him fall backward and curl up tight and uncurl, his head whipping back & forth in a frenzy. As I watched, he arched his back so violently I though he was going to snap in two. Then he flopped dead. I was glad. I noticed one detail. His canteen was leaking and water dripped drop by drop onto the grass. Another trooper appeared by his side and peered into his face. Then he wrenched off the man's cartridge belt, so roughly he flipped the body over on its side.

The sky was clouded over and it was just starting to rain, so at least we didn't have the heat to worry about. The shooting had moved on down the line. Just as the rain came pelting in I saw someone spread a poncho over the body, which struck me as funny in a sick kind of way.

Mortar shells were whomping in now, but not in our area. I started crawling forward, and came to a sort of bottleneck between two fields. I crawled up onto the other field, on a higher level. (I was moving parallel to our line of defense, crawling past the feet of various troopers.) The cover was good enough, and since I saw no further casualties it seemed reasonably safe to travel. What I was after was some more action. I had missed everything on Hastings and didn't want that to happen here. Watching one man die wasn't enough, not when there were fire-fights all around me.

A trooper came walking toward me, blood all over his chin and neck. He went up to three men under a tree and clapped one on the shoulder. The man he clapped was, it turned out, a medic, and as soon as the medic acknowledged him he pointed to his chest, indicating another wound, and only then did he let himself go—slumped down on the grass and closed his eyes. The rain washed some of the blood off him.

I crawled on, passing two more wounded and one dead, and finally reached our forwardmost position. I sat in the downpour against a tree and watched several Viet Marines having a big skirmish with somebody on the other side of the paddy. While I was waiting there who should show up but Capt. Barry Westervelt, the first American I'd seen in a long time. He said *Hi* in a casual way and sat down beside me. He had a radio on his back, and he said he was going to call in an air strike as soon as he pinpointed the enemy position.

To make a long story short, he discovered (just as he was about to give the go-ahead to the circling planes) that the force opposing us across the paddy was none other than —— Battalion, Viet Marines. He filled the air with horrible flaming Marine curses. I asked if it was —— Battalion, then, who had caused our dead & wounded.

'You got me,' he said. 'But I'll damn well find out.'

It's getting dark now. I only have one more thing to say. While Westervelt was straightening out the big mess, more mortar rounds landed nearby and I noticed that each explosion made him wince, even though he kept talking calmly into the handset. Seeing him wince made me realize that at no time during the day had I been frightened. Worse, the explosions and fire-fights seemed to make me almost somnolent. Why d'you suppose that is?

Early morning, the following day

Just now the first rays of sunlight touched the top leaves of the palm trees. Until then they were grey; now they're gleaming green. It's all happening in silence. There's a half-moon in the west. All around me in the fields the cooking fires are sending smoke up into the sky.

The troopers have an interesting sort of buddy-system. The basic unit is four men. One carries the pot, a blackened dented thing, the lid tied on with strips of palm leaf. Another carries the rice. Another gathers the supplementary rations during the march—wild berries, for example. He also does the marketing if they're near a town. The fourth gathers the wood at mealtime and builds the fire. When they halt for the night the pot carrier and the rice carrier build the communal hootch, a sort of elaborate lean-to. I'm not sure I have the arrangement exactly right, but you get the general idea.

Incidentally every time we pass through a hamlet the supplementary-rations guys start racing madly after chickens, the chickens all flustered and raucous, the on-looking troopers laughing. During the march I'm often surprised by these outraged little faces peering out from packs, and even though God put them here for one purpose and that is to be gromfed up whole by man, I still feel sorry for them.

Chicken-stealing is about the only way these troops can

get meat, but it's a lousy way to make friends with the populace. The other day when we stopped for lunch I saw a trooper chasing a goose, and an old lady chasing him in turn with a stick.

Speaking of chicken-stealers, what good does it do in the end to send three battalions into Viet Cong-controlled territory, even if they manage to find and kill a thousand VC? Whatever happens, the three battalions'll pack up and leave afterward. What are the civilians to think? And surely the VC will move back into the neighborhood. In what way has the Saigon government gained an advantage?

It's all very confusing.

We're not moving out till noon, I'm told.

I just moved out into the yard because the sun was crawling onto where I was, in front of the hut, and that sun is not to be sat in. I cut off three banana-tree leaves and spread them on the mud and was just sitting down when Capt. Westervelt showed up ('Opening up your office for the day?' he asked.) He sat down and we talked awhile, and as we were talking a plane flew over and a minute later I noticed a fluttering in the sky. It was leaflets, all hanging together like an enormous flight of doves. They were so high up it took ten minutes for them to touch to ground, and by then the breeze had carried them a long way north of us.

I asked Westervelt about yesterday's casualties.

'—— Battalion had seven dead, five wounded. I don't have the figures for the other battalion yet.'

'Was it an ambush?'

'You better believe it.'

He said we're opposing at least one North Viet battalion, probably two. He said one way they figure that is by the incoming mortar rounds: they were all 82 mm., and that's a battalion weapon.

Westervelt comes from Hazleton, Pennsylvania. Naturally we talked about the state for awhile. 'Ah yes, the mountains,' he said. 'On a clear day you can see half a mile.'

He said he hoped I hadn't written down any of the 'language' he used over the radio yesterday. On the spot I read him what I had written (*he filled the air with horrible flaming Marine curses*) and he fell over backward laughing. 'I was pretty sore,' he admitted. 'It could've been a disaster if I hadn't canceled the air strike in time.'

I've learned so far that he's married, has three kids and his wife expects a fourth in twenty-four days. He said the worst thing that's happened to him since he got here was stepping on a nail while fording a stream. He was laid up for several days. What made it so bad was that it was his very first day in the field. 'Very humiliating,' he said. 'It was a VC nail, of course.' He's a graduate of the Naval Academy and played end on the football team. He's tall and looks like a siege tower when he moves among the Vietnamese.

I forgot to write about our withdrawal yesterday.

Two of the dead were carried back across the paddies on bamboo beds taken from huts nearby. I watched one of these processions from a knoll, the bed vivid against the green shoots of the paddy, one trooper at each corner, the corpse on its back like a prime minister on his way to the pyre. It was a solemn and impressive sight.

The backtracking column was all straggled out, with

long empty spaces between clusters of men, and more than once I found myself alone. This was an unpleasant experience, knowing that one or two North Viet battalions were nearby.

During one stretch I found myself with four troopers carrying another body on a bed, plus a North Viet prisoner who was carrying the troopers' weapons. We were traveling beside a deep powerful stream. On the opposite bank was an aggressive-looking water-buffalo, prancing and snorting at us threateningly. The Vietnamese watched him as we moved along, obviously dreading the moment we'd have to cross over. (Me, I kept my eye on the prisoner with the weapons.) Fortunately the animal lost interest and dropped behind.

Getting the body across the stream was tough because the banks were steep and slippery and the current powerful. I gave them a hand. The poncho-covered body kept sliding as we climbed the banks. I noticed that every time it did, one of the men adjusted the poncho to keep the face covered. Once it came onto my shoulders and neck, and I learned to my surprise that I've lost my fear of corpses. In Korea they terrified me and I had nightmares about them, but maybe that's because I saw them only in the dark.

I can say the following things in Vietnamese now: rice, eat rice, salt, where's the well? drink water, I'm hungry, I'm a civilian, slow, fast, how much? give me, thank you, and a few other things. These are all phrases that'll be useful when I'm captured. And I can say *Choi oi* like the Vietnamese do when they're amazed or disgruntled. The first time I heard it was when Capt. Bizelle was buying a can of sweetened condensed milk in Quang Tri and thought the vendor was asking too much. I heard him mutter *Choi oi* to himself and later asked him what it meant. He had a hard time putting it into English. Finally he settled on 'Great Scott!'

During the past two days, First Sergeant (his name is Le Quang Huu) has been giving me all sorts of foraging tips. At first he thought I was a glutton because I was always hanging around while the troops ate, watching them and looking as if I wanted to dip my bill in various pots. It got sort of farcical. They began feeling sorry for me and offered little tidbits, like banana, holding them out encouragingly as if I were a chimpanzee. Anyway First Sergeant showed me how to boil cinnamontree leaf for a tasty drink (that's what *he* thinks anyway) and how to chew the bark (if you care for that sort of thing). He also showed me sugar cane. We'd been passing great fields of it and I didn't know what it was. It looks like corn stalks with a purple tint. You chop off a section and peel the hard bark and then chomp into it and suck the juice. One of life's great taste sensations. Some troopers carry sticks of it in their packs. Good for quick energy, in case you have to chase a chicken.

None of this has any food value, though, and that's what interests me. The best thing he showed me was *cu san*. You boil the roots and after it's cooked it looks like a banana but tastes like a sweet potato. It has a sort of wick running through it, so it also resembles a yellow candle. Very tasty.

(Did I mention that bamboo toothpicks are passed out after every meal? According to Terry Suggins you're supposed to cover your obscene mouth with your left hand while you pick with your right. I haven't observed anyone doing that except Terry Suggins. He probably read it in some Welcome To Veetnam pamphlet.)

* * *

Many trenches and tunnels in this neighborhood.

There's no question we landed in the headquarters area of a big North Vietnamese Army unit. Seven radios have been captured, two typewriters, a portable generator, a cache of money, and pen & ink maps of the whole area, showing not only every paddy but even the principal dikes. I've also seen a stack of notebooks, a bundle of miniature flags (yellow hammer & sickle on a red background) and, most interesting of all, hundreds of snapshots taken from captured packs, showing parents and girlfriends, graduating classes, and individuals in full North Vietnamese Army uniform.

This morning a patrol from —— Battalion found a rice cache, enough—it is estimated—to feed two battalions for a month. They also found a tunnel network.

No infantry action today but plenty of air strikes. Major Hanna, the senior advisor, had what he calls a turkey shoot. 'Beaucoup bodies,' he told me.

I crossed the paddies with Major Hanna and a bristling escort. Each paddy is on a different level, and rainwater pours continuously from one to another by means of sluiceways in the corners. Some of these have bamboo basket-traps wedged in them. On yesterday's crossing one of the troopers pulled one up for me to see. There were five minnows flashing around inside. He kept it as part of the daily foraging.

It was wonderful seeing Bizelle & Suggins again. They're certainly in their element. They both look happy. They sort of *gleam*. What they've been up to, they've been interrogating the peasants (in separate groups), and a story emerges: all yesterday and last night they were forced to carry dead & wounded North Viets up the mountain trails into the valley on the other side. Bizelle says the villagers' clothing is stained with blood. The villagers claimed that most of the enemy survivors were wearing bloody bandages. Hanna, Bizelle and Suggins are delighted with all this. 'It makes up for yesterday's bad luck,' said Hanna, referring to the troopers firing on their comrades.

Later he told Bizelle he wanted to see all the bodies he reported. Bizelle looked shamefaced and said he actually found only parts of bodies. 'But there's a long trail of blood,' he added. 'And you can see where they stacked them before taking them up the mountain.'

'You've no idea how many?'

'I didn't measure the density of the *gore*, no sir, if that's what you mean.'

Suggins said, 'There're hands and feet and hunks of meat all over, but the main housing groups are just gone.'

'Jake, I want some bodies. I must have an accurate body count. I told Colonel Khan we had beaucoup bodies. I shouldnt've done that.'

When we recrossed the paddy, Major Hanna took me over and showed me a dead North Viet, as if he thought my purpose in life was to view corpses. This one is down in a pit on its knees, its back up against the dirt, its face a swarming mask of flies, glittering green and gold in the sunshine.

It occurred to me that there's something queerly reasonable in all this, Hanna showing me a corpse. After all, he's been a Marine for many years and during this time his raison d'être (let's face it) has not been to build schools exactly, if you know what I mean. And so it's natural in a way that he'd want to show me the result of his life's work. It all makes perfect sense, as long as you acknowledge death as one of man's causes.

I heard Hanna make his final report to Khan over the radio, and he said an estimated fifty North Viets had been killed by air strikes. 'But I've only been able to confirm thirty-four so far,' he added. If I wanted to be nasty I'd ask him how he arrived at that figure, but he might take me around the corpse circuit again.

Next morning, 11 a.m.

I'm having a lousy day so far from itching. I slept with my boots off the other night and the mosquitoes really got me, and the bites have been aggravated by all the boot-rubbing in sweat. My feet and ankles are nothing but blotches of exquisitely itching bumps. It's my own fault; I was too lazy to rig my net.

I just counted thirty-seven separate bites.

The itching has begun to demoralize me. This morning I resorted to one of my Spillanes, which I keep for bad times: *Vengeance Is Mine*. A very satisfactory piece of writing.

I'm back with —— Battalion again.

This morning someone scanning the mountain through binoculars spotted two men (one with binoculars) looking down at us. This mountain is almost 3000 feet high, standing out sharp-edged and green against the morning's clear sky. The sun rose behind us, but we were still in shade. The mountain blazed in the early rays. Major Tran Buu Trung took my pad and drew me a picture of the mountain and made an X to show where the enemy were, then gave me his binoculars. I never did find them, but apparently they were perched in a tree overlooking a

trail. Capt. Bizelle pinpointed their location on his map
and called in the coordinates to the artillery several miles
to our rear. You could hear the faint boom in the distance,
and Bizelle said 'On the way.' The first round landed, and
he radioed a correction. To everyone's amazement and
delight (including mine, God forgive me) the second
round landed right on target. 'Beautiful,' he yelled over
the handset. 'Fire for effect!' Moments later the impact
area was smothered in puffs of grey smoke, the report
reaching our ears seconds later. It was fantastic shooting,
when you consider that the cannons were six miles away. I
asked Bizelle how many shells were fired altogether and he
said forty-eight. I asked how much each shell cost and he
said forty-two dollars. That figures out to $1008.00 per
gook.

Everyone was excited. Bizelle said I should've been here
yesterday when Hanna called in a barrage on some North
Viets who were trying to scale a rock face on the mountainside.

'It was so perfect,' said Bizelle, 'I damn near got an
erection.'

Another wild dawn this morning. It got me: the purple
sky, the black mountain emerging, the soft bird calls and
jungle scents. Then I saw the soldiers around me.

The itching is making me irritable. I walked to the well
this morning and shaved and on the way back got lost and
laughed at when I asked for directions, which I had to do
three times. The Vietnamese are big laughers, and a lot of
it is not what you'd call friendly. Anyway this morning I
lost my temper and turned on the one who was nearest and
threw back at him his inane laughter, which brought a
satisfying look of confusion on his face. My contribution

to the war effort would be to haul off and kick some of these teeny weeny asses around here.

So you see I'm as warlike as anyone.

You should see the elaborate shelters these troopers put up just for overnight. (This subject is usually dull when you hear it from some Scoutmaster, but something else in actual practice.)

I've adopted two comfort items. One is a pair of rubber shower-shoes, or sandals. Every Viet Marine carries a pair tied to his pack. When we halt for the day, he'll take off his boots, put on his sandals, and flap around in them till dark. Terry Suggins gave me his extra pair. The other item is a hand towel which Bizelle calls a sweat rag. You dip it in paddy water or stream as you pass by, and wrap it around your neck. That really cools you off. He gave me one.

Bizelle knows I'm interested in foraging. An hour ago he showed me how to fix banana palm for eating. He chopped off the top of a man-high tree and trimmed the outer bark off with his knife, leaving a shiny smooth green cylinder about five feet long and five inches in diameter. Then he peeled off layer after layer, each a clasping sheath, each less green and more yellow than the one before and each softer, until at last he got down to the edible core. This he sliced into a hundred wafers and gave to his cook to boil lightly. They were crunchy and delicately delicious. (I recall grandly ordering 'heart of palm' in a fancy restaurant in Newport Beach and thinking I was really living.) Anyway I picked up one of these wafers when it was still raw and took a close look. The innards were involuted in a fantastic way. I bent it, cracking it, and pulled out an end and unraveled it. It took a long time and when I was through I had a loose jumble of miniature ribbon in one hand. Bizelle told me he used to have a banana palm in his backyard in San Francisco but one night he had guests over and got a little smashed and chopped the tree down, because he wanted to show them how he learned to fix it when he was fighting the Huks. He said this was an embarrassing memory because the guests were civilian neighbors he had invited over to get acquainted. He had wanted to show them that Marines were as civilized as the next person. He said his wife was mortified.

Afterward he showed me a tea bush. It turns out they're all over the place, tough stiff-standing things with thorns. Troopers walk up and strip off three or four tender leaves near the top and simply drop them in boiling water.

I wish I could convey Jake Bizelle to you. I think you'd find him lovable despite his way of life, which is death. I feel bad that he has no kids, because he'd make a good father. (However I can visualize a teenage daughter being constantly embarrassed and saying *Oh daddy* all the time, because he's loud and friendly and completely uncool.) He talks in a gruff way, flopping his hands around in aimless gestures. He sweats a lot and is always puffing and wheezing and wiping his big pan with the rag. He tells me he and his wife are thinking of adopting a Vietnamese orphan.

Around 4 p.m. same day

Major Trung and his headquarters group are halted in and around a big bamboo house, open on three sides. Inside there's a Confucian altar and a lithograph of the

Buddha tacked to the wall. We're waiting for the rain to stop, I guess; or maybe we're stopped for the night.

Bizelle is presently prancing hugely around the courtyard in the downpour, wearing nothing but his loud blue shorts. He's lathering himself all over, or trying to, with a cake of soap. 'I never felt so good since I was a kid,' he just shouted. Here's a guy who really knows how to enjoy himself. I wish I was like that. Right now I'm sitting here on the porch cursing under my breath at the young Vietnamese lieutenant beside me who's singing—in a madly fruity voice—a medley of ancient American songs like *When I Grow Too Old To Dream* and *Silver Threads Among The Gold*. I wouldn't mind if he'd sing some Vietnamese songs, but oh no.

I think we need a Christian breakthrough here, but I'm just not up to it.

Bizelle just yelled, 'Where else can you have so much fun and get paid for it?' Several troopers have stripped and joined him in the rain. You should see the scars on some of these guys. Major Trung's cook must have ten holes in him. They've been fighting a long time, whereas our boys go home after twelve months.

All during the march this afternoon I kept smelling decomposing flesh, little clouds of stench that vanished a few steps onward. We passed two bodies that Suggins described as the worst he's ever seen, but nothing could've made me look at them. I've seen enough dead Vietnamese to last me forever.

A few minutes ago a peasant woman came to Trung with a complaint. It seems she was driving a cow along the trail when a couple of enemy soldiers stopped her and took the animal away. Trung and the woman and Bizelle squatted down over the map and she described where the incident took place. Trung and Bizelle think they've found it—near the junction of a cart track and a mountain trail. There are three huts a few hundred yards from the spot (all huts are marked on the map). At this moment they're being obliterated by artillery. The reasoning is that the huts are probably being used by the cattle-rustlers for shelter. I asked Bizelle if there might be civilians in the huts and he said the people of that hamlet have become refugees. I didn't want to embarrass him by asking how he knew that. It's too late now anyway.

It's true there are refugees following us. At least a hundred are camped down the trail. Right now Suggins is organizing a distribution of rice, donated by the troopers. The people have no rice of their own—the North Viets took it all. Bizelle pointed out that for a Buddhist to leave his family burial plot is no easy matter, since ancestors are worshipped as minor deities.

I asked him the basic question: why are these people leaving their homes and burial grounds to come out with us and start from scratch? He said some are scared of what the enemy'll do when he comes back, after we've left. Agents will put the finger on those who gave us information, and those who were hospitable to us. Others just don't like living under the Viet Cong. They are forced to carry supplies and dig tunnels, and most of their harvest is taken away. Bizelle says all three of our battalions have refugees behind them, with more coming in all the time.

The terrain changed radically during our march today. The paddies and the jungle patches ended and we crossed a span of fast-flowing brooks, many with waterfalls. The ground was like moss and there were clusters of black boulders along the way. Eventually we climbed up onto a breeze-swept plateau, and everyone grinned and opened his sweat-sopping shirt and got cooled off.

Half a mile later we saw a wooden sign stuck in the ground. There were two sentences, freshly painted, one in English and the other in Vietnamese: *140,000 Americans Were Lost in Korea—Don't Let This Outrage Reoccur.* Half a mile further on we saw a luxurious park of pines, isolated and fenced off, singing in the wind, and in the middle of it a concrete monument with a bas-relief star on three sides. A Viet Cong monument, Bizelle said. A little further on we saw the entrance to a hamlet—bamboo gates with a bamboo star on top. And a hundred yards beyond, another sinister sign: *240,000 French Expeditionary Corpses Were Routed.*

Just now three more refugees wandered in: a man carrying a small girl on his back, and a toothless old lady. The girl is wearing her father's conical hat, which is so big it nearly covers her shoulders, but I got a glimpse of the stunned blind look on her face and the bloody rag stuck to her forehead. The old lady is carrying a pole with their belongings wrapped in cloth hanging from both ends. I watched them stumble around the courtyard for a minute or two, apparently too confused and shy to ask for help, until finally one of the troopers got up and led them down to the refugee camp.

Next morning, same spot

It's strange waking up at night and seeing, all around you, slowly-moving stripes of yellow light and shadow from distant flares. The flares make a ghostly wailing sound when they go off. Bizelle tells me it's the canister-cover tumbling through the air.

Major Trung smokes a water pipe—one puff after every meal. I don't exactly know what a water pipe is, but he smokes one. He puts a pinch of tobacco in the shallow bowl of the little metal box, lights it, and sucks in one mouthful. It makes a gurgling sound.

He and I had a talk last night. He showed me a couple of souvenirs some trooper gave him. One was a miniature Viet Cong flag, the other a watercolor showing Lenin stepping out of a rowboat, shaking hands with Stalin on shore. After that he went out to the cane field and brought back a bundle of stalks. We chewed and sucked them while his one-eared bodyguard, Pvt. Quat, stood like a statue in the courtyard.

Trung doesn't speak much English, but I learned a couple of things. He came south—from a village near Hanoi—in 1954. He couldn't tell me specifically why but he gave me a general idea. He said the citizen of the North was too heavily taxed. 'You have good crop, they take,' he said. 'No good to try bigger crop. They take.' He also resented the way the government took small children away from their family and sent them to 'Communist school,' and they rarely saw their parents after that.

I asked him why the Viet Cong hated the Americans. He said: 'VC say American come Vietnam, take-take-take like French, no give. Say American have no *plan* for Vietnam people.'

As a Northerner, he spoke disparagingly of the people of the South. After several minutes of listening, I gathered that he believes the Northerner to be quick, sharp and energetic, whereas the Southerner is lethargic. He said the former always plans for the future, while the latter does not.

I couldn't resist asking him what he thought of my plan to get captured so I can see the 'other side' of the question and write about it. He took it in stride. He pulled out his box of matches and tapped it significantly. 'VC see one side.' He turned it around and tapped it again. 'You-me see two side. But VC, only one side. Comprenez?'

I asked him how long he thinks the war is going to last. '1980,' he said with a grin, his gold front teeth reflecting the glimmer of a distant flare.

Yesterday we saw some punji pits. When Bizelle pointed one out I nearly laughed, it was so bluntly vicious. (A punji pit has several poison-tipped stakes sticking up from the bottom of a camouflaged hole, usually set in the middle of a path.) What I couldn't understand was, aren't the local civilians far more likely to get caught in them than Saigon soldiers or Americans? Bizelle straightened me out on this. It seems the civilians are the ones who made the traps in the first place, so naturally they know where they are. 'Whenever we want to find out if a trail is punji-pitted or a road mined,' said Bizelle, 'all we do is send a few local types ahead of us. If they balk, we know why.'

More food notes:

I learned how to identify and cook *rau muong* yesterday, which is bean shoot. I also learned about *sim*, a wild berry that's all over this area. Next I want to learn about bamboo shoots, which we often have with our rice.

The other day we had something that intrigued me; it was a glob of soft white stuff, with a wonderful flavor.

There was no one around who could speak English well enough to tell me what it was. I had to find out—it was so exotic, so Oriental. Well, we had some again last night, and Bizelle identified it for me. Mashed potatoes.

Around noon

Luck of the Irish.

I'm writing this at Col. Khan's command-post, on an island of trees in the middle of a big paddy. For the past hour there's been a series of sharp fire-fights in the knolls to the south. The unit engaged is —— Battalion. The battle broke out only a few minutes after I left. I had abruptly decided that the show was over, the VC long gone, and I wanted to catch the re-supply helicopter out.

So much for my sense of timing. As a writer I guess it's lousy (after all, I did come here to see the Viet Marines in action) ; but for purposes of safety and survival it's terrific. Apparently —— Battalion walked into a large-scale ambush. There are 9 Viet Marines killed so far, and 46 wounded.

I can hear Bizelle's voice over the radio right now (he's talking with Major Hanna), so I know he's okay. No word about Terry Suggins.

I recall a couple of things in retrospect.

The two advisors never travel together when the battalion's on the march. This morning, as Suggins was about to separate himself from Bizelle, just as the column was starting out, I heard Bizelle tell him to stay away from the point, to stick close to Capt. Lam, one of the company commanders. Suggins said *Yes sir,* and walked down the cart-track and disappeared. It turned out that Lam's company was the one hit first and hardest.

The other thing is, telling Bizelle only this morning—as I was about to leave—how lucky I am. He had radioed Hanna that I was coming across the paddy, and asked him to watch for me. In their radio lingo they gave me a code name ('Bravo, this is Leatherneck Niner. Our friend Mickey Spillane would like to come over and see you. Over.') When it was time to go Bizelle told me to keep my head down for the next few days, because Friday the 13th is upcoming. I told him I never paid any attention to it, that I'm just naturally lucky.

'Lucky at poker?'

I lied and said I was.

'Next time we meet, I'll have to clean you out.'

We shook hands hurriedly and he ran to catch up with the column.

The distance to Khan's command-post was about a mile. I was three-quarters of the way across when the ambush was sprung. I couldn't believe it hardly. I kept looking back at the knolls and the isolated stunted trees, aghast. I couldn't see much except flashes and puffs of black smoke as mortar rounds landed. In one of the lulls I heard the sharp stinging notes of a bugle, blatting echoes across the paddy.

Suggins is safe, Hanna just told me.

Press center, Danang

I saw an air strike before I left. A hamlet nearby was obliterated because some North Viets were supposed to be sniping at us from there. I also saw (through binoculars) a line of enemy riflemen seven hundred yards across the paddy and the white smoke-puffs of their shooting, a cross-breeze carrying it off after each volley, the scene reminiscent of Civil War musketry in Brady photos. I saw several North Viets racing madly across another part of the paddy (as madly as you can race in ankle-high water) after the first plane's bombs sent nearby huts and palm trees high into the air. All this was strangely unfascinating, and I was surprised at my lack of interest.

This reminds me that when I was shaking hands with Major Hanna, just before I went to the landing zone, I blurted out: 'I'm sick of all this.' I was more startled than he was. I hadn't really meant to say that at all. I pondered it on the trip to Danang, because it mystified me, and figured out I had started to make some heavy-handed joke about living in the field getting to be too much for me; but it ended up a sort of *in vino veritas* thing.

I waited at the landing zone with three dead troopers. They were laid out on boards, side by side. One was wrapped in a poncho, the section over the head cinched tightly because (I was told) the head was a mess. The other two were wrapped in gay patterned cloth. The helicopter landed and the bodies were loaded aboard, their weapons and gear thrown in after them. I climbed in and we lifted off.

A feeling of exhilaration surged through me, knowing I was escaping the hard times below. I looked down at the island of trees dropping away and felt sorry for everyone down there. It was delightful to be up and out of the heat and trudgery, up in the cool blue sky.

The only space I could find in the cabin was at the feet of one of the corpses. Even though he was shrouded, I knew what his face looked like because I was there when they brought him in. He was killed by a 75 mm. recoilless rifle, I was told. When they carried him in, one leg was thrown up over the other, bending the wrong way, like the leg of a rag doll with all the stuffing gone. Now, in the helicopter, the leg was alongside the other. One shriveled yellow toe stuck out of a hole in his sock. I reached down and tweaked it a couple of times, just to prove that corpses don't scare me any more. The only thing else I noticed was the wind billowing out the cloth wrapped round the rest of him, making it like a big peasant skirt.

We landed at Tam Ky where the bodies were unloaded and laid out on the dusty ground. There've been very few sights I've seen over here that would make unusually interesting or powerful photographs, but I saw one then, as several women in *ao dai* and conical hats came over, some carrying babies, and hesitantly asked to see the faces of the dead. One of the Vietnamese medics undid enough of the cloth to expose the faces of the two who had faces, and the 'photograph' was when the women bent over, clutching each other fearfully and peering down to look.

I rode back to Danang in an Air Force helicopter, a fast one called a Huey, sitting right behind the pilot. It was great fun watching the fertile deserted land roll by below, the ocean off to the right. I saw Danang when we were still many miles to the southeast. I saw Monkey Mountain and Marble Mountain on either side of it, and several freighters anchored in the bay.

You'll never know how glad I was to get back to the press center with its iced pineapple juice and hot meals, cold showers, movies, drinks and most of all mail . . .

This is a very pleasant spot here, the press center. In the morning you can see fishermen rowing by, two to a boat, standing up with one oar like Venetian gondolamen.

Sometimes at night big ships glide past while the outdoor movie is on and sometimes a crane barge and tugs with yellow lights. In the distance you can often see a few orange-colored flares, hanging like chandeliers over the plain.

The official score so far for Operation Lien Ket 52 is 341 North Vietnamese dead, 47 captured. Friendly casualties are described as moderate. There were 19 dead Viet Marines when I left. The most interesting figure, though, is the estimated 700 refugees following Col. Khan's headquarters group.

I had a bad night last night. My mind was all a jumble and I can't say for sure what was bothering me, but I have a free-association: this morning when I came back from breakfast the sheet on my bed was pulled up around the pillow, stretching it like a shroud around a corpse, and when I saw it I jumped a foot in the air. My heart didn't stop pounding for five minutes.

August 23rd, press center

The other day I went into a little café and ordered *caphe sua da*, which is iced coffee with sweetened condensed milk. (Capt. Bizelle had that in Tam Ky.) Later I ordered a glass of papaya juice. It was served with a saucer of shaved ice and a long spoon. You're supposed to dump the ice little by little into the glass—at least that's what I saw one of the other customers do. This café was typical of the cafés of Danang and looks more like somebody's back kitchen than anything else. After I paid up and left, I walked down the street and found a shop where they repair eyeglasses. Mine had been bent out of shape on Lien Ket 52. The guy in the shop held them over a pan of glowing charcoal to soften them, then straightened them. After that I bought some writing paper in an odds & ends shop. (All shops, by the way, are open to the street; you get the impession of a series of square caves.) Then I bargained with a vendor over a can of *sua*. She wouldn't part with it for less than sixty piastres, so I said *Choi oi!* and marched off. Last of all I got a haircut in a shed by the road with two stools and one barber.

All this may sound simple but it wasn't. It's a nervous thing launching yourself alone in a strange city, ignorant of the language and customs. What made it hardest for me was the curious stares. A small crowd followed me wherever I went, mainly kids. The whole time I was getting my haircut the front of the shed was clogged with onlookers. And try sitting in a café enjoying a cold drink, or trying to, while the proprietor and his wife and three kids plus four customers watch your every move, and when you do something clumsy, like knocking over your stool as you rise, they all go skyhigh in laughter. And it's not hard to be clumsy in one of these cafés, either: the stools and tables are made for midgets. Even the Vietnamese are too big for them.

Anyway I felt ridiculously brave and adventurous doing all these ordinary things, especially since there were no other Americans around (Danang is off-limits to the military).

Did I mention that the national footgear is shower-clogs? (like the kind Terry Suggins gave me). The only trouble with them is, they flap around absurdly until you get used to them, and when you walk in the dust beside the road they'll scoop up a big flop of it and flip it in a grey cloud which comes down all around your head and shoulders. That is a spectacle and encourages raucous laughter among the natives. It's a nice piece of business, though—if you happen to be a clown.

But I have to admit I feel good about my intrepid solo into downtown Danang.

August 30th, press center

The other day, desperate for something to write about, I went along on an air-delivery mission and watched five Marine parachutists jump out the rear of a C-130 a thousand feet up and float down within the perimeter of the Special Forces camp at Tra Bong. On the second pass, rolls of concertina wire were pushed out. It was the Marines' job to collect the parachutes off the rolls and bring

them back to Air Delivery at the Danang airstrip. About
the only thing that impressed me was the sudden violence
of the jump. The men didn't go one at a time like they do
in the movies, but all at once. They stood crouched at the
lip of the ramp watching the jumpmaster over their
shoulders, and when he gave the signal they simply turned
their helmeted heads and leaped as one. You never saw
such a crazy thing.

When we got back to Danang I asked Gunny Olienyk if
I could make the next jump with them. It looked easy and
I told him so. He smiled tolerantly and said there was a lot
to it. He took me over to a long shed to check me out. First
he got me a can of beer and showed me a rare collection of
Playboy centerfolds, covering one long wall, starting with
the first issue and ending with the last. He led me solemnly
from picture to picture as if we were doing the stations of
the cross. After that he spent a half hour showing me how
to get into the harness, how to help your assistant strap
you up, how to hook up and jump, how to control your
fall by pulling on the straps, how to land and how to
gather up your shroud. He promised to call me the next
time an air delivery was on, and that's one of the reasons
I've been hanging around the press center so long. My
master plan is this: once I've made a jump with Air
Delivery I'll be 'jump qualified' in an informal sense and
maybe I'll be able to talk myself into making jumps with
other, more interesting outfits.

Actually there's only one other Marine outfit that
jumps and that's Force Recon, a small, elite reconnaissance team. That's my goal.

When I heard nothing from Olienyk for several days I
went out to see him. It turned out he'd gotten cold feet.
'You'll have to get permission from higher up.' I asked

him how high. 'General Robertshaw himself,' he said. Robertshaw commands the 1st Marine Air Wing, of which Air Delivery is a part. I already have an appointment to see him tomorrow.

. . . I happened to hear of an outpost called Nui Tron on an isolated mountaintop, manned by Marines and Montagnards. I flew down to Chu Lai in a DC-3 and got a helicopter lift to Quang Ngai; but there was nothing going out to Nui Tron for awhile, and rather than wait around for hours I came back here. The reason was not so much impatience as a bad cold.

The following morning I was lying on my rack reading *The Long Wait*, one of the master's greatest works, when who should come banging in through the double-doors but Humphrey Flayhav. There were three other corpsmen with him. They were smashed, all four of them, even though it was eleven in the morning. You can imagine how sociable I was, what with my cold and the interrupting of my greatest pastime. The fact that they were boisterous and frolicsome didn't help any either. Anyway I got up and took them over to the barroom and grudgingly bought them a round, hoping they'd buzz off after that. I had one myself, hoping it'd help unleash some of my devastating personal charm. For about fifteen minutes I sat sulking as they rioted beside me, but after a second drink I took a look around and everything was different. I made a discovery: Doc Flayhav is neither horsefaced nor humorless. (Never judge a man by how much you dislike him.) Then one of the other corpsmen, Fred O'Neill of Gary, Indiana, asked me for my autograph for his daughter Annie and that cheered me up and I began to forgive them for being alive.

O'Neill is a paunchy, tired-looking guy with a sagging sour face who talks quietly out of the side of his mouth. He was a corpsman with the First Marine Division in Korea and was wounded. At first I didn't like him too much because I thought he must be cynical, with a puss like that; but when we started talking I saw I was wrong. Anyway he and the other two corpsmen make up a Medcap team, and he invited me to come along on one of their outings the following day.

Medcap is short for medical civic action program and although it's an important and maybe even significant part of U.S. policy here, it's hard to write interestingly about. Essentially it is American medics dispensing medical aid to villagers—the first step toward gaining the friendship of a Viet Cong-controlled or a neutral hamlet. The next day the four of us rode out to a jumble of pasteboard shacks on a plain of glaring white sand overlooking the ocean north of Danang. This was Medcap's first visit to that hamlet. They had no Marine escort; just the three corpsmen and an unarmed driver. Fred O'Neill said 'Bring along a bodyguard and you're asking for trouble. Your average fire-team of grunts'll just antagonize the villagers. You know how grunts are around gooks.' So far the team has had no trouble, even though they've been going into 'unsecured' areas for some time.

The first move was to find the hamlet chief. That was easy since one of the team, Ken Boggs II (Darlington, South Carolina), speaks Vietnamese. The chief, an old Ho-bearded gent, sent word around that anyone under the weather should come to his house and the American *bac si* would fix 'em up. The corpsmen unloaded a foot-locker full of supplies from the rear of the ambulance and carried it inside. Then everyone stood around nervously

puffing on cigarets, waiting for the first patient to show
up. O'Neill peered out at the neighboring shacks and said
'How many VC d'ya suppose're sitting in the back rooms
waiting for us to blow?'

After a few minutes a scarecrow of a lady came up
carrying a baby with sores all over the top of its head. One
of the corpsmen, M. J. Dolmajian of Fresno, California,
took the baby very casually and went to work washing its
head with soap & water. Soon there was a crowd of people
outside, waiting to see the corpsmen. You never saw a
more pitiable bunch in your life—cripples and harelips
and kids with cataracts. Most of them, though, just had
bad coughs or festering sores. And yet, being Vietnamese,
the crowd was cheerful, the kids full of mischief. It was
wonderful the way the corpsmen waded into them, working quickly and a bit roughly, swabbing out pus-filled
eyes, squirting worm- and cough-medicine into reluc-
tantly opened mouths, disinfecting all manner of sores.
Some of the patients had wide rings of yellow, blue and
white paint around their wrists and ankles. 'Chinese medicine,' Dolmajian called it. 'In other words the local witch
doctor.'

'Dangerous stuff,' said O'Neill, 'because sometimes he'll
rub buffalo dung into open sores.'

He said the most frustrating thing is the inability of
the team to teach mothers to keep their kids clean. All
three men spent a lot of time washing crud off babies'
sore-studded heads and passing out mini-bars of soap
(donated by Holiday Inn) while Ken Boggs explained
how they're to be used. It seems that the sores are caused
by scratching mosquito bites, and because the skin's so
dirty infection follows.

The men passed out candy vitamins too. Outside in the

glaring sun the Marine driver, Pfc. Al Sherman (Tucson, Arizona) was passing out molasses candy and being mobbed in such a frenzied way I really felt sorry for him.

By this time the men had taken on distinct personalities. Stormy Dolmajian, as everyone calls him, is very sure of himself and it goes good on him. He's a rugged-looking fellow, full of nervous energy, with a bristle of black hair and a breezy American manner that made the patients relax under his hands. He chewed gum and popped it loudly from time to time. Both he and O'Neill have been in the Navy a long time and plan to stay in. Boggs is getting out in a couple of months, and plans to go back to the University of South Carolina and study law. He's a virginal-looking fellow and a laugher. He laughs at everything and anything, and yet it's not inane. It's the laugh of a friendly monster. He laughed all the way through sick call and the villagers seemed to like him and occasionally laughed with him. I'm sure I've mentioned before all the laughing and giggling and general tee-heeing that goes on among the Vietnamese. Well, Boggs and they got along very well. (Fred O'Neill just glowered sourly and worked on, and the patients were a little afraid of him.)

It was a pleasure to hear Boggs speak Vietnamese. He does it with the flair you need to make yourself understood. Vietnamese is like French in that you have to ham it up unashamed, otherwise you sound ridiculous. (That's what Terry Suggins told me.) You also have to sing it, since words take on different meanings according to inflection. Suggins wrote down an example in my notebook: the word *ma* can mean either appearance or rub or mother or tomb or ghost, depending on how you do it.

Pretty soon there were no more patients and we took

off. The team will return in a week, and O'Neill said the second visit is the worst because if the hamlet is Viet Cong-controlled there'll be trouble.

An unusual thing happened on the way back. We were barreling down Route 1 and saw a group of people up ahead, just off the road. We stopped. The group was gathered around two people stretched out on the ground, and I thought *Ahah! more corpses! At last I have something to write about!* But they turned out to be alive: two women laborers who'd been working in a gravel pit. There had been a cave-in of some kind. One woman had a broken leg, the other a fractured skull. You could clearly see the dent in her forehead, with a cut beside it down to the bone. Her eyes were open but she was delirious.

It started to rain. There happened to be a Marine sentry-box just down the road, and while Boggs borrowed the sentry's rifle to use as a splint, O'Neill used the phone to summon a Medevac helicopter. I asked Dolmajian if the lady was dying. 'Could be,' he said.

I went over and watched her. Her black pajama top was open and you could see her little padded bra all stained with blood. She had a plain peasant face, the face of Asia—the face you've seen in newsphotos of famine, flood and flight.

Coincidentally a Navy doctor showed up and after taking a look at the woman ran over and grabbed the phone from O'Neill: 'If we don't get this woman to a hospital right away, she's had it.' Just then a literal bolt of lightning struck the ground with a terrific crack a few hundred yards away, and somehow the charge reached the phone in the doctor's hand; he threw it down violently and started rubbing his arm. The Vietnamese who saw it burst into gales of giggling laughter, pointing at him.

I just can't get used to this trait of theirs, this cruel laughter at others' mistakes and misfortunes. It makes me want to bomb them back to the Stone Age.

Eventually the helicopter came and took the woman away, and we drove the other to the hospital in Danang.

The following morning, which was yesterday, I accompanied the same team to a Catholic orphanage a few miles west of Danang. This is a regular weekly stop. The orphanage is attached to a big church that rears up out of the jungle like some temple in a Kipling tale, its surfaces filmed over with mossy green slime. Ken Boggs II introduced me to four nuns, childlike creatures in white who hid their faces and giggled (what else?) while Boggs did his jolly monster laugh.

The team held sick call then, and I noticed how good-looking the kids were. Most of them were racial mixtures, which probably has a lot to do with it. Even dour Fred O'Neill halfway acknowledged their looks, when he pointed to one grinning elf and said 'There's always gotta be an ugly one in the crowd, though.'

Just as we were ready to leave—me with no material whatever (what can I write about *orphans?*)—an imposing middle-aged nun showed up and O'Neill told me out of the corner of his mouth that she was 'the honcho nun.' This non-giggler smiled at me and took my hand and, in French, invited us all up onto the porch for a glass of 'citron,' which turned out to be some kind of -ade. The thing that impressed me most was the way she held onto my hand as we walked up the steps—and I remembered Terry Suggins saying that Vietnamese are great people-touchers.

We all sat around a low table on plastic chairs and

sipped our -ade, O'Neill scowling sourly, Dolmajian pop-
ping his gum and Boggs monster-laughing as the nun
beamed. It was a grand cultural-ethnical event. Nobody
said a word, which I liked a lot.

Then the nun asked Boggs to come look at a certain
bedridden girl and I went along with them, keeping tight
control of my humberts. We entered a cool dark dormi-
tory and there, all by herself, was Heartstrings Hannah,
the orphan of your mooniest dreams. She looked to be
about nine years old, and was stretched out on her sleeping platform in blue pajamas. She stared at us. She was
not cute. She didn't smile or do any of the conventionally
winning things that launch GI's on furious orphanage-
building campaigns. All she was was beautiful, in a common plain Oriental way you'd never notice unless you
looked twice. The honcho nun told Boggs she had lost her
appetite and just wanted to lie around and do nothing.
Boggs brought Fred O'Neill in and he decided she ought
to go to the hospital. The nun said okay. She and her little
nunlets got the girl dressed up in a rumpled cotton dress
and shoes that were too big for her, naturally, and combed
her long black hair.

On the trip to the hospital she rode in back with us,
sitting prim and blankfaced under Dolmajian's protective
non-sentimental arm (the road was rough and we banged
around a lot). O'Neill reached over and felt her arm and
said 'One thing for sure. She don't get enough chow.' I
stared at her fantastic profile and thought about how
having no parents is possibly the world's biggest drag.

I just got back from seeing the Air Wing chief of staff,
Col. Doyle, about the parachute jump. He said he'd let me
know. At least he didn't say no outright, as I expected.

Just returned from another project, brief but fairly juicy. I visited one of the 'combined action' companies (CAC 121) in which a squad of Marines plus a corpsman live isolated in a Vietnamese village. Their mission is to make friends with the villagers and help them solve their most pressing community problems.

CAC 121 is commanded by Cpl. Fredrick Sims of Fairbanks, Alaska. He and his eleven men live in three sheds on the outskirts of Hoai Duc, a few miles northwest of Danang. The feeling hit me right away that the unit's morale was poor, and I soon found out why. First of all the parent unit, —— Battalion of the Third Marines, is leaving in a few days for Okinawa for rest and refitting; but the men of CAC 121 have to stay behind. Second, the villagers have stolen a lot of their personal gear. Only the night before, a transoceanic radio had been taken. So the Marines weren't feeling awfully tender toward their yellow brothers. I got the impression they were guarding their sheds more than anything else.

CAC 121 has been in Hoai Duc for several weeks. The villagers have accepted their material help, and a few come to sick-call every morning, but there's no real communication between the two groups. The situation is aggravated by the Marines being isolated and vulnerable to Viet Cong attack. (There have been many attacks on other CAC's. On the jeep-ride out to Hoai Duc a village was pointed out to me where a Combined Action Company —the Marine part of it—had recently been driven out.

There was a definite lack of hospitality toward me when I arrived; the men were too busy brooding. Cpl. Sims was a bit more accessible. Right away I found out (souvenirs on the wall) he's a nut on Hong Kong, and got him going on that. Before I knew it I had a can of beer in my hand and he was telling me his dream of glory, which is to open up a liquor store there. He took out his wallet and showed me pictures of the Chinese dragon-lady with whom he spent his recent R & R. The two are seated at a table in some clip joint, him in his short-sleeve Hawaiian shirt, looking like an earnest schoolboy, she in *cheong sam*, old enough to be his mother and big enough to carry him over the threshold, if it comes to that. 'She's crazy bout me,' he said, googling. He told me she's just waiting for him to return. He's planning to marry her. He's twenty-two years old and doesn't know nothing.

Later I met Sgt. Huynh Chi Ngoi of the South Vietnamese Army, CAC 121's interpreter. He took me on a tour of the village. He showed me the Catholic church and the Chieu Hoi center. (Chieu Hoi means open arms; this is a big government program inviting the Viet Cong to defect.) We walked through the market, a large open courtyard crowded with women in rag-turbans squatting on the ground, their wares before them. Ngoi bought me a rice tortilla. After that he took me to the Buddhist temple beside the river and introduced me to the head monk, who showed us around inside. It was almost bare in there, no chairs or benches, just a couple of tom-toms and Chinese scrolls on the walls. On the altar were hand-tinted photos of monks who immolated themselves in Saigon and Hue. In the place of honor, below the statue of Buddha, was a photo of the Venerable Quang Duc's heart. After that Ngoi and I walked along the path beside the river and he showed me some saucer-boats drying in the sun. They were made of woven bamboo, coated with sap. Down below us, in the middle of the river, two families were collecting sand, dumping it in canoes tethered to the bank. Ngoi said this is the principal occupation of the villagers; the sand is used for cement. Last he showed me the hospital on the hill. It was more like a small-town jail than a hospital. Inside, he pulled back some curtains and showed me five patients lying on boards in their clothes. He also showed me a table where women have their babies. He and Cpl. Sims saw a baby born the other day. Ngoi got sick. 'Very bad squeamish,' he explained.

When we got back, Sims showed me two current CAC 121 projects. One is a rice storehouse next to the sheds, guarded by the Marines and therefore safe from Viet Cong taxation. The other is a dispensary where the corpsman holds sick-call every morning. The material for both buildings was supplied by the Marines. There are other projects I never got a chance to see: the new paint job on the schoolhouse, the new cement lining in a couple of wells. All this is nice but it's hard to see what good it'll do in the long run. The villagers take what we give them, *but*—in what way do our presents gain their allegiance for the Saigon government? They know the Americans are going to leave someday, just as the French did. The Viet Cong will return to Hoai Duc, and they will never leave.

Late in the afternoon Sims got a message by radio that a Marine company three miles away needed an interpreter, on the double. The outfit was —— Company of —— Battalion. Sims, Ngoi and I drove over there, following a cart-track most of the way. The track abruptly plunged into a dry creek bed and then climbed up to the horizon. Bunkers of —— Company dotted this upgrade. There were many Marines there, staring down at a crowd of peasants. In the center of the crowd was a straw mat, and sticking out from under were two charred feet, the toes curled. Also sticking out was a bamboo pole, to which the body was tied and by which it had been carried to the spot.

The company commander came down the slope and explained the situation to us. The villagers were claiming that the man, a civilian, had been killed by a —— Company patrol and thrown into a fire—to destroy the evidence.

The patrol leader, a red-faced corporal with bad teeth, was called over and ordered to tell Ngoi what had happened, so Ngoi could tell the villagers.

'Well, we spotted this VCS'—Viet Cong Suspect— 'running behind a hut and opened up on him. The hut caught fire from one of our tracers. The VCS was still alive when we got up to him and we finished him off.'

A couple of minutes later I sidled up to this corporal and asked what he'd meant by finished him off. He didn't know I was anything other than a Marine (I was dressed like one) and answered unhesitatingly: 'The corpsman shot him in the side of the head.'

Just then the new widow showed up carrying a dirty little baby and followed by two small kids in floppy hats. One of the Vietnamese bystanders raised the mat so the woman could see the remains. She started making hoarse noises in her throat and sat down a few yards away, with her wretched, mosquito-ravaged baby gumming away on her. The other two children leaned against her and looked around bewildered, fingers in mouth.

At first glance it was like a statue of a Negro boxer tipped on its back—the clenched hands in the defensive position, one foot advanced. On closer inspection you saw that the flesh was like well-done charcoal steak. The face had been burned away entirely. In the right temple you could see a small clean round hole, and a much larger ragged pit on the other side where the bullet came out.

A dignified white-robed elder came shuffling up, holding an umbrella to shade himself from the sun. He stood looking down at the body for a long time. The widow was keening to herself.

Ngoi began asking the villagers questions. Some said they had seen the murder, and had pulled the body out of the fire after the Marines left. In all his questioning and walking about, Ngoi never looked at the corpse, and his face was grey. Very bad squeamish, I imagine.

Lt. Harold McNulty (Wilkes-Barre, Pennsylvania) showed up. He was the battalion 'civic-action officer,' also the legal-affairs officer and paymaster. He commented to me that the body was probably a Viet Cong plant: 'Every time some old cadaver turns up, the VC tell the villagers the Marines did it, and encourages 'em to soak us for as much as they can.'

I didn't know what to think.

I noticed Ngoi breaking into stiff tight-lipped grimaces, like an actor in a samurai film. At the time I thought it was because he was squeamed by the body. I learned later it was something else.

After some questioning of the patrol members it came to light that there were possibly *two* burning huts, widely separated, and the patrol had been involved with only one, and the man *they* shot was shot in the chest, and therefore the black horror at our feet was some other fellow. Or something like that. It was too confusing to keep straight. Who then was this man? Someone suggested he was struck by a stray bullet.

'It's entirely possible,' said McNulty earnestly.

He told Ngoi to tell the widow the Marines were deeply sorry and there would be an investigation and she would receive monetary compensation.

The widow was chanting loudly now. Ngoi walked over and tried to break in. One of her toddlers was pressing up against her, wanting to have his mosquito bites scratched. Just then the dead man's mother showed up. She pushed her way through the crowd, a harried old hag, and saw the remains. She let out a shriek, and fell down and began beating the dust with the palms of her hands, moaning and wailing. The widow came over and sat down beside her, and they moaned and wailed like the 'tragic duet' in some opera. The Marines couldn't help laughing.

Then the old lady fainted dead away. The villagers tried to bring her around. One woman cradled her head in her lap and spat betel-nut juice in her mouth. Betel-nut is a mild narcotic used by most Vietnamese peasant women. Over the years it blackens the user's teeth and turns the lips bright red. You see splotches of spat betel-nut juice beside the roads and streets and trails of Vietnam, and it looks exactly like blood.

Finally we drove over to the district headquarters. McNulty took me inside to meet the district chief, a 1st Lieutenant in the South Vietnamese Army. We sat in his office and drank tea. McNulty told him about the charred body and asked him if he'd help with the investigation. The district chief said he would. Later McNulty told me the man was a 'VC-hater.' McNulty was present recently when five Viet Cong prisoners were brought before him. He ordered them shot. McNulty protested. The man explained that if he sent them to the prison compound in Danang they'd be detained a few months, given an indoctrination course showing them the evils of Communism and the wonderfulness of capitalism, and released. To save them from that he shot them.

That night Ngoi and I were invited to dinner at the house of the local bicycle salesman-repairman. We had rice and *nuoc mam* and papaya salad and beer. Ngoi didn't say a word through the whole meal.

There was an 'ambush' scheduled for later that night. The Marines had talked a few citizens into sitting near one of the village gates. Cpl. Sims explained that this was the first step in forming a 'home guard.' They gathered in the marketplace at 8:30. There I met Zombie, a shopkeeper who'd been wounded by a mine and had just returned from the hospital. I met Hawkeye, whose right eye is permanently open because his eyelid and part of his brow were blown away. I met Frenchy, whose father was a Legionnaire. I met 'Sergeant Lung,' who coughed every few seconds and is dying of tuberculosis.

The ambush never came off. The citizens simply faded away into the night. Sims was calm about it. 'That's the third time it's happened,' he sighed.

I went back to the sheds and started drinking beer (which I bought from Sims). There were cases of it stacked against the wall. I had noticed he polished off at least ten cans since I arrived. ('It's a life-saver,' he told me. 'It's the only thing I really enjoy out here.') I decided to drink myself to sleep. There was nothing else to do.

Later on, Sims got a message that a tank unit was under attack a couple of miles away and a platoon of reinforcements would be passing through Hoai Duc in a few minutes. He was told to send a couple of his men to meet them at the bridge and guide them out to the position. I went along. It turned out that no reinforcements were needed. The platoon (from Kilo Company, ——— Battalion) was used instead as a blocking force, strung out across a rice paddy, waiting for the withdrawing Viet Cong unit to blunder into them. We lay there till dawn, and I think there were times when all forty Marines were sound asleep; the paddy droned and buzzed with snoring. The Viet Cong, if they came near at all, must've had a good laugh.

There was one small bit of action around 4 a.m. A machine-gunner on our right flank—where there was a tiny hamlet—fired a short burst. I assumed it was a nervous Marine shooting at shadows; but word was passed that a Viet Cong Suspect had been killed. Strange that such a tremendous event as a man's death could occur so close by and we could all go numbly back to sleep. You become callous to violent death as to anything else, I guess.

Later that morning I asked Sgt. Ngoi for his version of the charred-body episode. He surprised me. He put on that terrible samurai face again and, speaking softly, told me the villager's story was true and the Marines had lied to cover up a murder. He didn't try to hide his bitterness and anger.

'Marines all the time shoot VCS first, ask question later. But many time dead fella only farmer!'

I found Cpl. Sims and told him I wanted to go over to ——— Company and talk to the patrol members (particularly the corpsman who 'finished him off') and he said okay. Ngoi was already scheduled to go there that morning and explain all the 'solidium' arrangements to the widow. 'Solidium' is a word McNulty kept using to refer to the compensation awarded the widow. Just as we were about to leave, Sims got a message from battalion headquarters. It seemed that Lt. Col. Loessner had found out I was present during the incident, and was furious at Sims for having taken me along in the first place. He told him not to let me out of his sight, and that I was not to be allowed to visit —— Company.

McNulty showed up half an hour later, his pug Irish face full of concern. I was all packed up and ready to leave: I wanted to get back to the press center and write this up. I was tired of the unfriendliness of the CAC 121 guys and disappointed at the insignificant progress they'd made with the villagers. I also felt slightly oppressed, what with the battalion commander keeping tabs on me.

McNulty drove me to the —— Battalion headquarters, where I had a talk with Col. Loessner. The lieutenant had begged me to see him, to chat awhile and let him know I wasn't going to complain to Westmoreland or anything. He advised me not to mention the charred-body incident at all. I had no such intention—what good would it've done?

Loessner was sitting alone in his hootch, a stocky man in a tee-shirt, chewing balefully on a cold cigar butt. He looked mean as hell, and challenging. McNulty nervously introduced me as a former Marine. The colonel relaxed broadly and offered me a cigar. We talked awhile—or rather he talked and I listened. He said two things that impressed me. First, he wanted to make sure I understood that his three CAC's were *military* units. 'I use them as outposts,' he said. He scoffed at the whole civic-action concept. To him the CAC's are tactical units tactically deployed. The other thing that impressed me was his opinion on how to win the war: invade the North and take over. Without the support of Hanoi, he said, the Viet Cong would wither away. He's forty-three and doesn't know nothing.

I've been sitting here trying to think of some kind of wrap-up comment, but what can I say? The widow was given the equivalent of 65 dollars, a couple of bags of rice, a box of canned goods, and a can opener. She was also promised money to build her husband's tomb. His name, in case you're interested, was Nguyen Dzu.

That one incident undid whatever good the CAC's have accomplished, and will keep it undone for a long time to come.

I'm beginning to wonder what good the Marines have accomplished in Vietnam. Certainly they have killed and maimed a good many Viet Cong and North Viet soldiers; but soldiers are not the real threat. To defeat the other side they must kill the people.

September 11th, press center

Did I tell you I've been trying to visit the Arvin prison compound in Danang? (Arvin is short for Army of the Republic of South Vietnam.) It seems that writers and news people aren't allowed to interview prisoners—but I'm working on a couple of angles.

The other day I met a civilian official named Mortimer J. Lessy (Boston, Mass.) who is the coordinator for the Chieu Hoi program in this area. This is the 'open arms' policy started by Diem in 1963, aimed at getting Viet Cong to turn themselves in, in return for a food & clothing allowance, resettlement of their family in a New Life hamlet and other benefits.

Mr. Lessy invited me to his house for dinner. He lives in a small stucco house in the Catholic part of town, near the bay where the big ships are anchored. Through his front window we watched them riding the tide, lights blazing. Lessy shares his house with Mr. Williams, a policeman from Bloomington, Indiana, who trains local cops. His wife and kids are in Taipei on the island of Taiwan. I asked him why they were so far away instead of in, say, Bangkok. He said Bangkok is too expensive now that it's an R & R center for American troops. He said he had wanted to settle his family in Manila but, being a cop, naturally checked up on the crime rate and found it to be high. What finally decided him was hearing about a good school for American kids in Taipei. Williams drank a can of beer with us but had to leave after that, so I didn't get to ask him about his work.

Lessy was quiet and reserved. He said his greatest pleasure was meeting people from other cultures—and that was the only personal remark he offered. Our food was served by his manservant, Nguyen Tran Thinh, a former Viet Cong sergeant. After the meal, Lessy invited me to accompany him on a 'County Fair' the following morning.

Here's how a County Fair works. Long before dawn a company of Marines surrounds a Viet Cong-controlled hamlet. At dawn a company of Arvins moves into the hamlet and gathers all the civilians in one spot. Then the hamlet is searched. Anyone found is captured or killed. Tunnels and caves are blown up. The civilians are fed C rations, given medical attention and lectured by the ralliers. (A rallier is an ex-VC now working in the Chieu Hoi program.) The ralliers tell the civilians about the good work the Saigon government is doing on their behalf, and give them reasons why they should quit supporting the National Liberation Front. Whenever possible, one of the ralliers is a former resident of the target hamlet—and is incidentally expected to expose anyone he knows to be Viet Cong.

Mr. Thinh was to be one of tomorrow's ralliers. He grew up in the target hamlet, Chau Son.

Lessy picked me up early the next morning and we started out for Hill 55, headquarters of the Ninth Marines, a few miles southwest of Danang. A fantastic thing happened en route. We were traveling in two jeeps, Lessy and me in one, the three ralliers behind us. We came to a one-way bridge and were let through, while a Marine convoy waited on the other side. A mile or so downroad Lessy noticed that the ralliers' jeep was not following us. We stopped and waited and finally it came along—with an extra passenger—and we continued on to Hill 55. The new passenger was a young peasant woman and it turned out—get this—that she was a Viet Cong agent one of the ralliers had recognized and put the finger on. She had been sitting on the fender of one of the trucks in the convoy. They found messages on her from a village cadre (political leader) to several officials in Danang.

Of course there was a good deal of guffawing about this at Ninth Marines headquarters, especially that she had hitched a ride on a Marine truck. I tried kidding a lieutenant about it but he got stuffy; the others on the hill thought it was a laff riot though. While we were standing there, the regimental commander came out of his bunker and told the lieutenant to take the woman down to the prisoner-collection point. The lieutenant began rounding up the three ralliers too, until Lessy straightened him out. By then everyone had fallen down laughing.

I was surprised to learn that Chau Son was less than a mile away. You could see it clearly from 55, one of those islands of trees and huts in the middle of a rice paddy. It impressed me to see a Viet Cong hamlet right there under the guns of a Marine regimental headquarters. It was sort of absurd.

The County Fair was already well under way. You could hear occasional bursts of fire from Chau Son and explosions as tunnels were blasted. The five of us were put aboard a tracked vehicle called an Otter. Five minutes later we were crunching across the paddy, and I couldn't help feeling that this alone was ruining whatever friend-making progress the County Fair had accomplished so far. (Some farmer is going to have to put in a lot of time & effort to rebuild the dikes we flattened.)

Naturally the first thing I saw when I climbed out was a corpse. Lessy and I were taken to it immediately, as if this was the sole purpose of our visit. It was lying on its back at the edge of the hamlet, beside a tree-line. On the other side of the trees a river flowed placidly. This man had tried to sneak out of the hamlet, we were told, just as the Arvins moved in. He had obviously been unaware of the surrounding company. The Marine who shot him was sitting on the ground a few yards away, a bland-faced kid with his dungaree jacket open, his neck and chest all red from sunburn. He was an ordinary-looking American boy, the kind you might see wiping your windshield at the service station or packing your groceries at the market.

I took a good long look at the corpse and it scared me. I didn't want to end up like that, and I was afraid I might. (I was thinking of my visit to the Viet Cong.) The charred body of Mr. Nguyen Dzu hadn't really bothered me—it was an object of surrealism and hard to take seriously.

But this.

You could see where the bullets went in and where they came out, and what's more you could see the boy who did it. Another cruel tableau in the sunlight. What got me was not the sin of it—that didn't come to mind at all—but the sheer violence of it. The young Marine told me the man had come running along the tree-line carrying a French submachine gun and that he only heard him at the last moment. The corpse had a hole in its chest so big and deep you could see one of the ribs and the red meat around it. That scared me. So fucking violent. There was also a neat little hole between the eyes. This particular bullet had blown the stuffing out of the right side of the head and the eye was not where it should have been; it looked like a big brown jewel in a limp yellow dishrag. And there was the usual obscene cowflop of brains as well.

I asked him how many rounds he had fired. He broke into a smile that was a combination of modesty and pride.

'I dunno,' he said. 'Just one short burst.'

He said the man started shivering as soon as he fell, and he imitated it for me, shaking his head and arms. 'So I went over and finished him off.' That phrase again. I asked him how he had done it.

'Shot him right between the eyes.'

I wonder where you draw the line. Do you say, Go ahead and kill your gook but don't burn him up afterward? and don't shoot him between the eyes if he's still alive? These boys are here to kill gooks and let's face it, there are no gradations. You either do it or you don't, but whether you do it in a gratuitous way and whether you happen to enjoy it are beside the point, militarily speaking. And I think it's too much to expect an American just out of Hick City High to distinguish between guerrillas and civilians; they all look alike, they all dress alike, they're all gooks.

By noon four prisoners had been pulled out of tunnels under the hamlet. Two were amazingly young-looking. If you had seen them youd've said they were twelve or fourteen years old. But when they began talking their faces came alive and you could see they were intelligent, even sophisticated young men. For some reason almost all the Viet Cong and North Vietnamese I've seen have been tiny, even smaller than the average citizen.

Later I watched a Marine, a couple of Arvins and a

prisoner pull a corpse out of a tunnel. The entrance was concealed in heavy brush near the lip of a trench. The hole went straight down for eight feet and at the bottom became horizontal. And there was a second tunnel down there, its mouth four feet down. They went off in different directions. The corpse was crumpled up at the entrance to the lower one. A few feet along the trench where I was standing was a group of women, all in black. Under the prodding of a couple of Arvins they were digging into the side of the trench, the soldiers wanting them to break through to the higher tunnel—for what purpose I don't know.

The prisoner climbed down into the hole and tied a rope around the dead man's neck, and climbed out again. The Marine and the two Arvins hauled the body to the surface, the rope cinched around the neck like a hangman's noose. The black shorts had been worked down over the buttocks by the dragging and the skin was scraped white, but there was no blood (dead people don't bleed). There was a dried smudge of it under his nose, but all told he was a comparatively decent-looking corpse. He was killed, I learned later, by the concussion of a nearby explosion.

The three men were all sweaty and breathless by now. The body hung teetering on the lip of the trench, the legs still partway in the hole. They didn't know what to do next. Finally the Marine said 'Kick the fucker down there,' and he and another man standing by gave it a shove with their boots and sent it tumbling and flopping down into the trench. The women working nearby glanced over at it, and were prodded back to work by the Arvins. Undoubtedly they knew this man, and maybe some were related to him.

A minute or two later I saw a Marine lieutenant snap a

photo of the corpse with a Polaroid Land camera and afterward show it around.

A few minutes later I happened to notice some Marines standing in the middle of a small paddy at the edge of the hamlet. I walked out and joined them. A corpsman was working on a wounded Viet Cong, who was laid out on a board. One end was propped against the dike so that his head was higher than his feet. He had been shot in the leg, so I guess it should've been the other way round—but as it turned out, nobody gave a damn anyway. I edged myself in and managed to sit down at his shoulder. He was in bad shape, unconscious but rolling his head from side to side and groaning. I asked the corpsman how the man was doing. He said the wound was arterial and had been pumping blood in gushes when he found him. He didn't say how he was doing. This corpsman, a red-faced fellow with black eyebrows and a hawklike beak, was Cole M. Blaylock, Jr., of Provo, Utah.

He was wrapping gauze around the man's knee when the company commander showed up, a burly number with curly red hair and a camera hanging round his neck.

'You want me to keep him alive, sir?' asked Blaylock.

The captain stood there and thought it over. Another Marine said: 'He's supposed to be a cadre or something."

'Who says so?'

The man turned and pointed to an interpreter, a Mr. Khong. He was called over. 'Is this guy a cadre?'

Mr. Khong nodded.

Blaylock, clamping the gauze, shook his head and said 'I hate to waste supplies on him, even if he is a cadre.'

'What'll it take to save him?' asked the captain.

'Albumin's about all. He's run out of blood.'

The captain thought it over some more, then turned to Mr. Khong. 'Think you can get some useful information out of him?'

Khong nodded.

'Okay,' said the captain, turning back to Blaylock. 'See what you can do, Doc.'

Blaylock broke open a cardboard container and pulled out a bottle of tea-colored albumin, some rubber tubing and a needle. He had a tough time getting the needle into the vein. The wounded man got violent and tried to push himself up the board, and I helped hold him down. I was glad to be of some small assistance.

Just then Mr. Thinh began speaking over the bullhorn to the assembled civilians, and Mr. Lessy called for me from the edge of the hamlet. I went over. There were about thirty people—women, children, old men—huddled together, some of them eating C rations. They didn't seem awfully interested in what Mr. Thinh was saying.

The cadre croaked. After Thinh's speech I went back and saw the paddy was deserted, except for the guy on the board. The Marines had left him out there for the villagers to bury. Because of the rice shoots, almost ready for harvesting, all you could see was the top of his head and the end of the board.

A few minutes later someone showed me a photograph of him, taken by the lieutenant with the Polaroid.

Mr. Lessy said afterward that he was pleased with the County Fair. 'It's the best one I've seen yet.' I wonder what he meant by that.

The following day, having nothing better to do, I flew down to An Hoa with a bunch of newsmen to watch a road-opening ceremony. This was a big deal as far as the workers at An Hoa were concerned, but for the newsmen it was routine. I found nothing to write about, although I looked hard for corpses. Oddly enough there weren't any. The only fun I had was watching a salty CBS man named Al Christie at work. He was twice as bored as any of us, but he worked—went around taking notes, interviewing officials and making sarcastic remarks. His long-suffering cameraman plodded along after him, rolling his eyes back in his head from time to time. The relationship between Christie and the escort officer was something. The officer had no sense of humor but was eager to please the unpleasable newsman.

'We'll have to hurry,' said the officer, 'if we're going to hear the Marine Band.'

'Oh, we don't want to miss *that*,' said Christie.

During the ceremony he pointed to a crowd of peasants and said to his (Italian) cameraman, 'Hey Linguini, I want some shots of all those funny-looking people in pajamas.'

'*Shh*,' said the alarmed officer, looking around miserably.

I guess I've made him sound unpleasant but the truth is, he was charming. He had the knack of being able to say almost anything without offending you. He was like a caricature of a hard-bitten, cynical reporter. Christie is going home to Los Angeles in eight days. I asked him if he'd be glad to get out of Vietnam. He gave me an are-you-kidding look and said: 'I hate this place. It scares me.'

Me too.

That night I took Mr. Lessy out to dinner at a restaurant that was more like a shed than anything else. Very crowded, but the atmosphere friendly enough. Lessy and I were the only Westerners there. The waiters were young boys in ragged shorts and tee-shirts. We ate *banh hoi*, which is lettuce and beef and raw vegetables on a network of very fine noodles. Vietnamese servings are small and I was hungry, so I played the Bignose Pig and ordered a second plate.

After we parted I strolled around town. The street-lights of Danang are few and dim, but I saw some sights. I passed an open shop where rows of girls were sewing on ancient treadle Singers. I saw men pushing four-wheeled booths, the candles behind the glass illuminating the corpses of chickens. I saw isolated clusters of joss sticks sprouting from the side of the road, glowing in the dark like punk. I saw a soup vendor limping from house to house, knocking two tubes of bamboo together, making a strange hollow sound. I got caught in a sudden shower and stood for a few minutes under the overhang of a closed-up motorcycle repair shop. Two little boys in shorts stood there too, grinning at me. After they ran off I saw a huge rat scuttering silently toward me, heading right for my shower-clogged feet, and it didn't change direction till I slapped them on the ground. Then two young men appeared and looked me up and down. They didn't appear to be armed but I was nervous anyway. *Maybe this is the moment I get captured*, I thought. One of them sidled up close and reached inside his shirt, and I was ready to give him a shove and run like hell; but he pulled out a cross at the end of a neck chain. 'I Catholic,' he said proudly. After they left, an old cripple beggar-lady showed up, leaning on a tall staff. She wouldn't go away, even after I handed her some money. I couldn't see her face because of the conical hat she wore and because she was much shorter than me. She held out one palm and chanted something over and over. I finally said *Di-di*, which means go away. But she wouldn't budge and the whole thing was becoming nightmarish—so I did the di-diing. It was still raining hard, and I ducked into the first lighted shop I came to. It turned out to be a bookstore, small and crowded. I pretended to browse, and need I say that every customer in the place either glared or leered at me. I was convinced the shop was a front and I had blundered into a meeting of the I Corps Committee For The Liquidation Of American Writers. I got back to the press center finally, rather breathless.

Next day I happened to hear that another County Fair was taking place, with the same Marine company involved (Alpha Company, 1st Battalion). I decided to go along.

I found Corpsman Blaylock sitting in front of a hut with his boots and shirt off. A few minutes after I started talking with him, a shot rang out some distance away and Marines were shouting for a corpsman. Blaylock grabbed his medical kit and took off, sprinting in his bare feet out to a pagoda in the middle of the paddy. There was a lot of shooting going on and I decided to stay put, but I was full of admiration for Blaylock—the way he raced out there unheeding, completely exposed to the sniper.

Things got complicated very quickly. A skirmish line was formed to drive the sniper or snipers out of range so a Medevac helicopter could land. During the push a Marine stepped on a mine and had his arms & legs blown off. The first I knew of it was when I saw four men dragging a heavy-laden poncho. They stopped near me to catch their breath and wipe the sweat off their faces. Whatever it was inside the poncho was so small it never occurred to me it was a human body—I assumed they were dragging ammunition or something. Just making conversation, I asked them what they were carrying. All four of them turned on me with a direct bitter glare.

I followed them as they dragged their burden out to the pagoda, where a landing zone was being set up. One of them was carrying the dead man's helmet. On the camouflage cover was written *70 More Days To Go*. The seventy had a line through it and the figure *60* above it. That had a line through it too, and the figure *50* on top. The shape inside the poncho was like some great beetle. Blood kept splashing out into the water of the paddy as the men dragged the bundle along. As I told you, dead people don't bleed, so there must've been a pool in the folds.

The Marines kept the poncho closed, so I went away frustrated. When they set it down against the pagoda they sort of shored it up, as you might arrange the wrapping on an old crumbling fruitcake. Despite my crude remark above I really did want to see the remains, not for ghoulish reasons, but to learn if I'd react as coldly as I did to all those Vietnamese I saw on Lien Ket 52. In other words, whether the fact that this was an American Marine would mean anything to me emotionally.

I did get a look, though, at the wounded man inside the pagoda. The bullet had smashed into his elbow, breaking bones, grazed his stomach and punched a neat hole in the palm of his hand. When I got there he was lying on his back, dreamily instructing his buddies about mailing letters and taking care of his transistor radio. Blaylock told me he'd recover, but that he might lose his arm. I was impressed with Blaylock's bedside manner; he was tender toward the morphine-goofy kid. It was in sharp contrast to the way he had treated the cadre two days earlier.

When the helicopter came there was a lot of shooting and the sound bounced around inside the pagoda. I learned later the helicopter was hit twice, despite the heavy fire the Marines were pouring into distant tree-lines. There were no additional casualties.

Later I met the young Marine who'd shot the Viet Cong on Friday. I caught up with him on the other side of a footbridge across the same river that flows past Chau Son—which was only a few hundred yards away. The company commander had sent a message for him to wait for me there. His name was Pfc. George Pike of Fort Worth, Texas. I asked him to tell me again how he killed the Viet Cong. This time he left out the part about the shivering and the hole between the eyes. I tried to refresh his memory but he played dumb, so I dropped it. His company commander had mentioned that Pike wouldn't let himself be photographed with the body. Now I asked him why not. He had trouble answering—got very tongued-tied and started to blush. I was all set to hear some big guilt-ridden statement for posterity. What he finally blurted out was this:

'Heck, I dunno—just bashful, I guess.'

September 13th, press center

You'd never guess what I was doing an hour ago.

I think I mentioned I was waiting to see Colonel Doyle of the Air Wing to find out if I'd be allowed to jump with Air Delivery. Well, he said no. I felt sort of relieved—I mean, what kind of nut would want to jump out of an airplane anyway? Also I had learned by then that Force Recon doesn't make jumps; they send their teams in by helicopter. So having one jump in my background wouldn't help me get on one of their missions—which is one of the projects I'm working on.

I have a friend at the press center named Capt. Lloyd Steigelman (St. Louis, Mo.) who incidentally was wounded in the riots last spring. When he heard what Doyle said he drove me to a place called ——— at the airbase. He wanted to introduce me to someone. 'This guy's a wild man,' he said. 'If anybody can help you jump, this guy can.' By this time I no longer cared about jumping but I went along anyway, what the hell.

His name was Major Boyd Ellis (Winona, West Virgina), a tall stooped fellow with a bony hatchet face and gleaming slanty blue eyes. That's a lot of adjectives, I know, but he's a vivid fellow. He's forty-five but looks a good deal older. Steigelman remarked afterward how pale he was and it's true: he has the skull-tight whiteness you associate with old men.

I liked Major Ellis right off the bat—although his extrovert manner, nervous rasping voice and heavy-handed kidding didn't exactly put me at ease. But then I am never really at ease except . . . (and I wanted to tell you, I've made some small progress in the matter of kidding. It is almost essential to know how to kid around here. No one is ever serious, and earnestness is a sure way to drive people away. So I'm learning how to kid around.) The three of us stood there kidding around awhile, life coming to a complete standstill—or so it seemed—and then Steigelman casually mentioned my peculiar desire. The major didn't even blink.

'No problem,' he said. 'Take you up tomorrow.'

Suddenly parachuting was the last thing I cared to do. But it was too late now. Steigelman left, and the major had me try on a harness and crash helmet he dug up for me. His instructions about the actual jump were unnervingly vague. 'All you do is jump out and let your gear take over.' Then he climbed up on top of the desk and leaped off, to show me how not to land. 'Don't try to land standing up, otherwise you'll find your thigh-bones sticking through your shoulders.' He sat on the edge of the desk and pushed himself off, showing me how to actually leave the helicopter. He did this several times—he's a very physical fellow. (I learned later that he runs around the edge of the airfield every day, and that he ran the Boston Marathon a few years ago and finished.) He told me how to control the direction of drift, in case I found myself heading for the ocean or a barbed-wire fence or something. After that we walked over to Weather Control. The officer at the illuminated meteorological map of Southeast Asia told us there'd be six to eight knots of wind at 1200 feet tomorrow at eight o'clock, coming from northwest to southeast. (1200 feet was to be the height From Which.)

The major gave me a lift back to the press center, and the last thing he said before he drove away chortling was 'Don't forget to say your prayers tonight.' This kind of thing kept turning up all through the evening, as one pressman after another heard about my jump and tried out his black-humors on me.

For dinner I had a big steak. Later I watched a movie and every so often I'd remember with a jolt. It wasn't the idea of jumping that scared me as much as the fear of being terrified.

I slept well last night, surprisingly, and woke up feeling good. I went outside and took a look at the weather. There were a few clouds but not the rain kind, and you could see some stars. There seemed to be no wind. Glad of that.

I met Major Ellis at —— at seven o'clock. I had two questions to ask. Was I going to jump alone? No: there would be three others, four counting the major himself. The other question was, what would be my signal to jump? 'I'll make a shoveling motion with my hands,' he said.

We went into his office and sat down. He asked me if I wanted a cup of coffee. I said no, that my heart was banging too hard as it was.

He grinned. 'Nothing to be nervous about. The worst that could happen is, your chute doesn't open.'

I thanked him a lot.

We had half an hour to wait. We made small talk. I asked him when and where he made his first jump. '1944,' he said, 'when I had to bail out over China.' Right. I asked him about his second jump. 'When I got shot down again over China. That was in '45.' We chatted on and on—I've never chatted so much. It was like two people in a hospital waiting-room, when one is about to have an operation on his bowels.

Major Ellis was no more nervous than usual. He got himself a cup of coffee from some other part of the building and brought it back. He sat down and pulled a fifth of Calvert out of a desk drawer and poured some in his coffee.

'Sure you don't care for a shot?' he asked, grinning like a shark. 'Steady the ol' nerves?'

I said no thanks. (I took a shot once when I was scared about going out on a Korea patrol, and it made my legs all rubbery.)

Next he pulled out a package of Day's Work plug tobacco and offered me a chaw. The last time I tried that I ended up puking in a wheat field.

Finally it was time to go. We walked outside and down the edge of the airfield to where an old patched-up H-34 helicopter was waiting, with its Vietnamese crew. The three other jumpers were there too—all U.S. Air Force enlisted men. Ellis went over to talk with the pilot, and I put on my harness by myself. When he returned I asked him if it looked okay. He gave it a cursory glance and nodded. I figured he'd give me a closer inspection just before the jump. He didn't.

He put us aboard one by one, as the rotor blades began whirling. I got in first, then the three enlisted men, and the major last because he was the jumpmaster and had to sit beside the hatch. The rotors were whirling fast now, beating the air fiercely. The craft started rising by inches and I watched the big rubber wheel change shape as the weight was taken off. We were airborne.

It was definitely Too Late now.

There were still the same non-rain clouds in the sky, but

only in the west; the rest was blue with an early-morning haze over everything. We flew a couple of miles down the coast, the beaches and surf rolling below. Below was a spit of sand a mile wide running north-south for several miles. On the east of it was the ocean; on the west, the Han River with Danang on the other side.

The first jumper gave his cord to Major Ellis. This cord was yellow and had a lockable hook on the end of it. The other end was attached to the main parachute. Major Ellis locked the hook onto a taut cable running under the canvas seats we were sitting on. The jumper stood up at the hatch and waited as the helicopter banked and headed in across the sandy expanse. Major Ellis gave the signal and the man jumped out headfirst. I was too stiff and strapped up to bother leaning over to watch his chute open.

We circled out over the ocean again and headed in for the second pass. So far I felt scared but brave, if you know what I mean. I had decided at breakfast that the way to avoid terror was to neutralize my imagination and follow instructions like an automaton. When the major said *get ready* I would do so without hesitation, without reflection. When he said *jump* I would jump with an empty mind. I believed this was important. Otherwise I might find myself rolling on the cabin floor screaming, kicking and biting.

The second man jumped out and Ellis pulled the long yellow cord back into the cabin, hand over hand, as he had done with the first's.

I still felt fairly solid, so I decided to allow myself a moment or two of mind: I wanted to review a couple of touchy details. I must remember not to panic and pull the reserve-chute ripcord right away, I told myself, because the main chute will not open for what'll seem a long time. And I must remember that if, after the chute opens, I find myself being crosswinded toward the ocean or river, all I have to do is turn myself around by yanking on either toggle until my back is to the wind, and that'll slow down the drift.

Then I saw two things that bothered me, and my imagination started up before I could do anything about it. First I saw one of the jumpers below, floating softly under a red & white canopy, and he seemed to be dropping toward the river. Then I noticed how narrow the spit of sand was—or so it seemed from our lofty viewpoint. It was easy to visualize myself coming down either in the river or the sea.

I calmed down by remembering that Major Ellis, knowing I was a beginner, would surely drop me in a safe spot. Then my mind went blank again.

The third man leaped out headfirst and disappeared, and Ellis pulled in the long yellow cord. I automatically scooted down the canvas to where he'd been sitting, because it was my turn next. I found myself facing the yawning hatch. There was no guard rail or anything like that; just a big square hole in the side of the cabin, six feet by six feet. I looked out on the vast expanse of yellow sand and green sea below. There was nothing much between me and it but the law of gravity, and sweetheart, did I ever freeze.

It was the most amazing thing. It happened instantaneously: I felt a cold terror wrench my stomach. I think it was the fear of death itself. It was such a profound feeling that I think I know now what it's like to face death—not like in Korea with some guy dropping mortars on you or a sniper sniping at you from a distance, but face to face with the thing itself. You may think I'm overdramatizing, but I can't imagine being more scared than I was then. If I ever have to face death, actually, with time to realize it's going to happen and me helpless to do anything about it, at least I know I won't go to pieces but will merely stand stolidly.

Then I figured: buddy, if you're this scared just looking out the hatch, you're in *real* trouble when it comes time to jump. At that moment we were turning into the approach and the helicopter was tilted to starboard and I was therefore higher than the hatch. Here is how I fought my fear. Instead of leaning back into the canvas seat to compensate for the tilt, as you'd ordinarily do, I leaned forward, sort of tempting the gaping hatch to suck me out. And that was enough to pull me together.

We were directly over the drop zone but Ellis still hadn't hooked me onto the cable. He turned and yelled something in my ear but I couldn't understand him. I think he was explaining why we had to go out over the ocean again and make another pass—which is what we proceeded to do. The bad thing about this, of course, was that I had to wait that much longer. I noticed that even though I was seated, my legs felt weak and heavy.

Major Ellis finally put out his hand and I slapped the hook in it, and he bent down and clamped it onto the cable and inserted the locking-pin. He stood up and gestured me to get ready.

Too Late Blues.

What I was supposed to do now was sit on the floor and scoot over to the edge and slip my legs partway over the side and wait there till I got the signal. I didn't know then why he gave me this position to jump from rather than the upright leap of the others, but I found out later. It was so he could shove me out if I turned chicken at the last moment, the bastard. Anyway I did all this without hesitation or reflection, like a good automaton. The only visual recollection I have is of the fat wheel; it was just below and to the left of my feet. I didn't dare look beyond it.

'*Jump*,' he shouted, and I pushed myself into the void and started plummeting, my eyes shut against the giddiness of it, my stomach up in my throat. Then a long time later I felt a tug as the straps suddenly tautened, and there I was, your self-perpetuating Hero, floating soft and stable under a white canopy.

I had one more shock to undergo: the moment when I opened my eyes and looked down. Instant vertigo! The problem was, I had nothing under my feet. For thirty-five years I've had something under my feet. Now there was nothing. For about three seconds I hung on to the straps for dear life, afraid to move lest I jar something loose. Me, for instance.

But then I knew that everything was going to be all right, and I unloosed one hand and gave Ellis a thumbs-up sign just for the sheer joy of not being dead. The helicopter was above and behind me, but I knew the major was watching me as he had the others.

It was quiet up there now, with a slight breeze. I was still too high to know where I'd land, so I experimented with the toggles, pulling one and turning slowly to the left, pulling the other and swinging back.

Then I began to see where I was going to land—and here's something I almost hesitate to put down because it seems made up: I was heading straight for a barbed-wire fence. What made this especially farcical was that it was the only fence for miles around. I couldn't imagine what a barbed-wire fence was doing in the middle of a sandy waste, but there it was. A couple of hundred yards further on was a tree-line with some buildings on the other side. I guess the fence was some kind of boundary marker, huh? Anyway I pulled down on the toggle and slowly changed the direction of drift.

Then I noticed, still far below, several figures racing across the sand toward the spot where I was heading. I couldn't figure out who they were or what they were up to. A few moments later the ground started rushing up at me and I concentrated on not letting my thigh-bones go through my shoulders, and for some reason I was relaxed when I hit the sand and found myself tumbling over and over, amazed at how hard I'd hit.

When I sat up and looked around, blinking sand out of my eyes, I found myself surrounded by grinning little boys, all tough and cute in their caps and ragged clothing, all brown and barefoot. They started brushing the sand off my face and helped me up and out of the harness. I loved them all madly! I grabbed them and pulled them against me, pinching their cheeks and ears. . . .

(no date)

. . . Yes, I'm serious about the Viet Cong thing. But that doesn't mean I'm just going to say goodbye and walk out into VC territory. I'll wait until I can make some kind of formal contact with them. I'm working on a couple of angles now. The toughest part of the project may be finding a VC official; they don't exactly wear badges.

I'm having the following translated into Vietnamese. Then I'll have it printed on a waterproof card, and carry it on me when I go.

Greetings!
I am a civilian.
I came to Vietnam to write a book about the war.
I've already written half of it—the half concerning the Saigon government and its allies.
Now I want to write about the Viet Cong.
Many Americans will read my book.

Please understand I don't intend becoming a prisoner, just a visitor in temporary custody.

. . . Despite all the tales you hear of indiscriminate beheadings and disembowelings, the Viet Cong rarely kill civilians without a political reason. The seemingly wanton acts of terrorism you read about are deliberate, meant to show the people the Saigon government is unable to defend any but the select few. Each act of terrorism reminds the citizen of the shadow government waiting to take over, a government that promises to serve the people rather than the other way round. You may ask, Is killing civilians serving the people? In a way it is, yes, because the civilians they kill are usually corrupt oppressive Saigon appointees.

I can't see any political advantage in killing a lone American civilian. But I can see a certain propaganda value in treating him well and sending him back the way he came.

Here's a list of the things I'll carry with me when I go:

Civilian shirts, pants, cap, sandals, poncho, canteen, shaving gear and mirror, sweater, toothbrush, money for rice, the card quoted above, water purification tablets, malaria pills and vitamins. And a paperback copy of *The Last Parallel*, with my picture on the back—which will help convince them I'm really a writer.

. . . Just remember that whenever I take a risk over here it's only after I'm convinced the odds are on my side. You didn't see me running out to that pagoda with Corpsman Blaylock, did you? Okay. You can be sure that when I do this, it will have been set up in a way that satisfies me as far as safety goes.

September 23rd, Saigon

This is the same hotel where I spent my first night in Vietnam. It's called The Oriental and reminds me of a French colonial prison. I came back here because I had a case of the glooms, and this place being familiar I thought it'd suit me better than something new. Maybe that doesn't make sense. Anyway it turned out to be a mistake, because the last time I was here I had been with you only a few hours earlier, and being here again brings all that back too vividly.

I'm on my way to a new project—the Australian Task Force. They have 4500 men in Phuoc Tuy province, roughly forty miles southeast of Saigon. I'll be there tomorrow.

The only thing I have to tell so far is, my first meeting with an Australian. He was Major Douglass Buchan (Doncaster, Victoria), the press liaison here. His office is across the river in the Chinese section called Cholon. I couldn't understand a word he said. There was considerable politeness on either side, but not much communication. He finally had to write down the where & when of tomorrow's flight. The hardest thing was keeping from laughing. My right thigh is blue because I pinched myself every time I started going over the edge. It was heightened by my just having read a review of a book called *Let Stalk Strine*, which means Let's Talk Australian. Its author makes fun of the way his countrymen talk. He says, for example, that Orpheus Rocker means psychopathic in Strine. Rise Up Lades are sharpened steel wafers, usually stineless, used for shiving. Sander's Lape means in a state of suspended animation, as in 'Doan mica noise, Norm, the kiddies are Sander's Lape.' Bare Jet is a phrase spoken by Strine mothers and daughters, as in 'Jim make yer Bare Jet, Cheryl?' 'Nar marm, nar chet.' And Gunga Din means locked out, as in 'I Gunga Din, the door slokt.'

When Major Buchan began speaking to me in perfect Strine, I had to start pinching myself and visualizing tragedies. He must have noticed me twisting and coiling in my chair, because he stopped and gave me a look of inquiry. What could I do then but whip out the review, which I had in my wallet, and hand it over? He read it and smiled politely. I was sure I had offended him, but when it was time to go he said 'Trust you enjoyed your first lesson in Strine.' (At least I think that's what he said.) He told his driver to give me a lift back to Saigon in the Land Rover, and naturally I climbed in on the left side and found myself behind the wheel.

'Care to drive, sir?' the corporal asked with a straight face, as the major smiled politely from the doorway.

All in all it was a shambles.

Tonight I had dinner at the Continental Palace Hotel, on a terrace overlooking the colorful sidewalk with its picturesque Vietnamese beggars. The menu was in French. I ordered a little bit of this, some of that, and a lot of the other. Afterward I looked over the elaborate dessert menu and ordered that exquisite Gallic dish known as *bananes*, which I figured would be thinly sliced bananas, say, in some kind of insouciant sauce, probably hot. At least that's the way I pictured it. It didn't turn out that way, though. The Viet Cong terrorist who was my waiter plocked down a dish with one small green banana on it, which I humbly peeled and ate in two bites.

Later, greeding for a real shot of dessert, I bought a large bag of assorted cookies, and took a walk in the darker part of downtown. Saigon by day is nothing much to write home about, a moldy place with a lot of trees and traffic, but at night it's exotic enough. You get an occasional whiff of jasmine and ginger, and every house looks like an opium den. I saw an isolated ladies' shoe store, closed up for the night but with a glowing display window. It was incongruously American-looking. Further down the block I nearly tripped over a sudden legless beggar in the dark.

September 24th, Nui Dat

The Australian base camp is hidden under tall rubber trees. They were sprayed recently, but the insecticide was too potent and the leaves are falling. Every time you walk from tent to tent the dead leaves crunch underfoot, like it was autumn. (Sickening nostalgia too when I remember it is autumn in the States.)

Before dinner I was having a drink in the officers' lounge (a tent) when the camp commander walked in: Brigadier Geoffrey Sandhurst. Someone barked *Gentlemen, the commander* and everyone rose. The general sat down and was served a Scotch & water. I was introduced. It was like meeting a king. Everything was hushed and solemn, and I had a definite farting-in-church problem.

At dinner several young officers tried being sociable but since I couldn't understand them it was a bust. In desperation I whipped out my *Let Stalk Strine* review and passed it around. To my horror everyone got tight-lipped and one fellow asked if I didn't think the whole business was exaggerated.

'O tremendously,' I said.

Off to a great start.

September 25th, Nui Dat

I flew by helicopter this morning to Vung Tau (my stomach flopping over each time I thought about the parachute jump) where I watched a graduation ceremony of thirty Aussie soldiers and thirty young Vietnamese civilian men who had lived together for three months, learning each other's language.

It was moving to see the lads from Down Under in their magnificent slouch hats standing in the sun with their partners, exchanging jocularities. It got me thinking about how all men are brothers, even if they don't know it. I wondered how many of the white-shirted fellows were Viet Cong agents. After all, the Aussies plan using them as interpreters.

Pvt. C. M. Lupton (Wollongong, New South Wales) stepped forward, gave an arm-cracking salute to the Brigadier, and read a speech in Vietnamese, the paper shaking violently in his hand. Then Le Ngoc Chuong (Vung Tau) read a speech in English which was incomprehensible due to a strong Strine accent. After that the Brig himself arose, twirled the ends of his mustache, and told what a terrific job the Australians are doing killing gooks, with special emphasis on the recent battle of Long Tan. He ended by saying the close association between his troops and the populace (as symbolized by the sixty young men before him) will result in even more dead gooks.

They served pastry and soft drinks afterward, turning the affair into a great success.

This afternoon Major Smythe came rushing into my tent to ask if I wanted to go out on an operation. It turned out to be a routine sweep by a squadron of armored personnel carriers—just a nice ride hither & yon about the countryside. Some of the terrain was like Kenya, with magnificent umbrella trees and white birds rising in the distance. You could almost see the impala leaping.

The squadron passed through a village, exchanging the characteristic thumbs-up greeting with the kids. Sgt. Ron Roberts (Melbourne), the commander of the APC I was riding, kept shouting *Gooday, mate* to them.

Again struck by the beauty of Vietnamese children. Photos never seem to capture it; you have to see 'em in the flesh, running beside your vehicle. They're prettier than flowers. Someday when it's all over I'd like to drive from village to village, just digging the kids.

Late in the afternoon we stopped in the middle of the plain for a 'brew,' which means tea. Sgt. Roberts pointed out the distant site of the battle of Long Tan, in which 245 Viet Cong were killed and 18 Australians. The battle took place in a rubber plantation on August 18th, the two units running into each other inadvertently.

We sipped our tea and watched kids driving their cattle home from pasture, an idyllic scene at twilight. They rode atop water-buffaloes, each kid with a big conical hat hiding his face. Every so often one would glance up and the face would knock you dead. Often you couldn't tell if it was a boy or a girl. Didn't really matter.

On the way back to Nui Dat, Roberts suddenly jumped to the ground with his pistol drawn, jacked a round into the chamber, and rushed over to what looked like a corpse in the ditch—and it seemed as if the prop department was already on the job, setting out the usual objects for my viewing pleasure. It turned out to be an old retired scarecrow.

September 26th, Nui Dat

Just back from an all-day patrol with a platoon of A Company, —— Battalion, Royal Australian Regiment.

There's a lot of flat jungle west of the camp. That was our zone of reconnaissance. It was the first true jungle I've ever seen. Green light filters down dimly, and the vegetation is fantastic: vines seem to reach out and grab you like something malevolent; thorns jut from tree trunks like daggers; lordly trees with skirtlike buttresses and long vines like boa constrictors—the kind of trees Tarzan used to swing from. The sudden screeching of animals high in the canopy made us jump many times.

Unlike the Marine columns I've traveled with, the diggers creep along slowly and quietly. One man counted his steps, and every few hundred yards the patrol leader (Lt. Kurt Helstrom of Glengowrie, South Australia) would consult him to find out how far we'd gone since the last consultation. It turns out that 150 paces equals 100 meters, roughly. The diggers travel light: no helmet or flak jacket, and sparse ammo. They wear floppy bush hats, the brim hanging down all around, with a thin red ribbon intertwined in the band.

We ate lunch in silence in a dense patch of jungle. I was impressed with the way they deployed beforehand. The three squads arranged themselves in a 360-degree perimeter and sent out three-man clearing patrols to make sure the ground in front of each squad was deserted. When they returned, five minutes later, a one-man listening post was set out in front of each squad. Only then did the main body break out the rations.

I had heard that Aussie patrols stick to the jungle and

avoid the trails. It's true. Leftenant Helstrom's columns never went near a trail today, although the map shows several in the area we covered. Maybe this is why the Australian Task Force has had such piddling contact with the other side—sniper fire, booby traps, an occasional mortar round. Long Tan is their only battle so far, and it was an accidental meeting. One can't help visualizing the superbly-trained Aussies, proud of their reputation as jungle-masters, searching diligently through the forest gloom while Uncle Ho's nephews parade up & down the paths in perfect safety.

9 p.m. the same day

Just back from a weird supper in the artillery mess tent. Lt. Col. W. J. Oliphant (Brisbane) the gracious host. We ate roast mutton by candlelight, the candles in silver candelabra, on a pure white tablecloth. Chianti with the meal, brandy in snifters afterward. Every so often the guns of the battery would roar, shaking the tent, the shells trailing a long shimmer of sound; but inside all was mad decorum.

'Rather grim,' snapped the colonel, glaring at the circle of gnat corpses around the base of the candelabra. 'Deal with them, subaltern.'

'Right away, sir,' said the officer on my left, brushing them off the tablecloth.

Unfortunately that is the only dialogue I recall; I'm afraid I was rather dazzled. Col. Oliphant was charming and witty, but overpoweringly so. All I could do was smile fixedly and feed my face.

* * *

Major Smythe, the liaison, is a handsome dashing fellow of, I would say, considerable shallowness who outbritishes the Brig himself. A few minutes ago he told me at length the 'score' of the Task Force to date. It seems the Aussies have killed 321 gooks, with 12 probables, wounded 59 and captured 31. They've killed 95 Viet Cong Suspects (let's not ask any embarrassing questions about that). 106 weapons have been captured, 330 grenades, 28 mortar rounds, 15,000 bullets, 200,902 pounds of rice and 11 pounds of salt. Smythe recounted all this in a marvelously pompous manner, as if the figures meant something. The best thing he said, though, was this: 'The Task Force has pacified 120 square miles or ninety percent of Phuoc Tuy province.' (In other words the Australians, like the Americans, have already won the war. When the gooks find out, then we can all go home.)

Incidentally one of my tentmates, Jack Moseley of the *Melbourne Dispatch*, tells me the major is suspicious because I never use the typewriters in the press tent, never file stories to Saigon 'like the other blokes.' (There are several reporters here, including one from Malaysia, one from Norway, and a Scotsman who works for Reuters.)

(no date)

I'm writing this in a rubber plantation a few miles north of Nui Dat. The nearest town is Binh Gia, site of a great Viet Cong victory of 1965 when two South Vietnamese battalions were destroyed—one of which was the 4th Viet Marine Battalion.

Early this morning Smythe woke me up to say that agents had seen two Viet Cong units outside of Binh

Gia and an attack was being mounted against them. Did I want to go along?

I caught up with C Company, —— Battalion, at a private airstrip in the Gallia plantation. We boarded some armored personnel carriers and started off amid neat rows of trees (each with a clay cup collecting latex).

After a mile or two the APC's slowed down, tailgates were dropped, and everyone clambered out grim and warlike. The first thing that happened was, a VC mosquito bit me on the hand. I saw the contact, and learned they sink their beaks into you the moment they land; they don't stop to think about it.

The Viet Cong were long gone, of course. What would you do if you were VC and heard two squadrons of armor coming toward you a mile away? C Company might've had a chance of contact if it had walked in.

I've been traveling with the artillery officer, Lt. Ian Rowe of Freemantle, South Australia, a small slender fellow with blue eyes, a red face, a neat blond mustache. He puffs on a big Sherlock Holmes pipe and looks very serious. This morning during our futile stalk he came back to ask if I admired spiders, then took me over to view a fantastic bat-spider hanging above the trail (we were entering a village at the edge of the plantation). It had bright yellow protuberances like folded batwings. It hung perfectly still and viewed us back.

We stopped for lunch in the village. The people stayed inside their huts, patiently waiting for the invader to depart. You could catch a glimpse of a hand or foot in the shadows, but little movement. Rowe and I sat down in a clearing where a water-buffalo was tethered. 'You done it wrong, I feel,' said one of the diggers nearby, and I found I was sitting in the center of the world's largest cowflop. C

Company has been out on so many consecutive operations that the men haven't been able to do their laundry—but I smell worse than them, now.

Watching the men around me eating, I suddenly noticed the magnificent Aussie beak! It is generally of grand size but not gross, and always finely molded with distinct planes. But big. Such enormous bills! I notice too that small mouths are common, and that almost everyone has blue eyes. Many mustaches too. The Aussies are as big as the Americans; no undernourished Beatle-types like I expected. A robust hearty lot.

I mentioned to Rowe the formal dinner I ate with Col. Oliphant, who happens to be his boss. Rowe got a cold look in his eye. It seems he doesn't approve of the goings-on at the artillery mess—thinks it makes the unit look ridiculous.

'Next thing you know he'll have us wearing scented hankies up our sleeves.'

He says the colonel barely scraped into the twentieth century. 'He calls helicopters heavier-than-air flying machines, for instance.' He also said the colonel calls his officers by the names he thinks they should've been given. Naturally I asked him what he was known as. He puffed bleakly on his pipe and said, 'At first I was Sordid Subaltern. Now I'm Desmond Trueheart.'

Halfway through the afternoon, when I was convinced there was nothing resembling an enemy within five miles and we were on a sort of merry outing, a shot rang out and the atmosphere got sinister. A brief fire-fight broke out and when it died down I went forward, and a marvelously arty panorama came into view. Massive rainclouds rolled across the horizon like battle smoke, and in the near distance a lifelike scarecrow loomed atop a bamboo pole like a crucifixion, dressed in black pajamas and conical hat, the sleeves flapping ominously in the hot breeze.

One Aussie had been wounded, shot through the chest, and when I saw his grey face and glazed eyes I knew he was through. There was the usual bucket of blood all over the place. He had that small Australian mouth I was talking about and a prognathous jaw, and he blubbered loudly with each exhalation.

Major Fred Gough, the company commander, sat down beside him and spoke comfortingly, even though it was obvious the boy was out of reach. Gough cracked the old joke about how unfair it is this fellow is heading back to all sorts of rear-echelon luxuries 'while us blokes have to stay out here and plod.' The boy just kept making that slow rhythmical blubbering. All you could see was the whites of his eyes, and as he approached death—or death approached him—the blinking increased rapidly.

Funny what gets you. The dying Aussie didn't get me at all. I dunno why. Maybe it's just that there's nothing unusual or unexpected about a soldier dying: I mean, it's one of the things they do, soldiers. What got me was when I glanced around and saw the remarkably stricken and grieving faces of those standing by.

Anyway he died before the helicopter arrived. When Major Gough stood up he muttered bitterly, 'He was a Nasho too.' That's slang for National Serviceman, which means he was drafted. About half the guys in the Royal Australian Regiment are Nashos.

A little later they found a civilian hiding nearby and dragged him in. He was questioned by one of the lads I saw graduated in Vung Tau, who said he couldn't understand a word he was saying. The prisoner was batted around a good bit and finally shoved down. One blond porcine leftenant made a big show of wanting to shoot him and ask questions afterward. Everyone was so worked up with good old-fashioned blood-lust that no one saw the obvious, that he was an idiot child from the nearby village, badly wall-eyed and more frightened than any whipped animal. The Aussies were quite nasty with him, throwing him around like a sack of potatoes, him babbling in falsetto. Major Gough finally came over and took a look at the cowering creature.

'Why, it's only a poor fool,' he said.

He told two of his men to take him to the edge of the clearing and let him go. The three of them went off, the boy stumbling along in the middle, the Aussies roughly guiding him with the muzzles of their rifles. When they reached the edge of the clearing they stopped, and he went jiggling slowly on into the forest, like a child going out to play with the fairies.

Next day

I'm writing this beside the road (Route 2) during lunch break.

We slept in the rubber plantation last night. The company Sergeant-Major, Alfred Coombs of Sydney, rounded up some rations for 'our learned guest' as he calls me, and strung my hootch against one of the armored personnel carriers. An APC is a juggernaut kind of machine, perfect for crunching people. My whole night was one great flinch.

I've noticed it's almost impossible to get an Australian

to talk about himself. They all seem articulate and gabby —amazingly so compared with Americans—but almost nothing they say concerns themselves. (Whereas the ordinary Yank, he'll reveal his most personal worries and enthusiasms right off the bat.)

Sergeant-Major Coombs sat with me as it grew dark, and told me about the guerrillas in Malaya and how they were put down. He believes the Viet Cong can be crushed the same way. But the British-Australians outnumbered the guerrillas in Malaya 10 to 1 and the guerrillas weren't indigenous (they were Chinese) and therefore got little support from the populace.

When he said goodnight he rose slowly to his feet—he's not a young man—and began kneading his leg. 'I think I'm going in the fetlock,' he groaned. And that's the only thing he said that could be called personal.

This morning the Aussies entered the hamlet of Ngai Giao and searched every hut, blundering around inside while families sat in silence. They looked everywhere, poking into the thatched roofs, overturning pots and sifting through personal belongings. Major Gough told the interpreter to tell the people the Australians were their friends.

After that we moved on down the road, flankers breast-stroking through the grass on either side. Sergeant-Major Coombs flogged them along with his blaring sarcastic voice.

'Is it rude out there, son? I wouldn't want you to excel yourself.'

We walked together for a few hundred yards, and I happened to mention my interest in foraging (talking about my Selfe like a typical Yank). He began pointing out paw-paw trees and pepper trees and coffee bushes. About the latter he talked at length; it seems his best friend runs a coffee plantation in New Guinea. He also pointed out some tapioca, and I had to laugh. *Cu san*, the sweet potato-like stuff I ate with the Viet Marines, turns out to be plain tapioca—than which there's nothing more common in Southeast Asia. A few minutes ago he showed me how to slice it up and fry it in margarine (Aussie rations include a tin of margarine). He said that's how he used to prepare it in Malaya.

Just before we halted for lunch we came across hundreds of Viet Cong leaflets, strewn all over the road. They had obviously been planted there only a short time before. It's interesting to know we're being watched. Most of the leaflets are written in jargon familiar to me from Korean days—all about fat cats and running dogs and puppets of Wall Street. One pamphlet, though, was entitled *Bertrand Russell Calls On GI's To Stop Fighting The People Of Vietnam*, and started out like this: 'I am Bertrand Russell, speaking to you over the radio of the forces of the National Liberation Front of South Vietnam. I am speaking to you, American soldiers, in order to explain how your government has abused your rights in sending you to occupy a country whose people are united in their hatred of the United States.' He goes on to repeat the usual crap about poison gas and so on, and winds up like this: 'When Britain occupied the United States in the eighteenth century, American farmers fought with pitchforks in their bare hands, although they were hungry and in rags. They fought for eight years and they defeated the British Empire in their own country.' He closes by saying he plans to form a war crimes tribunal.

Nui Dat base camp

Major R. N. Frisbie (Adelaide, South Australia) is the civil-affairs officer of the Task Force. I've been making the rounds with him for two days, trying to find some good material. It seems hopeless—except for the ready-made stuff you see every day in *Stars & Stripes* ('Quick Action by GI's Saves Ailing Vietnamese Woman' or 'Marines Hardboiled? Ask Orphans of Tuy Loan!')

I met Colonel Tran Van Quat, the province chief, at his headquarters in Ba Ria. We drank tea and talked, but nothing happened in the way of material; it was too formal. Afterward I was subjected to the kind of briefing I'm constantly trying to avoid, complete with wall map and pointer. Col. Quat graciously explained how he is winning the war in Phuoc Tuy province.

Later, Major Frisbie told me something of the overall aims of his work. 'My job is to gain a psychological advantage in one form or another. I am not a humanitarian. I sell whatever government there is to the people of this province. Its merits are of no concern to me since I'm a military officer.'

Lots of luck, pal.

Can you imagine a Chinese Communist officer trying to sell the people of Huntingdon, Pennsylvania, on the merits of the government in Washington, with that government controlled from Peking?

Anyway Frisbie showed me some of the results of his work. I saw a marketplace under construction outside of Hoa Long, paid for by the Aussies, labor by the noggies (the Aussie equivalent of gooks). I also saw thirty civilians in another place filling sandbags with dirt, for which they are paid 1 piastre a bag.

'What we're trying to do,' he explained, 'is to teach these people to help themselves.'

Awhile back he organized a soccer match between some kids in Binh Ba and a few Aussies. The kids won, 17–0. (Now there's a *Stars & Stripes* story if I ever saw one.)

Frisbie is presently involved in a rat-killing campaign, and the pile of tails is building up nicely. The papers back home are calling him the Pied Piper of Hoa Long, but that has nothing to do with the rats. He is often photographed with local kids, and has set up weekly helicopter rides called Boomerang Flights for the best-behaved students in the Hoa Long school.

This morning the major drove Jack Moseley and me up to Binh Gia to see the display of weapons captured in the battle of Long Tan. They were lined up under the market roof, with space at one end for the Royal Australian Band. The first set was greeted with a deafening silence by the puzzled guerrillas, who had never even seen a live kazoo player, let alone an entire marching band. Several young men came up and handled the weapons admiringly, and Moseley suggested that some of them probably took part in the battle.

During the concert we watched three randy diggers talking with girls in an open sewing shop, trying to get laid. We also saw a fat young thing, her face ghost-white with powder, offering her pudginess to strolling soldiers—until her father suddenly appeared, went into a Kabuki-like outrage routine, and yanked her away.

'They say we're making whores of their women, beggars of their kids and guerrillas of their men,' said Moseley.

At the foot of Thi Van Mountain

Early morning briefing: Major Gordon Taggart showed his company a map drawn by a patrol the day before. The patrol climbed Thi Van and saw three huts ('big enough to sleep twenty men each') and several Viet Cong wearing green scarfs. On the way back they ran into two VC and killed them.

As we boarded the trucks at Nui Dat, Sergeant-Major Browne handed me a red ribbon to intertwine in the band of my newly-acquired bush hat. Major Taggart snapped a picture of me.

The convoy drove through Ba Ria, turned up Route 15, and halted near the tiny hamlet of Phuoc Hoa. During the forty-five-minute trip you could see the target mountain isolated on the broad plain. Thi Van is 1300 feet high and three miles long. According to a map I saw, it's the southernmost mountain in Vietnam. The Mekong Delta begins on the other side of Route 15. (East of the road is dry land, west is marsh.)

An American 155 mm. battery was already set in on the dry side of the road, commanded by Capt. 'Smilin' Sal' Rizzuto of Chicago. As the column started into the plain I heard Rizzuto say to Taggart: 'Don't forget our birth-control pill. Whenever you need it.'

'Right, thanks.'

'Best birth-control pill in the world.'

'Right.'

'Weighs only ninety-five pounds.'

'Absolutely. Call for it if I need it.'

'Don't forget.'

There were charcoal-burning ovens all over that part of the plain—smoldering mounds of earth with thatched roofs on stilts, and several chimneys. This is how the people of Phuoc Hoa make their living—cutting trees and burning them for charcoal. The peasants weren't being very picturesque this morning; they all stayed in their huts.

First break:
In the jungle now, a mile from the base of the mountain. Still flat ground. Maddening how the Aussies avoid each beckoning path or cart-track. When we come upon one, the temptation to turn onto it is strong; but back we go, never faltering, into the tangle of creeper and thorn.

A big explosion behind us. Word radioed that Rizzuto's gunners have stumbled onto a booby-trap of some kind. Two men wounded. Local guerrillas'll remember this as a great victory, I imagine.

Writing this in our harbor-for-the-night, near foot of mountain. We ate lunch in a clearing a mile back. Major Taggart showed me how to prepare the dreaded cereal block. You crunch it into powder in your canteen cup, add water and boil. Result: sweetened porridge.

Then a sudden driving rain. We stood around in classic dejection poses, water dripping from hatbrims. Twenty minutes later the sun shone through and I saw my shadow—very unwelcome, knowing how hot the sun'll be when the clouds clear off. Feel an 'ant' crawling down my temple: it's the first bead of sweat. In a few minutes face and neck'll be covered with them, and clothes'll stick to you oilily.

At dusk, a single rifle shot from Thi Van Mountain.

Taggart takes a compass bearing and calls battalion head-quarters. 'Bearing, 5300 mils. Estimated distance, 1000 meters.' Writing in dark now. Everyone expecting action tomorrow, once we start climbing mountain.

Next day, on the mountain

A mosquito last night started playing his violin, and I knew he was after me. I lay there wrapped in my net. Pretty soon it was a duet and then a trio and then a quartet. I lay still on my phosphorescent pallet. One of the players stopped, and I knew he was on me somewhere. I twitched violently. This went on till midnight. This morning my knees and elbows are four white bumps that itch maddeningly. Taggart was right: mosquitoes *can* bite you through the net. Tonight I'll string mine like the diggers do, instead of wrapping myself in it.

Around 1 a.m. a mortar barrage 'of unknown origin.' Nobody hurt. None of the rounds landed near us.

Just before dawn the monkeys started chittering and hooting and shrieking. Impossible to sleep.

At 7 a.m., headquarters relayed an agent's report that a Viet Cong mobile-battalion is known to be in the vicinity of Thi Van.

We crossed a wide cart-track and saw the prints of Ho Chi Minh sandals in the mud. Naturally they were identified as 'VC tracks.' (Couldn't possibly be woodcutters from Phuoc Hoa, could they? Oh no.)

This afternoon C Company, climbing the mountain to our south, ran into a field of mines and a handful of Cong, whom they chased away with small-arms fire. 13 Aussies were wounded. According to the account Taggart got over the radio, the enemy did no shooting. Major Gough told Taggart he believes the explosions were set off by remote control.

'A bloody waste of manpower and blokes,' said Taggart. (And a big victory for the other side. This is the kind of 'battle' that guerrillas can go on winning indefinitely.)

We started climbing the mountain around 10 a.m. The jungle is so dense you have to turn sideways and edge your way through, bending and twisting to do it. The stands of bamboo are the worst.

A sudden miniature oasis, with a flat black monolith and a placid pool in the center.

Further on, a tunnel in the vegetation with a stream for its floor and golden sand on the bottom. We followed it sloshing for a short distance. It curved around a steep bank and a miniature beach. We halted in column for a break, and I saw a crab the size of a silver dollar lurking underwater, ready to ambush one of the skittering water-striders.

The columns often stop while the forward scouts hack out a passage with machetes. We stand in one spot waiting, sometimes for several minutes. One is almost forced through boredom to study the details of bark and bush and insect life—like some kind of nut naturalist. In this way I've learned that the local ant has a hind half that looks like a gold shot. I've also seen fantastic butterflies and iridescent birds.

About a third of the way up the mountain we found a tin-roofed hut for storing rice. It was empty except for a few grains in the corners. The terrain is steep at this point, with ominous boulders overhead in the gloaming. We ate lunch around the hut, because there was an earth shelf there. We didn't know it then, but there were thirty or so Viet Cong nearby. Neither side was aware of the other's presence.

After lunch we sat around reading. It was startling to see everyone settle against a rock or tree to read. I whipped out my faithful Spillane (*My Gun Is Quick*) and got lost in it. Then it started to rain. When it rains in the jungle it takes a long time to filter down through the canopy.

Finally we had to put our books away and start climbing again. The man in front of me (Pvt. M. J. Thomas of Penola, South Australia) stopped and gave a thumbs-down signal, which I passed to the man below me. I didn't know what it meant, so I asked Thomas.

'Enemy,' he whispered.

He started climbing again and I followed. After a few yards we came to another, larger rock shelf, open to the sky. The rain had stopped.

The diggers ahead of us were all deployed in defensive positions, except for a few creeping to & fro. I worked my way in among the trees. The further along I crawled, the more tense the men. Then I heard talking up front, unbelievably, and laughter. It rang through the forest. It never occurred to me it was Viet Cong. I imagined it was our forward scouts gone sloppy or something.

I crawled up beside two nervous diggers behind a rock, and asked what was going on (I passed them a note with the question written on it).

'Noggies,' whispered one.

I crawled back and found Major Taggart, and stood by as he briefed his three platoon leaders. There was going to be an attack, and when that sunk home I began to get excited. (For a few moments I was more preoccupied with my excitement than the attack, because lately I've been worried over my apparent lack of nerves. I haven't been getting excited when I should, and it bothered me.) The briefing was short and beautifully organized. Taggart knew from his map there were three possible enemy escape routes. He told the first leftenant to block the one leading north, up over the mountaintop. The second was to block a certain draw leading northwest, also up and over. The last platoon (under Lt. Angus MacLennon of Pascovale, Victoria) was to block the only route leading down the mountainside. It was this latter unit that would make the actual assault.

'Advance until you're able to get off aimed shots at the enemy,' said the major to MacLennon, 'or until they come into your position. Your mission is to kill as many Charlies as possible. Tell your blokes to keep their shots low.'

Incidentally a goofy-looking private interrupted the briefing to breathlessly report finding a rice cache. Taggart snapped at him ('Oh, stuff and nonsense, Pritchit!') and he slunk away.

I followed MacLennon—a big fellow with a red handlebar mustache—and sat by as he briefed his three squad leaders. Then I followed one of them (Cpl. J. M. Dunn of Holsworthy, New South Wales) and listened to him brief his seven men. I noticed how much rougher each briefing was than the preceding, starting off with Taggart's formal Duntroon jargon and ending with Dunn's impenetrable slang. The reason I chose Dunn's squad is because it was to be the turning point of the platoon, and there'd be less climbing to do.

MacLennon offered me his Owens submachine gun in

exchange for my pistol, but I told him I wasn't going to do any shooting. His jaw dropped.

I had a few minutes in which to do some thinking, and as usual it did me no good. I asked myself what a believer should do in a situation like this. Is he to try and prevent the attack from being made? Impossible. Is he to warn the other side? That would probably save many lives. But who has that kind of guts? The truth is, I'm a writer first, a human being second, an American third, a believer last. All my life I've wanted to witness an assault in mountainous terrain. I doubt if there's a greater show on earth.

Anyway the attack was called off at the last minute ('Oh, *bugger* it!' muttered the major) and we climbed down the way we came. Even though I was disappointed, one part of me was gleeful we had escaped with our lives, both sides. It's interesting to think how close those Cong'll never know they came to disaster.

No one knows why the attack was called off.

I recall a time in Korea when a certain raid was called off and I went outside and cried in frustration (and it was only that, because in those days I had no fear of death).

Next day

As soon as we reached the plain, a U.S. air strike was called in, interspersed with some of Smilin' Sal's birth-control pills. It was a terrific display of power, but I don't think it had much effect. The diggers of B Company weren't impressed either, since the bombs landed in the wrong place.

The day ended abruptly as it always does in Vietnam and we bedded down. Around nine o'clock there was a final barrage, sensational in the dark—a Night on Bald Mountain.

Such black nights! Literally can't see hand before face. Gives a sense of claustrophobia.

Last night I had The Nightmare again. I dream I wake up in blackness to find the Aussies gone, and me stranded in Noggieland. I've had the dream three times. It always wakes me up, and the reality is like the dream—until I hear breathing, or someone turning over. Last night I lay awake a long time, listening to the jungle's strange noises. I heard a dog-bird. It made a horrible hoarse bark. I thought it was a tiger, or maybe some kind of wild mastiff. Sergeant-Major Browne told me this morning it was a dog-bird, but he may have been putting me on. I do think it was a bird, though, because each time it barked it was farther away—farther than a running animal could travel in the interval.

Then everything got quiet, and I began hearing soft and phony-sounding bird calls, like a bunch of guys doing lousy imitations. I know it wasn't Viet Cong, because they don't go creeping around whistling to each other in the dead of night. Many people would say they do, but then most people (soldiers too) have an unrealistic view of warfare, overlooking the fact that the enemy is human and although he may be renowned as a night-time jungle fighter he's not a fucking idiot.

Even so I lay there starkly staring, with my boots laced up and my pack within grab, just in case we were being surrounded by fucking idiots.

An hour before dawn a gibbon started up, making a sound like a slide-flute. It was the most exotic, languorous, eerie sound I've ever heard: very long-drawn-out, swooping in a slow descent and then climbing high, holding it, and at last dropping off again, always slow and silky. That sound evokes one's most romantic dream of Indo-China, if one has never been there and doesn't know how unromantic it really is.

The men've spent the morning hacking out a landing zone. The helicopters just now brought in our re-supply. Each craft drops down quickly from a great height, hovering while the gunner & crew chief heave the boxes off in a frenzy. I guess too many helicopters've been shot at lately.

I'm almost ashamed to list the goodies each of us got, besides the usual rations, but here they are: a can of cold milk, a can of cold beer, a can of cold Schweppes Bitter Lemon, a hot hamburger in a roll, a ham & cheese sandwich, an orange and an apple.

Lots of mail for everyone. I watched a young private named R. J. Fowler (Sydney) sit down against a tree and, with a beatific smile on his face, his lips moving, read a letter from home. He glanced over at me and said: 'The cat had kittens in my room! In my top drawer!' and I thought: at last I've found one who isn't impersonal— maybe I can make a strike. But Pvt. Fowler, alas, turns out to be as inscrutable as the rest. One interesting thing, though: he has a grandmother who lives on 15th Street in Santa Monica, and an aunt in Goffstown, New Hampshire. He got a letter today (besides the one from home) from that grandmother, and that made my homesickness worse somehow.

It's plain that Australians are made uncomfortable by personal questions. And if there's one thing I try to avoid, it is being obnoxious. So I have a bit of a problem here.

* * *

Just now Major Taggart got word why the attack was called off yesterday. It seems a radio message was intercepted, in Vietnamese, its point of origin triangulated as the very spot where we were forming our attack, saying in effect: *Enemy on Route 15, heading this way. Send 200 porters to help us carry away our equipment.* Battalion headquarters decided that if 200 porters were required to carry the equipment, there must be a lot more than the thirty VC our forward scouts saw up there. So they ordered us out of there fast.

I had a talk just now with the digger who got closest to the enemy yesterday. His name is Pvt. J. H. Curry (Huonville, Tasmania). As an interview it was pretty lousy. He only said one thing that wasn't in the nature of a cold factual report. He was telling how, after he and his buddy saw the VC milling around the huts, his buddy left him there alone for a few minutes. 'He's a bit of a gossip—always gotta be telling the other blokes the news. So he ups and leaves me—the bloody *bawstid*—me and thirty noggies!' Curry was left lying atop a flat rock overlooking the clearing where the huts and the VC were. It turned out that a sentry was sitting at the base of the rock. Curry became aware of this only when the man got up and walked toward the huts. He was wearing a white shirt and khaki pants, Curry said, and armed with a Garand rifle.

Northwest face of Toc Tien Mountain

We're camped around a big two-story pagoda. We got here around noon. On the way, the artillery officer called in ninety-three 105 mm. rounds on some huts he spotted up the slope. It was interesting to note they were still standing when the smoke cleared off. The barrage cost approximately $4000.

The walls of the pagoda have been blown away on one side, and there's a big polychrome Buddha inside. There are books strewn all over the tile floor, hundreds of them. Outside there are lily-pad pools and mossy grottoes with stone tigers and elephants. A flight of crumbling masonry stairs leads to a gallery and a tower room that looks out in four directions. There's another flight of stairs leading from the front of the pagoda straight down the mountain-side.

There are some other huts a few hundred yards up the slope. Angus MacLennon noted that one of them is large and seems lived-in. 'Some bloody religious maniac, I suppose.'

'Doubt it,' said Major Taggart. 'Pagoda wouldn't be the mess it is.'

Major Fred Gough's C Company is working the mountain to our southwest. Word just came that they've searched the area where the Viet Cong were seen (by Curry and others) and found no bodies or blood trails. I'd like to know how much that air strike cost.

It's late in the day but, if I have time, I'm going to try and write a piece about close calls I've had lately. I had one so close this afternoon I think an angel may have saved me.

Here's number one. When we stopped for lunch the other day (when I was with Gough's company) I sat down at the lip of a blown-out bridge that had been replaced with several logs. This was on Route 2 near Ngai Giao. Sergeant-Major Coombs fixed my tapioca and walked away, and that's when I moved over to the spot. After lunch the company moved on, searching huts and checking identification papers. During the afternoon I heard an armored personnel carrier had struck a mine in the road. At the end of the day we boarded a squadron of APC's and headed back toward Nui Dat. Sgt. Roberts pointed out the crater near the edge of the road where the mine had gone off, and it was where I ate lunch.

Here's number two. Major Taggart sent a patrol up the slope to investigate the huts, and at the last moment I decided to go along. The patrol had already left but the tail-end was still in sight, so I hurried after them. I wasn't watching my step. Hurrying and not watching one's step are the two dumbest things you can do over here. Suddenly two strong hands grabbed me from behind in a violent teeth-rattling way. A young digger from out of nowhere had saved me from putting my left foot down on one of the bombs dropped in the air strike the other night. It was a CBU (Cluster Bomb Unit), one of the most unstable duds bomb-disposal teams deal with. It's an odd-looking object, about the size and shape of a 1-pound can of coffee, yellow except for the folded aluminum fins at one end. It's manufactured in America.

The incident reminded me of one very similar. I was on my way home from prep school, in 1947 I think it was, and I got stranded in East Stroudsburg, Pennsylvania, because I'd gotten off the train for a stroll (the porter said there was time) and I saw the train pulling out and ran for it. A tall man wearing a hat appeared out of nowhere (it was night) and pulled me back in time to avoid being hit by a freight rolling in from the blind side. Like the young Aussie this afternoon, he walked away without a word.

I saw the Aussie's face. It was an unmemorable one—

almost: I recall it well enough to recognize him if I see him tomorrow. It's too dark now to go looking for angels.

The patrol itself was fairly interesting, if you like that sort of thing. We found medical supplies, propaganda, tax records (how much rice taken from each hamlet), and one long hut with benches and a blackboard. We found some caves beneath boulders, with many Viet Cong artifacts inside, the whole site reminiscent of rock-dwellings in Arizona. There was a magnificent panoramic view from up there: Route 15 far below at the outer edge of the scrub-covered plain, and beyond that the Mekong Delta stretching away into haze.

Next morning, beside the pagoda

There was a B-52 strike last night—many miles away, yet it rattled our hootches.

I've been strolling around the perimeter searching for *him,* or *it.* Lt. MacLennon said I was like a bloke looking for a lost dog.

At Battalion Headquarters, beside Route 15

The operation's over. A squadron of APC's came across the plain for us, following a cart-track part of the way. One APC hit a mine. On the trip back, us aboard, an APC hit another mine. During the wait I walked up and down peering into faces. I finally gave up.

. . . I'm worried about my lack of nerves again. The incidents with the mine and the dud bomb didn't make any impression on me emotionally. I look back coldly.

. . . We rolled across the plain toward Route 15, a white statue of the Buddha looming off to our left out of trees. We crossed a marsh, the APC's wallowing like hippos, and found dry land and the highway on the other side. The traffic on 15 was nutty. Two red Hondas with young couples aboard, like Malibu kids on their way to the beach. A two-toned Chevvie station wagon. A brand-new red Volkswagen. I could hardly believe I was in Vietnam. (15 runs between Saigon and Vung Tau, a resort on the ocean—but even knowing that, the traffic seemed incongruous.) Then a gaudy bus bristling with pigs and ducks and people in conical hats. But the craziest thing of all: a long string of young men in red, green, yellow or blue tee-shirts and shorts, pedaling furiously on racing bikes. A bike race!

Life a funny thing, as Sonny Liston said.

It's late in the day and I'm sitting atop Sgt. Roberts' APC, waiting for the convoy to start back to Nui Dat. There are kids playing nearby.

Vietnamese kids are always saying everything is number one or number ten, just like Korean kids years ago. I think they keep this going because the GI's respond so strongly. Many GI's assume this number one-ing and ten-ing is the prattle of primitive minds.

This afternoon I met the battalion intelligence officer, Capt. Eric Andrews (Liverpool, New South Wales), a Rhodes scholar and author of a just-published study of the German Army and the Nazi Party. Andrews is a tall, deliberate kind of guy with a face like a priest. We sat down beside one of the charcoal-burners and chatted about this and that. I found him instantly sympathetic and easy to talk to. I blurted out my plan to visit the Viet Cong. I hadn't realized how scared I was until I started talking about it. He suggested I go to Phnom Penh and look up the Viet Cong representative there. He warned me I'd probably have to wait a long time for an answer, though. Visas to Cambodia are handled through the Australian embassy, he told me, located on the seventh floor of the Caravelle.

Nui Dat, same night, in the press tent

Idyllic scenes at dusk on the convoy back. Kids fishing at the edge of the Delta. A saffron-robed bonze washing his motorscooter in a stream. Crossing the bridge in Ba Ria, looking down on sampan families eating supper. The town breaking off suddenly into paddy fields and an isolated row of huts, each with a tiny kerosene lamp out front. Is it true they're 'to ward off evil spirits'?

I'm disappointed the digs're so impersonal, so mature, so well-balanced and sensible. They seem to have no hidden madness like the British.

A wild raging lust for a drink as soon as I got back. I ordered a can of Singapore beer and a double Scotch—the beer for thirst, the Scotch for wassail. I sat in silence in the corner, listening to several Aussies and three U.S. Air Force officers tell jokes. The Aussie jokes were dirty as hell but witty, some brilliantly so, whereas the Americans' were embarrassingly crude. I was surprised that many of the Americans' jokes were racist. More surprising was the realization the Americans were doing unconscious parodies of the boorish, bigoted, violence-obsessed Yank. The Aussies seemed to accept them on those terms, graciously, as if these were typical Yanks. Snobbery in reverse: I found myself mortified by the behavior of my countrymen across the room. They were so loud, for one thing. The Aussies told their stories smoothly and softly and casually, whereas the Americans leaned forward all red in the face, blurting out theirs like kids behind the barn. And the payoff was invariably violent.

Next day

Rather grouchy because of poison ivy, Vietnam version, all over hands and forearms. Now I know why Aussies travel with sleeves rolled down. I also have a good case of jungle rot—a sprawling fungus Down There, or rather on either side of it. Fortunately Down There isn't involved.

The most exquisite scratching.

Had a bad night. My cot is broke, thanks to burly hearty hard-drinking Jack Moseley, who blundered in one night while I was away and fell against it, got up and fell against another, breaking it too, finally settling down gently on the only remaining one in our tent, which happened to be his own. Now mine sags sickeningly to starboard, and I fell out twice last night into the muck, once while I was having The Nightmare. That and the crotch itch and the mosquitoes biting me on my poison ivy nearly did me in, fair dinkum.

Morale very low. Severe homesick problem all day. The bar doesn't open till late afternoon, so I'm really stuck for kicks. What makes the situation especially serious is, I've run out of Spillane. I found an old Rex Stout and tried it. No soap. Nero Wolfe a good character, but Archie too fruity: does things like stick his tongue out as he walks past district attorney's office. Also the stuff's so well-written it's hard to read—sort of like the Australian character.

Next day

('What day is it, Jack?' 'Buggered if I know, mate.')
I visited the school at Hoa Long to see Tet Trung Thu or mid-autumn children's festival. Concentrated mainly on stuffing Selfe with cakes and cookies, and sulked when I failed to wangle a can of Schweppes Bitter Lemon (none left by the time I asked). The kids performed a dragon dance, teachers beating tom-toms. They'd rush up to you in scary masks, then withdraw in rhythm.

On the way to the party we saw three dead bodies beside the road, with a sign stuck in the ground. Lt. Illingworth translated it for us. *Here are three Viet Cong, killed by your local militia.* He pulled the Land Rover over to the side of the road so everyone could get out and take pictures.

A bit of humor from one of the Yanks at supper—the psychological-warfare officer. He saw a spider on the tablecloth and slapped at it, missing, and raised his hand for another try.

'Here, *here*,' said Major Frisbie, grabbing his wrist, 'let's try and win some hearts and minds here!'

But the Yank, gleaming madly, said 'It isn't often we psy-war types get a chance to *killlll!*' and cut the creature in two with his fork.

These Air Force guys, with their crude gabbiness, their enthusiasm and warmth, are so different from the Aussies. Compared with the Aussies, they come off like characters out of Dostoevsky.

Wednesday

I made the rounds today with Frisbie's assistant, Lt. Tony Illingworth (Alice Springs, Northern Territory). Only a couple of small things to report.

As we drove through one small village he said 'Charlie was here last night.' I asked him how he could tell. 'Watch the kids,' he said. 'See how they're ignoring us? You should've seen 'em yesterday—yelling and racing beside me, full of spirit, unafraid. Now look at 'em.'

Around noon we stopped at a small slaughterhouse. I got depressed by the hanging liver and lights and tongue and gonads, but mostly by a cow waiting to be killed. There was no doubt it knew what was coming. It had seen another killed just before we arrived. It was tightly tethered under all the hanging guts and glop. It hung its head low and its eyes had the fear of death in them. It was so nervous that when one of the butcher-women touched it going by, it kicked, harmlessly, and the whole butcher-family giggled.

All that scared me pretty bad. I don't want to end up with my various parts hanging from the rafters like that. You hear the most ghastly stories about what the Viet Cong do to civilians.

Battalion headquarters beside Route 15

Tomorrow C Company (Major Fred Gough) is going to climb the mountain again. Patrols have seen VC up there again.

Sergeant-Major Alfred Coombs greeted me with:

'Getting your story, son? Good on ya.' He was sitting cross-legged on the ground, cleaning his rifle, which he calls Tillie. ('There y'are, Tillie—all ready for a big day tomorrow.') He says the weapon is temperamental. 'Has her on days and her off.'

Lt. Ian Rowe is incommunicado just now, puffing his big Sherlock Holmes, staring broodily across the plain. If he were an American I'd ask him what's on his mind—and he'd tell me.

I had another chat with Capt. Eric Andrews. We talked about the pleasures of living in a college town. I told him about Huntingdon. Our conversation was interrupted when the colonel told him to take the helicopter up and investigate a column of smoke rising from the mountain.

The only thing that bothers me about Andrews is, what's a guy like him—a gentle scholarly type—doing in the gooking business?

Morning next day

A quiet party in the dark last night. Major Gough, his officers, the Sergeant-Major, the learned guest and a bottle of Scotch. The Sergeant-Major asked me about my writing and the others got interested, and I realize this morning, thinking back on it, that I am more impersonal than any Australian. I was willing to talk about journalism in general, but not my own brand of it.

Later, everyone asleep but Gough and me, working on a surprise second bottle, he uttered a surprisingly personal remark, telling how he used to work as a news-gatherer for a radio station: 'I often regret not following that up as a career.'

We're halfway up the mountain now, taking a different route than last time. We're halted for lunch in a sort of Hansel & Gretel village smothered in canopy, a brook running in among the thatched huts. It's a Viet Cong base camp, or was—only gnomes and such live here now. There's the smell of death all around, very strong. I started to get depressed again, but it turns out to be old monkey meat in a pot.

All day long the diggers've been turning up mines and booby-traps, and there are CBU's everywhere. We tiptoe softly.

A possible Aussie 'character' emerging. His name is Pvt. Rolf Bayswater (Mt. Isa, Queensland) and he loathes the Army and everything it stands for. Needless to say, he's a Nasho. Bayswater is quiet, and when he does speak it is usually to complain about the Army. The first time he made any impression on me was yesterday, when I saw him staring incredulously as I ate some Army biscuits with gusto. His face was so curdled with distaste I said I'd heard too many of them will kill you—just to get a rise out of him. 'Yay,' he said, 'or start you to barking.' Bayswater fits well in this Hansel & Gretel atmosphere. He wears his bush hat all peaked up in a point, with a feather sticking up in back, making him look like a giant troll. He and Major Gough have a routine going in which the major goads him into making anti-Army statements. Bayswater doesn't need much goading. A few minutes ago the major was fuming about the non-cooperation of some radioman at headquarters. 'All we need is a simple yes or no,' he muttered to himself. 'What's he waiting for?'

'He's in the Army, sir,' said Bayswater.

This morning the Sergeant-Major looked into my steaming canteen cup and said: 'I dunno what it is but it bloody well isn't tea.' He said it looked like something a bloody housewife might knock together. (I like it with lots of sweetened condensed milk.) The Sergeant-Major sat down and showed me the proper way to make tea in the bush. The general idea is, drink it straight and strong.

Next morning

The first thing I heard this morning was Rolf Bayswater's sarcastic 'Good *morning*, Vietnam.'

News came in last night that a patrol had run into some VC and killed four. This morning A Company spotted six—all wearing green scarfs and carrying packs—but couldn't catch them.

When we started moving, I found myself in the mood for a good rousing battle. I'm starved for something to write about. I know now how lucky I was on Lien Ket 52: material unfolded itself before me from one day to the next; I was writing constantly.

I came loaded down with rations this time—cans and packets bulging out my pockets and pack. Whenever we halt for five minutes I have a quick gromf. If we stop for fifteen I heat something up. The Sergeant-Major, noticing how often I eat, said just now: 'Having your tucker again, are ya, learned friend?'

I discovered a taste-sensation this morning. I took a

raisin bar and mixed it in with a can of corned mutton. Everybody made big puking noises when I offered them a bite.

The Aussie rations are superior to the U.S. kind. The meat portions are tastier, for one thing, and the variety is wider. You get steak & eggs, ham omelette, bacon & beans, Vienna sausage, corned mutton, corned beef, sausages & vegetables. You get a tin of Nuttelex margarine and a tin of rich cheese (unlike the processed plasticized concoction you get in C rations). You get Swallow's biscuits and tubes of jam. You get Cadbury chocolate bars and Horlick's 'candies fruit ration'—tangy wafers. You get fruit slices by Brockhoff, sweetened condensed milk by Tongala, soup powder by Robur. The real prize, as far as I'm concerned, is the tube of sweetened condensed milk. The diggers suck on it like candy. I eat a whole tube every day around three, which is about when my ass starts dragging. The Aussie heat-tablets are much bigger than ours and give off more heat longer. Here are the names of the cigarets the diggers smoke: Peter Stuyvesant, Craven A, Rothman's, Viscount, Country Life.

As I said, I'm a little short on material.

Next morning

We got re-supplied this morning, and one of the helicopters was shot down. I clearly heard the burst of machine-gun fire; the Aussies think it was the sound of rotor blades hitting the trees. They're wrong.

I climbed up to the site and found the crew all laid out. Medics were already at work on them. The pilot has a broken back, the co-pilot a broken leg and jaw, the gun-

ner a broken ankle. The crew chief is unhurt. The helicopter itself was burning fiercely on the slope above us, ammo
going off like Chinese firecrackers. The co-pilot turned
out to be a guy I had a couple of drinks with last week, Lt.
Murry. He recognized me and gave me a brave thumbs-up
greeting. I noticed he kept glancing at his hands to see if
they were trembling.

Later I watched the Sergeant-Major at work, distrib-
uting the rations, lashing his helpers with his voice
('Aren't you a bloody source of annoyance, though! And
you, son—when do I get a bit of honest toil from those
lily-white hands?') After the distribution he stalked about
blaring at everybody ('Come on, lads—you know better
than to sit down in one great fucking heap. Spread your-
selves!')

Major Gough got a pack of cigars. He gave me a
couple. We discussed why men like them. 'Oral gratifica-
tion, I suppose,' he concluded.

Later Sergeant-Major Coombs took me downslope a
hundred feet and showed me what he called a 'guerrilla
garden.' As an old Malaya hand, he had recognized it
from a distance, even though it is camouflaged and invisible from the air. He said that in Malaya whenever they
found one they'd set up an ambush around it. I asked him,
as casually as I could, if he had killed many guerrillas. 'I
lent a hand once or twice,' he said slyly.

Next day

We found another storehouse. There was an enormous
blind sow with her litter nearby, in a pit covered over with
camouflage. Her eyesockets looked like a pair of navels.

Major Gough told the Sergeant-Major to shoot her.

It was a ghastly harrowing business. The first shot went through her neck and came out the throat, the hole flushing blood all over the pale animal. She jumped up squealing and tumbled over into the dark gully, flipping and flopping heavily and splashing sheets of blood over the greenery. The forest rang with her shrieks. What bothered me more than anything was that in the murky green light she looked and sounded like a naked human dying hard.

She was still alive at the bottom, hard-breathing but silent in a shallow brook. The Sergeant-Major climbed down and put another bullet in her poor blind head. She wouldn't die: she kept trying to lunge away to safety. The diggers urged her on, wanting her to climb clear of the water so her corpse wouldn't foul the stream. The Sergeant-Major took aim and pulled the trigger a third time, but Tillie jammed. He glanced up at me sheepishly. I followed him as he climbed back to where Gough was sipping tea, and noticed that in making his report he had trouble saying the words dead and dying. ('She's not . . . *gone* yet, sir. She's definitely in the *process* of . . . of going, though.') Later, after someone else had put the sow out of her misery, the Sergeant-Major got very gabby, telling anyone who'd listen how his first shot was perfectly-placed and should've done the job.

Gough couldn't decide what to do with the piglets. Rolf Bayswater wanted to hose them down with his Owens gun. Finally the major said *Leave them!* and passed word for the columns to move out. Trouble is, the piglets'll starve without the sow. The only reason she was killed was so the Viet Cong couldn't have her. Therefore the piglets should die too, right?

Next day

Atop the mountain. The men have blasted a landing zone, but the Aussie pilot is reluctant to come down. 'Ask her if her husband's in the RAAF as well,' said Bayswater to the radioman.

Re-supply completed. I got a new pair of pants, which should keep all the jolly digs from saying 'I see you're having a ripping time of it, haw haw.'

Gough got a bottle of Scotch, which he's now cradling like a baby, cigar jutting from his mouth all gleeful.

Another great view of the Delta from up here. You can see ships in the South China Sea waiting to sail up the Saigon River.

Sounds of a fire-fight in the jungle below, and we got word that D Company (who had lain in a non-talking, non-smoking, non-cooking, hootchless ambush for three days) have killed 10 Viet Cong. Seven others are reported to have escaped. One of the dead was a woman.

Nui Dat (at last)

I decided to quit the operation when the battalion commander suddenly dropped down out of the sky and there was a helicopter door staring me in the face. I couldn't resist climbing in.

Here's a brief account of my last few hours in the field.

We started climbing down the southeast face of the mountain. An hour after we started, a spotter plane saw an estimated 40–50 Viet Cong in the valley below and called in artillery on them.

It started raining hard. The bamboo leaves lost their color, reflecting the grey of the sky. Big mists rolled in and the rain came down harder.

'The dry season,' said Bayswater.

The slippery slopes got steeper and at one point he tumbled a long way, and sat up unhurt at the bottom with a look of the most profound disgust. When I got to him he said: 'Aren't you sorry you turned down that job with the *Ladies' Home Journal?*'

That night, sitting around the blue flames waiting for water to boil, Major Gough glanced round and said 'This is a truly rude place, isn't it?' It had been raining all afternoon and we were going to have to sleep in wet clothes in a howling wind on a steep slope. We began talking about other rude places we'd slept in. Lt. Ian Rowe told about the time he rode from Bunbury to Perth in the engine of a freight train, and went to sleep on the foot-plate between engine and coal car. 'I was as comfortable as I'd be at a baroque music festival,' he said. A few minutes later he turned to me and said: 'I've always wanted to visit Altoona, Pennsylvania.' I nearly croaked. It turns out he's a railroad nut and wants to see the Horseshoe Curve. He also said that when he gets back on Civvie Street he's going to take a job with the Native Welfare Department in Wyndham. Regarding the aborigine he said: 'It is our task to educate, elevate, and finally assimilate the boong.'

He turned up this morning wearing a pair of 'glasses' he made out of vines. As I took off in the helicopter, the last thing I saw was Rowe peering up through his mad specs, sucking on his pipe and looking very wistful indeed.

I think he envied me my freedom.

It was good seeing Jack Moseley again and hearing his hearty *Gooday, mate!* He handed me a drink and a cigar, and a few minutes later he and his photographer pal, Bjorn Sjoberg, were teaching me how to play canasta. All this meant something to me, because we are civilians and naturally excluded from the camaraderie of the soldiers. (A journalist or photographer can get quite lonely over here at times.)

Moseley is having a feud with Smythe, calling him the Boy Major or Smith, and muttering *What swill* every time the fellow opens his mouth. I'm afraid I'm rather put off by him myself. It turns out he decided I was an impostor of some kind, possibly hiding out from the law. Moseley said he called Saigon and made inquiries about me. Evidently they told him I was okay, because he's been polite.

I wish I had the inclination to talk about him at length, because in his own way he is an unusual bastard, but all I'll say is this, that the depth of his shallowness took me by surprise.

I missed a couple of things while I was away this time. The Aussies cordoned off the village of Hoa Long and held their version of a County Fair. Moseley's account of it was side-splitting. He said the bewildered villagers were herded into one great mooing mass and from that point on it was a sort of assembly-line version of the road to paradise. 'First they had needles stuck in their arms, then their rotten teeth were yanked out. Then they had their throats swabbed and their clothes de-loused. Finally they were shown a propaganda film and released. Poor bloody noggies! I believe they thought it was some sort of reprisal!'

The other thing I missed was listening to the interrogation of a female prisoner. She had been captured by D Company, 6th Battalion, in a mountain cave. She had a radio. Moseley said she was young and good-looking. He and Sjoberg stood outside the tent while a couple of officers interrogated her, using the water-torture method. This involved forcing water into her until she talked freely. I'm sorry I missed that.

Danang press center

I can't tell you how wonderful it is to be back among the loud, friendly, enthusiastic, belligerent, vulnerable, passionate, childlike, responsive, dumb Americans.

Moseley, Sjoberg and I caught a helicopter ride to Saigon. (Riding in a helicopter is one of life's great experiences—a hundred times more fun than a plane. You are just high enough, just low enough, traveling just fast and slow enough, to see the clouds and the countryside at their best.) We ate lunch in the —— Hotel bar. Moseley says the hotel is owned by a Frenchman who pays taxes to the Viet Cong, and is therefore one of the safest places in town. After lunch Sjoberg went off to get his visa renewed, and Jack and I walked around. The streets are dead during siesta time—noon to three—the shops all shuttered up. Around two it started to rain. You could hear it coming a long way off, like a crowd of barefoot rioters pattering toward us. We ran, chased by the water, and made it to the Majestic in time. We watched the storm and the river traffic from the top-floor bar. Moseley plunged me into a whirlpool of homesickness by telling me he was going home in a week.

*   *   *

'Let's have some Chinese tucker, mate.'

We ate dinner at Cheap Charlie's, a Chinese restaurant. During the meal he interviewed me for his paper, taking notes and so on. I told him how big the digger's collective nose is, but he said he'd have to leave that out. He agreed his countrymen are impersonal.

'We have a saying: In Australia one has many acquaintances but few friends.' He said the Aussies are even more impersonal than the Pommies (British).

November 7th, press center

I know now that I love the Marines. Only a Marine or a former Marine could understand a right-wing statement like that. For awhile there—after the charred body incident—I didn't like them any more. But now, coming back to the Marine-run press center after a month of maturity, equipoise and equanimity, they seem the salt of the earth.

Since I'm queer for Marines I guess I have to have a favorite, and Steve Beauregard seems to be it. He showed up at the press center three days ago. He's having trouble with his hearing. He'll be going to Okinawa for tests in some hospital there. He told me his father is partially deaf. Of course he expects the worst—although he pretends not to give a damn.

Last night he came blundering into the room long after midnight, lifted up my mosquito net, handed me a glass of gin and sat down on the concrete floor for an intimate conversation on his favorite subject, Steve Beauregard. Every night he's been here he's gotten blind drunk on straight gin, and I recall him saying on Hastings it's the only thing he drinks. He's likable when he's drunk— friendly and open and generous. He just wants to share his glorious young ego with you.

He has a scar on each cheek, I think I told you. Imagine a young Neville Brand and you'll know what he looks like.

When he gets discharged he plans becoming a million-
aire importing Philippine cigars to Japan. This is somehow typical; every young Marine has some sort of big
deal all figured out.

Steve has nothing good to say about officers, and this
too is typical. It doesn't matter that Marine officers are
the best in the world; to him they represent authority, and
he's against that.

Speaking of authority, he told me again about hitting
his dad the last time he was home and that he has nightmares about it. Can you imagine an Australian admitting
a thing like that? In the first place an Australian would
never hit his dad; that'd be too personal. This is what's so
marvelous about Americans: we hit our dads.

It's a delightful and amazing thing to discover my
affection for Americans. They are a bunch of loudmouth
limes, goofy grapes and rootin' tootin' raspberries, and all
wondrously dumb. At least they seem dumb after those
Aussies who think like lawyers (all fact and no imagination).

November 8th, press center

It looks as if my next project is going to be Force
Recon. I'm looking forward to it. The monsoon season is
here, but the really rough weather hasn't started (although the sky is nothing but black clouds) ; and when it
does, the North Viets are expected to come south across
the Demilitarized Zone—despite the disasters of Hastings
and Prairie—and it'll be Force Recon's job to find them
first. (Just find them, not engage them.)

. . . I may go to Phnom Penh afterward and look up

the Viet Cong representative there. The big disadvantage is, I'd have to go to Hong Kong to get a visa and I'm seriously afraid if I went there (the first leg on the way home) I'd keep on going till I got to — East 85th Street, New York, N.Y., apartment 7B.

If the Phnom Penh thing doesn't work out I have a sort of last-ditch plan. Tay Ninh province is where one of the big VC strongholds is. It's also where the Philippine Civic Action Group is based. They're strictly non-military, concerned with malaria control and that kind of thing. My idea is to go down there and live with and maybe even work with them for a few weeks, letting the local guerrillas have a look at me, so that when I offer myself for capture I won't be associated in their minds with the United States military but with benign Philcag.

Also it might be smart to make my move during Têt, the lunar new year, traditionally a cease-fire period.

I've made friends with Dick Rosen of CBS. Have you seen any of his reports on television? He's fat and sleek and looks like an Egyptian potentate. He has great sleepy eyes and one of the world's finest grins. At first I avoided him because he seemed one of those dreaded Jewish intellectuals—the kind that keeps you on your toes and won't let you relax and be hazy; but it turns out he's a sentimental slob.

I've also made friends with Malcolm Asche of *The New York Times*—big and fifty and an instant father figure. (He made the mistake of calling me 'my boy' the other evening, so he's definitely In.) I asked him to be a sort of emotional sponsor in regard to my Viet Cong project, which simply means I'll write him for advice on various plans as I develop them, in return for his wise-old-Asia-hand encouragement. At the moment he's up at Dong Ha interviewing Marines for a series on Operation Hastings.

He and I sat at the bar the other night and got drunk slowly and had a great time, at least I did. The only thing I remember is we laughed a lot.

. . . Whatever you do, don't encourage me to come home early, or I'll be there like an arrow.

Let me tell you briefly about another, less imposing fellow I've met at the press center. His name is Leon Koontz and he was born in Pine Bluff, Arkansas. Leon doesn't have any real home at the moment, unless you could call the press center a home. He's twenty-nine but looks younger. Very small but wiry and well-built. Wears dark glasses most of the time. Outwardly he's a tough hard-bitten guy, pugnacious and profane. He speaks with a strong Southern accent, not the nasal kind but the melodious ear-pleasing kind, and uses some of the most scorching four-letter combinations I've ever heard.

After we had a few together he opened up enough to admit his real name is Napoleon Koontz. ('Aint that a bitch?') He told me he has a daughter, living with his ex-wife. The marriage lasted five years. Without using the word, he said he suffered during the separation and divorce, and afterward holed up in the remotest place he could find, which turned out to be Lynchburg, Virginia. There he was befriended by a crippled alcoholic and his wife, and through them got his first newspaper job. He loves Lynchburg as much and for roughly the same reasons as I love Medford, Oregon.

As I said, he's a tough customer; but I suspect he's

lonely & scared. He has reason to be scared; get this: he arrived in Vietnam two weeks ago with $85 to his name and he's pounding out stories on speculation, with no assurance they'll be bought. His last job was reporting for a Pittsburgh paper. He got restless and fed up, and quit, deciding on the spur of the moment to take the big gamble. His dream of glory is to become a world-roving newspaperman like, say, Bob Considine.

Leon has some sad facial twitches, and I imagine that's the reason for the sunglasses. He'll be talking to you—he talks a blue streak—with the cold unblinking stare you get when his eyes are naked, and suddenly the right eyebrow'll break in half, the forehead wrinkles turbulently, the eyes flick sharply to the right. It all happens in a flash, and before you know it everything's back in place; but what you've seen for an instant is a whipped little dog.

I sure hope he can write. Last night he wanted to show me some of his stuff. I said nothing doing and made my speech about never showing it to anyone but enemies & editors because otherwise you'll only hear you're the greatest writer that ever lived, practically.

November 12th, press center

. . . A few words about the Marine Corps birthday party. Beforehand there was a ceremony in which the oldest and youngest Marine came forward to receive the first two pieces of cake. Then, standing before the other Marines on the post, they formally took a bite. It is somehow appropriate that America's elite military unit celebrates its founding with cake. The French Foreign

Legion, they used to say *To our friends in the sands* and drink cognac. But the childlike Marines eat cake.

I'm still working on various plans to visit the Viet Cong. None of them are working out very well. Malcolm Asche is writing a letter of introduction to Wilfred Burchett, a journalist who lives in Phnom Penh and has acquaintances among Liberation Front officials there.

I'm afraid it's going to come down to this finally, that I simply walk out into Viet Cong territory and get captured. I shouldn't say 'simply,' though: people might see me heading 'the wrong way' and try to stop me, or some military unit might send out a rescue patrol. It could get awfully complicated and endanger others.

I just read about the market in Cumong Pass, 'the only place in Vietnam where a truce exists between the allied forces and the Viet Cong. Peasants from enemy villages can sell vegetables there' (quoting from an article in *Life*). I was thinking that'd be a good place to make my move.

But like I said, breaking loose from the allied side could be harder than getting captured.

November 18th, press center

Just back from Dong Ha and a mission with Force
Recon.

I had a hell of a time hooking up with them. If it hadn't
been for Malcolm Asche I wouldnt've made it. I think I
mentioned in an earlier letter he was gathering material
for a series on Operation Hastings. The last participants
he interviewed happened to be from Force Recon. These
Marines, three of 'em, were members of the patrol (or
*in*sert as they call it—the team is inserted by helicopter
into the zone of reconnaissance) that first spotted large
numbers of enemy soldiers south of the Demilitarized
Zone last July. This discovery led to Hastings. These
three came to the press center for the interview, and
Asche, knowing I wanted to go on an insert, invited me to
participate.

We sat around a picnic table overlooking the river and
had a few beers. This was the first time I ever watched a
pro interviewing people. I know now how sloppy my meth-
ods are. I sort of wander around picking up whatever I
can without pressing anybody—but then I'm not after
hard facts like Asche is, only impressions. Asche was
aggressive and blunt, not bothering to act like it was a
social event. For some reason this surprised me. I had
thought you should gloss it over that you're picking people's brains and in a sense making money out of them,
while they get nothing. Asche asked leading questions and

took notes, dominating the situation. When he'd gotten everything he needed he closed his notebook and smiled, and then it did become social.

The Marines stayed for dinner and I got friendly enough with one (Capt. Ray Barksdale of Ocala, Florida) to ask his help in getting out on an insert. That plus Asche's influence finally got me an opening. Even so, it was a tentative thing up to the last moment. I was told by the Marine press liaison here that the commanding officer of Force Recon would probably turn me down in the end, but that at least I could try and talk him into it. It turned out that the officers and men were hospitable and even eager to cooperate. That's the way it usually works: the grunts'll help you all the way; it's the rear-echelon people who hold you back.

This reminds me that the Australians never made me feel particularly welcome—but then I was a foreigner, wasn't I? I hate to say this, but the farther away I get the clearer it becomes that they're not a terribly impressive bunch. They seem so at first contact; they have a wonderful surface charm. But they are really a coarse, cultureless version of the British—the hated superior race they call Pommies. In general they strike me as a pretty lightweight crew. There is no madness in them, no passion, no vulnerability, and worst of all no imagination. Here's one small example of the latter: many of them thought I was cracked when they learned I paid $629 to come over here on my own.

Don't get me started.

The morning I left for Dong Ha the monsoon struck. It was like a blizzard, the wind driving a cold rain almost sideways, the trees bending and whooshing, the light making the rain like snow. It was demoralizing—hanging around the echoing Air Freight shed for hours and then Hue–Phu Bai, dreading how it was going to be out on an insert in weather like this. Besides that I was homesick in a heavy black way, worse than ever. At one point I was poised to turn around and go back to the warm luxurious press center and wait out the rain (I'd still be waiting). The only thing that stopped me was the knowledge that the enemy was expected to send another mass of troops across the Demilitarized Zone as soon as the rough weather began. And I knew that a Force Recon insert would be the first to discover them.

One last shot at the Australians.

I can trace the moment when my true feelings about them came into focus. It was during the Asche interview. The other two Marines besides Capt. Barksdale were: Capt. Ira Greene, Jr., of Ephrata, Pennsylvania, and Cpl. James Sohl of Mobile, Alabama. I recall how correct and military and sort of awesome they were, everyone using mad warlike expressions like *Say again?* (for How's that?) and *As you were* (for I take that back) and my favorite, *That's affirmative* or *That's a negative* (for Yes or No). But after the second can of beer they began loosening up. Capt. Greene's face turned red and stayed that way. Capt. Barksdale put on a tight little meaningless smirk. Cpl. Sohl just sat there giggling like Tommy Udo at everything. By the fifth can these three, as well as the two civilians, were glowing with a kind of goonish enthusiasm that is peculiar to American men.

I took a drop or two with the Aussies, you know, and my impression was that as they drank more, their already nearly-immobile mouths began tightening up until it was like being at a ventriloquist convention, and the content of their speech became more reasonable, more logical, more sensible, rather than the other way round. In other words the drunker they got the soberer they got.

Anyway halfway through supper Capt. Barksdale (whom I was calling Barky by this time) began telling me how much he enjoyed *The Honey Badger* and how he heard somewhere that Ruark was a son of a bitch, but that the autobiographical hero of the novel struck him as a fine fellow, and I said most writers have two personalities and their writing personality is often different from their social personality and this is why many writers start out in the first place, because they can only express their true personality by writing, and that's why many writers are wash-outs socially.

In short, I got drunk.

Where was I?

We landed at Dong Ha in a driving rain—at the same wretched airstrip I never figured to see again, the same stucco shack with *Dong Ha* painted on it, the same road leading down the long hill. This time the road was muddy and I followed it to the buildings and tents of 1st Force Reconnaissance Company. *Swift, Silent, Deadly* the sign said. Another said *Second To None* and showed a bed, a bottle of booze, a pair of boxing gloves. (Only cake-eaters could turn out something like that.)

Major Hart was out on an insert, but his executive officer, Capt. Holmes, took me into the headquarters shack and got me oriented on the wall-map, showing me where three Recon teams were at that moment, in positions overlooking infiltration routes. I don't know if you heard about Operation Prairie in the States but it was more or less a continuation of Hastings. It just ended. Hastings was the first North Viet attempt at massive infiltration, Prairie the second. They're expected to try again under cover of the monsoons. This is why Force Recon was sending all its teams to areas just below the Demilitarized Zone.

Holmes said Sgt. DeLucas' team was going out the following morning, and I could accompany them. He sent for DeLucas and told him to get me outfitted and find me a place to sleep.

Let me explain the name Force Recon. The *Force* part refers to the 3rd Marine Amphibious Force, which is composed of two Marine divisions plus supporting units, the whole contingent totaling 56,000. Both divisions have their own recon units; but Force Recon, an independent group, does the deep-penetration work for the whole contingent. Force Recon men are jump-qualified, scuba-trained, mountain climbers, and can sneak ashore in rubber boats, etc.

Staff Sergeant Jackie DeLucas (New Haven, Conn.) is animated and talkative—lots of personality. Short spiky blond hair and an open face. A happy man. ('A guy is either cut out for the military or he aint,' he told me. 'This here's the life for me.') He's been in the Corps eleven years, been busted twice, once for being drunk on duty, once for slugging a higher sergeant. He showed me a couple of scars on his arm from a fight he had in a Japanese market with a 'swabbie' (Marine slang for sailor).

'I'm real hard-core,' he explained.

The officers and NCO's slept in a long narrow one-story building that was once a French army barracks. DeLucas assigned me an empty cot there. He also assigned me a fully automatic M-14 with its stacking swivel and butt-plate taped up. (Fully automatic means that when you pull the trigger it goes *rat-tat-tat* instead of *bang*.) He gave me extra canteens, a gas mask, and enough rations for five days.

While he was helping me pack the rations he nodded toward the wall where he'd crayoned the lines of a poem he said was by Robert Frost. *Forgive, O Lord, my little jokes on Thee and I'll forget Thy great big one on me.* Underneath was an enormous photo of a girl's behind, and beside it he'd written *Wahoo!*

That evening after supper I sat in the small dank messhall with the stay-behinds and watched a segment of the *Combat* television series. It was about carrier pigeons and probably stunk, but since I had my beer and cigars I was in an exalted state and thought it outstanding. (I've discovered that one of life's pleasures is to watch a movie with a buzz on. It doesn't matter what the movie's about.)

The following morning dawned sharp and blue, surprisingly. I ran into Sgt. DeLucas at the four-holer and we sat there letting the first rays of the sun warm our faces. The flat countryside stretched away before us, blue shadows all elongated.

"Just like a morning on the farm, aint it,' said De Lucas, who grew up in Iowa.

After breakfast the team members and me smeared camouflage paint on our faces & hands, saddled up, and went outside to have our picture taken. This was DeLucas' idea; he had arranged it with a guy who owned a Polaroid camera. DeLucas gave me the picture as a souvenir.

I was surprised at the amount of gear they carried. While we were waiting for the truck I asked each man what he had, and wrote it down.

Sgt. DeLucas: automatic rifle, M-79 grenade launcher, 416 rounds, 24 M-79 rounds, 11 fragmentation grenades, 2 CS gas grenades, 1 green-smoke grenade, 1 radio battery, gas mask, binoculars, five days' worth of rations, four canteens of water.

Pfc. Leroy Grimes of Compton, California: automatic rifle, 360 rounds, 6 M-79 rounds, 4 frags, 2 gas grenades, 1 green smoke, gas mask, rations and water.

(M-79 rounds are beautiful objects with gold-colored tips. They're fired from a weapon that resembles a short fat shotgun. The rounds are 40 mm., which is about the diameter of a silver dollar.)

Lance Corporal James Hicks of Ironton, Missouri: automatic rifle, 360 rounds, 10 M-79 rounds, 4 frags, 2 gas, 1 radio, mask, rations and water.

L/Cpl. Wayne Jones of Bowman, North Dakota: automatic rifle, 420 rounds, 10 M-79 rounds, 6 frags, 1 green smoke, 2 gas, 1 radio, 2 white-phosphorus grenades, 2 thermite grenades (to destroy the radios if capture is imminent), mask, rations and water.

Pfc. Romeo Vasques of Santa Monica, California: automatic rifle, M-79 grenade launcher, 360 rounds, 24 M-79 rounds, 4 frags, 2 white phosphorus, 2 gas, 1 green smoke, 1 radio battery, mask, rations and water.

I carried the automatic rifle and a hundred rounds just to make DeLucas happy.

None of us had any changes of clothing. We all had ponchos. No helmets—everyone wore Aussie-type bush hats.

DeLucas held a last-minute informal briefing in the shabby messhall (the formal briefing took place the night before). Our mission was to traverse ground represented by four grid squares on the map, each boxing a thousand square meters. A subsidiary mission was, believe it or not, to collect a nut, a berry and a rock. When I asked DeLucas about this he shrugged. 'We get weird requests like that all the time. Maybe General Walt collects rocks, who knows?'

Anyway at the last-minute briefing he said: 'If we get hit, we aint leaving a soul behind, unless he's physically dead and I deem him so dead.' DeLucas is proud he has never lost a man. Team 12 has been surrounded twice but escaped intact both times. The gas masks and gas grenades were used in one of these escapes. 'Whenever we get surrounded,' he explained, 'we put on our masks and heave our CS. The gooks think it's poison gas and really bug out!' He told me incidentally that L/Cpl. Jones kissed the helicopter that extracted them on their last escape.

In the briefing he warned us to go easy on our water because climbing down to a stream is dangerous, since the streams in the area were in open valleys. 'We'll go for refills only as a means of last result,' he said.

Recon inserts avoid contact with the enemy. That's why I was surprised at the amount of gear they carry, particularly ammo: I always thought a recon patrol should be light on its feet so it could cover a lot of ground fast if discovered. That was the policy in Korea. Here the Marines are bristling with firepower on every mission, whether it's a battalion operation or a five-man patrol. The Aussies travel light—about 120 rounds per man and two or three frags—the idea being to avoid casualties by staying quick and mobile. I'd like to hear a debate sometime between an Aussie and a Marine on the topic, *Is the infantry officer's primary task to kill the enemy or preserve the lives of his men?* I suppose it's obvious he should try and do both; but there's no question that Marines are much more willing to take punishment.

The way I feel about it is, in World War II killing the enemy was probably the most important thing, but here you want to get your men home alive. Killing Viet Cong is like trying to wipe out the Mafia: you're wasting your time. Actually wiping out the Mafia would be easier since the people support it out of fear, whereas the guerrillas are supported out of fear *and* political conviction, plus other subtler reasons.

We were driven to the helicopter pad, where DeLucas briefed the pilots. I noticed they stared surreptitiously at the team with something like awe. Force Recon has a semi-legendary reputation; they're the Commandos of the Corps. Besides, camouflaged faces are impressive if you've grown up on war movies, as most of us have.

We climbed aboard a big Chinook and sat down on the sideseats. DeLucas' load was so heavy he went through to the floor. He waited down there all doubled up like an ironing-board, until the crew chief pulled him out.

We lifted off and headed west, following the Cam Lo River. In a few minutes we were over the area where I joined —— Company on Hastings. The only thing that looked familiar was the blown-out bridge, and I thought I saw the meadow where the lad from Pennsylvania told me about his dad and dead mom and the hills around home.

The terrain between Dong Ha and Cam Lo is generally rolling, but west of Cam Lo it gets mountainous. We kept going till we came to The Rockpile, where one of the biggest battles of Operation Prairie took place, and here we turned north, crossing the river where the mountains really rear up. The Marines consider this rough country, but even from the air I could see it wasn't as bad as the jungles of Phuoc Tuy province. It was woods, not true jungle. Unlike the jungles of Phuoc Tuy, though, there were no roads or cart-tracks—just dim dangerous trails snaking up and over the mountains.

As we began to descend, DeLucas passed out chewing gum. 'Everybody be watching out the portholes,' he shouted. (Once Barksdale's team was inserted in the middle of an enemy bivouac area.)

We dropped down abruptly—but the ramp stayed closed—and then clawed back up into the sky. This was a feint, in case there were North Viets anywhere in the area. I learned later our helicopter made five feints in all, each a half mile from the last—the idea being that the enemy wouldn't know on which touch-down we left the craft.

The ramp was lowered on the second landing. We jumped out and raced madly for the cover of the woods above us, as the helicopter climbed away. The clearing was steep and we had to jump over several fallen trees. Once in the woods we kept going for a couple of hundred yards and then stopped. The three helicopters (two gun-ships and the Chinook) were 'on station,' circling high above us after the feints were completed. DeLucas made radio contact in a low whisper, one hand cupping his mouth. I could barely hear him; it's amazing how sensitive the handset is.

'Skylark, Skylark, this is Toro,' he whispered. 'How do you read this station? Over . . . Roger. I read you five by five. Thank you. Out.'

The helicopters flew away to the east and the silence was terrific, the woods ominous. We lay there in the brush for an hour, just listening.

We spent the rest of the day creeping, stopping, looking, listening. Every time we came to an overlook we'd con the countryside through binoculars. One vista knocked me out. You remember last fall when your dad took us for that first drive? and we stopped on a high dirt road overlooking the valley where the Shakers live? Well, I never expected to find a duplicate in Vietnam, but there it was—a beautiful place with windswept grass. You could almost see barns at the far end.

During one of our stops I had my first run-in with the dreaded leech. I felt warm water running down my leg, and naturally thought one of my canteens was leaking. It turned out to be blood, and a lot of it. I always thought leeches lived in marshes only, but here we were in high country.

They fascinated me. They're weird-looking, like miniature snakes traveling on their tails, the rest soaring up like a cobra. They get wind of you and drop everything and come pulsing toward you in a frantic series of undulations. I wanted to laugh out loud the first time I saw them coming: they stumble all over themselves in their eagerness to suck your blood; you can almost hear them panting and slavering at the sight of you. The craziest thing, though, is when you find a whole gang of them closing in from all sides. You find yourself thinking about throwing gas grenades and kissing helicopters.

We spent a lot of time looking for them on our clothing, and whenever we found one we'd squirt a little insect-repellent on it. The leech'd go into a long death ballet, wreathing and writhing until it dropped off. The reason you go to all that trouble is that if you pull it off, the head'll stay in and cause infection. And if you try flicking one off your clothing, it'll clamp onto your finger. You can't feel it when they drill into you; they must exude some kind of anesthetic like mosquitoes do. After one has sucked on you awhile it gets bloated and sluggy, like a hunk of slimy snot.

It started to cloud up in the afternoon.

Around five o'clock we came across a recent bivouac area, just below the ridgeline, with human turds downhill not more than a day old. We found a fuse can with Chinese markings, a machine-gun magazine, a bottle of liquid soap and a tube of toothpaste. The brand name of the toothpaste was worn away, but along the bottom was *Hanoi, Vietnam.* We also found several cooking-fire sites in the area; each against a tree in a spade-dug hole. Each site was camouflaged against aerial observation by tying the tops of bushes together, forming a sub-canopy.

L/Cpl. Wayne Jones found a grenade—and provided a moment or two of excitement. Jones is a big muscular guy with an enormous head, snapping blue eyes and no front teeth; a characteristic friendly American farmboy. He had apparently never seen a 'ChiCom' grenade before and, thinking it was a hammer of some kind, began pounding it in the palm of his hand—testing it for weight and balance. The trouble with that is, this type of grenade is armed by pounding or tapping it against a hard surface. The first I knew of all this was when I heard DeLucas gasp, and saw him grab it away from Jones.

We stopped for the night on another ridge, just off the trail, well hidden but close enough to see anyone passing by. Behind us was a tall tree with a North Viet observation post at the top—at least there was a crude ladder and a platform, and who but they could've made it? Anyway Romeo Vasques went climbing up it like a big brown bear. A few minutes later he threw down a note saying he could see all the way to Dong Ha. When he got down I tried to go up, but froze halfway.

After we were all settled in for the night, I asked Vasques where he was from and learned that until recently he'd lived in the good ole Sawtelle neighborhood—on Corinth, just north of Santa Monica Blvd. In case you've forgotten, the new Bank of America is on the corner of Corinth and Santa Monica. He knew all about the Tivoli theater and Mrs. Karlson's Donut Shop and all the rest—but DeLucas made us cut out the whispering and watch the trail.

He set the night watches: three men awake, two asleep, changing off every two hours. DeLucas didn't assign me any watch and I didn't volunteer. I was dead tired and glad to sleep through, to get my strength back for tomorrow so I wouldn't be a drag.

We were all bunched up within reach of each other so in case of emergency we could escape holding on like elephants do, tail to trunk. There was no danger of someone dropping a grenade in our midst, because we were in heavy brush and would've heard him creeping up.

The night came on suddenly like it always does and the phosphorescent forest floor began glowing all round us. I slept comfortably, except around 3 a.m. when it rained a bit.

The second day the monsoon returned: a steady drizzle in the morning and a rain-wind that built up almost to gale force by nightfall.

During the afternoon something happened that should've scared me half to death but didn't. We were creeping along a wide trail when I looked down and saw, planted in the mud, a flat piece of metal with a little platform in the middle. It had originally been buried; the day's rain had partially exposed it. Somehow Grimes, Hicks and DeLucas, the three men in front of me, had missed it. What it was was a Bouncing Betty mine, the kind that jumps three feet in the air before blowing you to pieces, the kind that reduced that Marine on the County Fair to something resembling a beetle.

There's only one way to deal with a mine: avoid it. But I didn't do that. I kicked it. Nothing happened, so I moved on—after making sure Jones had seen it. On our next halt I asked him, whispering, what that metal thing was back there. He told me. Apparently he hadn't seen me kick it, though. When I say kick I don't mean I tried to punt it like a football: I just tapped the edge of it with the side of my boot, to see if was a piece of equipment or something.

Jones and me, we made a great pair.

I don't know how to explain it, except to say that my brain was disconnected just then.

I could've killed three of us and wounded the rest.

I hate to turn Freudian on you, but I just remembered a bad headache that second day. But no, hold it. Now that I think about it, it came on in the morning, before the mine thing. Anyway it was fierce. My morale plummeted, like it used to when I got one of my Beasts in Los Angeles.

That headache turned into quite an emotional experience. If I had thought of myself as hard, well, I learned then how mushy I really am. Big waves of homesickness came flooding over me and all I could think of was . . . It was the worst attack yet, and if they get any worse I'm in trouble.

In the midst of all this came a thought that made me feel even worse: that when the time comes to walk into

Congland, I won't be able to do it—that I'll chicken out for sure, because I'm too homesick.

All my loud plans and fancy talk. How mortifying.

But I'm okay now.

Anyway I guess I'll blame the headache for the temporary disconnection that let me idly kick a mine in my path.

I don't get scared when I'm supposed to. It doesn't bother me to think about the mine, even though it should. What bothers me is that it doesn't bother me.

I have an unrealistic sense of security whenever I'm traveling with troops in the boondocks. The only time I've been frightened was just before the parachute jump. Oh yes—gory corpses frighten me; I identify with them. Will I end up like that if I walk out into Congland? (The corpses have to be ripped up, though, to bother me.)

That night was as physically miserable as any I can recall. It rained on and off, and the six of us lay like pigs in a mudwallow. By midnight we were soaked to the skin and shivering, teeth chattering uncontrollably.

An electrifying thing happened that night, some time between three and four a.m. I had been alternately sleeping and waking, my metabolism slowing down enough to let me sleep comfortably for a half hour at a time. Whenever the cold woke me up I'd listen for the sound of rain on the poncho. If I heard (and felt) it, I'd try and go back to sleep. If it wasn't raining I'd raise the poncho and look around to see if any stars were out, hoping not only for a clear sky but dawn itself.

After one of these routine look-arounds I turned over

on my side, very slow and agonizingly because of wet clothing and the sloppy ground, and was putting my head down on the gas mask when I noticed something. The whole forest around me was glowing with phosphorescent leaves and bark, all strewn randomly—except for some spots in a straight line. I blinked and stared, and it looked as if some were flickering.

I reached for my glasses; but they were all befogged and I had to work to get them dry. When I finally put them on, everything jumped out clearly. There were men below, in column, on the trail, each carrying a tiny lantern, not thirty yards downhill.

I have no idea why they were traveling with lights, pinpointing their progress so clearly. It seemed insane, but I knew there must be a reason for it. The lights were spaced ten or fifteen yards apart and I could see five or six or seven at a time, moving generally north to south. (I was pretty well oriented to direction because all day I'd been peering at DeLucas' wrist compass.) The wind was howling in the trees but it didn't seem to affect the lanterns. My guess is, they were small candles behind a glass shield. They didn't seem to throw out rays, though, so it's hard to imagine them being used to light the path. What else could they have been for?

I felt safe enough. We were hidden in darkness and even if one of the Marines had snored, the wind would've covered the sound. The only thing that worried me was that someone might lift up his poncho and see what I was seeing, and DeLucas would call in an artillery barrage. But luckily Team 12 was all curled up beneath their tucked-in ponchos, and no one stirred.

The lanterns kept going by, winking in and out among the trees. At one point I had an urge to nudge DeLucas awake, to share this fantastic experience with him, and tell him the Frost-like couplet running through my mind:

> Whose woods these are I think I know;
> They must belong to Uncle Ho.

A little later I wondered if the column wasn't headed for the Rockpile or Camp Carroll for an attack, and shouldn't I do something about it. But I didn't. Whoever these invisible people were, they weren't going south to spread the gospel—that much I knew. But even so I couldn't do anything about it.

I counted nineteen lanterns before the last one faded out among the trees. I was so excited I lay stark staring awake for the rest of the night, about two hours.

At dawn it was coldly drizzling, and DeLucas whispered a startling remark.

'I don't give a fuck if the entire gook army's out there. We're gonna have some hot rations.'

I wondered if he'd seen what I saw. I doubted it, but I didn't ask. DeLucas is strictly Marine, an all-purpose gook-destroyer, and he'd never have understood why I didn't alert him to such a dream target.

He pulled out a bottle of cough medicine ('Guaranteed to make you cough,' he whispered) and passed it around. Everyone looked like sourdough prospectors wetting their whistles. It was terpin hydrate elixir, 40% alcohol, ferocious stuff, but it seemed to make the shivering and chattering lessen. DeLucas made me take a second swig, and it was then I first noticed how solicitous he was of me. He and the others had been calling me Mister, and now DeLucas began doing things that made me feel almost elderly. He made me a cup of cocoa and while I was drinking it reached over and spread his poncho across my legs. I felt like singing *September Song*. Then he noticed my hands, which were white and curdled like prunes. They looked like a dead man's hands. DeLucas pulled out a pair of gloves and insisted I put them on. He asked about my feet. They were dry, thanks to the Australian boots I was wearing.

We carried two kinds of hot rations: C's and long-range rations. The latter come in plastic bags, with dehydrated food inside. You open the bag, pour in boiling water, close it up and wait twenty minutes. The different kinds are: chicken & rice, spaghetti & meatballs, beef & rice, beans & meatballs. The Marines use C–4 plastic explosive to boil the water. The heat is intense and you can bring a cup of water to boil in ten seconds. The flame is so bright you have to hunch over it with a poncho to hide it. 'Pull up your chair,' said DeLucas, and we sat on our packs face to face, hovering over the flame like big bats, while the others trained their weapons on the approaches.

What a wonderful thing is a fire on a cold wet day.

After everyone had eaten we put on fresh paint and saddled up. DeLucas' pack was so ponderous he had to swing it on in a big sideways arc that would've knocked down a mule.

Some time that afternoon we ran across a hidden stream and stopped to fill our canteens. I spoke to L/Cpl. James Hicks for the first time, asking where his home was. I had been watching him throughout the patrol but never got around to speaking to him. I had scribbled in my notepad: *Hicks like a small stunned animal, silent and indrawn. If I were his parents I'd worry & watch him.*

Somehow he reminded me of a Mohawk Indian. DeLucas later told me a little about him. It seems that on the night of the Marine Corps birthday Hicks was to go out on an insert with his team (he isn't a regular member of Team 12; he's filling in for a sick guy) but he showed up drunk. The team took off without him and it drove him berserk: he saddled up, grabbed his weapon, and started out alone across the Dong Ha flats. Someone headed him off in a jeep and brought him back. 'He was gonna kill him a gook,' explained DeLucas. He's up for punishment now, but DeLucas says they'll go easy because he has a good record.

Anyway we were filling our canteens and I asked him where his home was. He looked at me and broke into the finest smile I'd seen since Dick Rosen's. I think he was relieved I had spoken to him. After all, I'd asked the hometowns of all the other guys, and I guess he felt left out. He laboriously printed his name, address and zip code in my notepad.

Around sunset we found an adequate landing zone for the extraction at 0930 the following morning. We settled down for the night on a neighboring ridgeline.

That night I had another dangerous experience—a nightmare from which I awoke yelling. The dream went like this: I was lying on a cot in a building like the French barracks in Dong Ha. It was dark in there, but I could see daylight through the window. A Vietnamese man, probably a VC, appeared in the window. He put his elbows on the sill, as if to rest a moment. He saw me and froze. The sun was shining on one side of his face, the other was obscured in shadow. The eye appeared to made of glass; it glittered in the sun, staring at me.

The next thing I knew, DeLucas was shaking me and I was in the middle of a yell. I woke up instantly and could hear the echo rolling around the ridges. Jones and Vasques were sitting up rigidly, clutching their weapons. I couldn't see Grimes or Hicks, but I imagine they were doing the same. After we got settled down again, the only thing I could think of to say was *I'm sorry*. DeLucas whispered back that it was okay, but he was probably wondering how the hell he ever got saddled with a cracking-up civilian.

(I'm definitely not hard-core.)

That's not all that happened that night. Just before dawn a rooster started crowing nearby—very near—and we almost jumped out of our skins. Was there a North Viet base camp behind us? If so, had they heard me yell? Of course they had. DeLucas decided we'd better stay where we were, well-hidden.

At dawn it started raining again and he said, 'We'll probably get extended a day or two' and everyone groaned. But we were lucky: by noon the weather had cleared enough to allow one-mile visibility, and the message came through: extraction in twenty minutes, helicopters on their way. We crept down from our hiding place and up to a tilted clearing on the other side of the next ridgeline. Overlooking it from the north was a massive red hillside, blasted bare from napalm and shellfire. You could see ruined bunkers and trenches. DeLucas said it was part of the Hill 400 complex, where heavy fighting took place during Operation Prairie. The ridgeline loomed starkly against the grey sky, and we stood facing it with our weapons. It somehow gave off the impression of being occupied.

We were lined up in the proper loading order, when

suddenly the three helicopters appeared over the hills to the south: two Huey gun-ships and an H-34. It was a dramatic moment. The H-34 swooped down and hovered two feet above the clearing, its rotors sending stinging spray into our faces. In less than ten seconds we were away, and I understood why Jones had kissed the helicopter that time.

Twenty minutes later the six of us were walking across the Dong Ha airstrip in a driving rain, and I was thinking about good ole Jake Bizelle and Terry Suggins and how splendid they looked that hot sunny day loading their little troopers aboard the planes in the swirling dust. It seemed such a long time ago.

There was an atmospheric de-briefing in a half-blasted stone building where the rubber boats were stored, the six of us sitting around a blanket-covered table in near-darkness while the Intelligence sergeant asked questions and took notes. DeLucas identified the magazine from a book of the world's weapons as belonging to a Russian-invented Chinese-produced machine gun. We turned in our nut, berry and stone too. I was surprised at how extroverty all five guys were acting, all giving the sergeant a raucous hard time. It didn't hit me till later that they'd been under terrific tension for three days & nights and were just blowing off steam. (I saw a lot more of this during the rest of the day and evening.)

Finally DeLucas rose and stretched and said it was time to shit, shower and shave, and everyone sort of growled and ran out to get their brandy. All teams get a brandy ration when they return from a mission, and you could hear these five howling animals hunting up the corpsmen for theirs.

But the corpsmen were gone. It turned out that the whole 1st Recon Company was moving south, and the advance party, including the corpsmen, had already left. 3rd Recon Battalion was replacing them, and their advance party was just arriving. I introduced myself to the commanding officer, Major Bill Pierce, and asked if I could accompany one of his teams some time in the future. He said yes.

That evening was the most enjoyable I've spent in Vietnam.

After supper James Hicks, of all people, invited me to sit down across the table from him and have some coffee. It was strangely moving the way this kid of twenty with brown eyes, shyer than any cow, folded his hands formally and made a big effort to be the gracious host. I teased him a bit, saying I'd heard he went out on a one-man patrol the other day. He sort of googled at that, gulping. I asked him if that was what usually happened when he got loaded—him wanting to go into action. He smiled and said no; ordinarily he just keeps drinking till he passes out, which I thought kind of sad. (For him the Corps may be a kind of prison, as it is to many Marines.) He said the trouble that night was he switched from whisky to gin to brandy.

Later that evening I went back to the drafty shabby messhall with my cigar and beer and watched the antics of the Force Recon fellows. There was a good deal of growling, I noticed. At one point Wayne Jones vaulted over a bench and fell on Leroy Grimes and bit his ear. Everyone seemed to take it in stride as an ordinary occurrence. Jones and Grimes rose somberly off the floor and resumed their seats as if nothing had happened.

But this started an outbreak of ear-biting, and I moved my chair closer to the door.

The movie turned out to be a *Batman* segment about the Mad Hatter. Watching it was some experience. When the theme song came on they all shouted the one-word lyric ('Batmaaaan') over and over in unison with the soundtrack, but violent and blasting like some demon-possessed chorus. It was a tremendously joyous sound, but when you remembered the tensions of their present exist-ence, and their youth, it was poignant too.

How seriously they took the melodrama itself! All the archness of the dialogue was lost on them, and they sat there goggle-eyed, following the action enthralled. And it occurred to me that they prefer their drama black & white like *Batman* because that's the way their life is—the good guys chasing the bad. And the truth is, despite all the crap about civic action and pacification and winning the heart & minds of the people, there's only one thing the ordinary grunt understands and that's killing bad guys.

When I came back to the tent (the new outfit had already taken over the barracks) I found Jackie DeLucas and the others sitting over three bottles of whisky, singing riotously, Romeo Vasques accompanying on his guitar. I didn't stay long because another movie was about to start, but they sang a song for me called *Recon Blues*, about a team caught out on the trail with a dead radio battery and 'surrounded by slanted eyes.' It had an eerie wailing qual-ity to it, like the best hillbilly music.

I went back to the messhall with my prop cigar and can of beer and sat through a truly outstanding movie called *Winter A Go Go*, combining rock & roll with skiing around Lake Tahoe.

The tent was black when I returned but I could hear

talking. I went in, found my cot, took off my boots and lay down under the blanket. Leroy Grimes got up woozily and turned on the bare light-bulb, 'so you can see what you're doing,' even though I'd already done it. I was amazed to see all the young animals lying under their nets stark naked. No one had a blanket over him, and it was cold. Apparently they were all whisky numb. 'All set?' asked Grimes solicitously. After he turned off the light he lost his bearings and said to himself: 'Gravity's pulling me to the right, so I'll just bear to the left.' Then he decided he needed a cold shower and stumbled outside.

DeLucas and Jones were having a conversation in radio lingo. Each had his own call sign. DeLucas was Motor Mouth, because he couldn't stop talking. Jones' call sign was Donald Duck, I dunno why.

'Donald Duck, Donald Duck. This is Motor Mouth. Over.'

'Motor Mouth, this is Duck. Go.'

'Duck, this is Mouth. How do you read me? Over.'

'Mouth, this is Duck. Read you five by five. How you me? Over.'

The inflection was stylized, like the way telephone operators talk. On and on they went. There was little in the way of content; their colloquy was mostly an exchange of formalities.

James Hicks was too drunk to be understood. He kept trying desperately to contribute something to the traffic, trying to 'get on the net' as they say. They called him Unknown Station and pretty well excluded him, until at last he managed to pull himself together. Then they turned the net over for one message, after formally paving the way in the most laborious manner. Unknown Station expressed himself in the voice of a rooster: 'Fuck

fuck fuck fuck fuck-KAW!'

Grimes came back and they began razzing him about being a virgin. His call sign was Gooney Bird.

'The only broads this guy's seen are in a Sears-Roebuck catalogue.'

'I seen 'em, I tell ya!'

Motor Mouth went on to tell how Gooney Bird was so infatuated with a certain girl on Okinawa 'he runs out and buys her a fifty-dollar radio!' Motor Mouth was scandalized.

On and on they went in the dark.

'Motor Mouth, Motor Mouth. This is Gooney Bird. Over.'

'Bird, this is Mouth. Go.'

'Be advised I have a message from Unknown Station. Will you relay? Over.'

And after the formalities were concluded, the forlorn message was always 'Fuck fuck fuck fuck fuck-KAW!'

Vasques was the only one who didn't participate; he was over in the corner trying to sleep. Along about one o'clock he made the mistake of complaining: 'Hey, why don't you guys shut up and get some sleep!' The others immediately turned on him, bombarding him with messages.

'Bean Bandit, Bean Bandit. This is Motor Mouth. Over.'

'Chili Guts, Chili Guts. This is Gooney Bird. Over.'

'Tortilla Twister, Tortilla Twister. This is Donald Duck. Over.'

They tried everything, but nothing 'raised' Vasques.

They were still going when I fell asleep.

*　　*　　*

When I got back to the Danang press center the next
day I found the following 'Situation Report' on the bulle-
tin board:

Late Sitrep
1900 16 Nov

*Third Division Marines battling near the DMZ today
reported killing 14 NVA soldiers in the first heavy contact since late September on Operation Prairie.*

*The battle is continuing 4000 yards south of the artil-
lery plateau at Camp Carroll, 12 miles southwest of Dong
Ha.*

*Two Marine companies and two companies of RVN
troops are in contact with what is believed a reinforced
company of communists.*

Could these be the lantern-carriers I saw?

(no date)

. . . I'm happy to say it's all over. I can't visit the Viet Cong, because there's no safe way.

I'm going to try and come home before January 23rd. . . .

I went to Saigon last week for three reasons: to get my visa extended, pick up Asche's letter of introduction, and arrange a visit to a patrol-boat base in the Delta.

I was feeling shaky on the flight down. The Viet Cong thing was looming ominously in the pit of my stomach. Only the day before, I'd gotten your letter saying *War Memorial*'s publication date was January 23rd, and I was feeling sad I wouldn't be with you on that day.

If I were paranoid I'd say things were conspiring against me the day I went to Saigon. When we landed at Tan Son Nhut the first thing I saw was a blue & white Pan-Am jet taking off, probably headed for the States. I had a morale problem for a few seconds. The next thing I saw, when I got to downtown Saigon, was a Singer Sewing-Machine Center. I couldn't believe my eyes. Furthermore it looked very much like the one in Medford (I guess they all look pretty much alike from the street) and I imagined I could see Mr. Metraw limping around furiously inside, puffing on his Camel—and for some reason that made me even more homesick than I was before.

But that wasn't all. A minute later I passed a magazine stand and saw the current issue of *Time* with Julia Child on the cover, and all I could think of was how you used to watch her in Huntingdon, taking notes, while I laughed in the background.

But I didn't feel like laughing then.

I needed to see a friendly face. I thought of Mal Asche but, as far as I knew, he was in Thailand. Then I remembered Dick Rosen and went up to the CBS office, hoping to bask in the sunshine of his ear-to-ear grin; but he wasn't in.

I wandered glumly over to the Continental Palace to pick up the letter at the desk. The clerk said Asche was in his room. I called and went up.

He already had two guests. One was Major En, who runs the school for 'revolutionary development teams' in Vung Tau. The other was Mr. Hoang, whom Asche had mentioned to me in Danang (and who Rosen said was an opium addict). He's a newspaper editor and a sort of Vietnamese Jewish intellectual: he has the kind of mind and temperament that won't give a slower person a break. Hoang is a nervous wild-eyed man with a desiccated face. He speaks English perfectly.

Asche produced a bottle of Scotch, some glasses, some cigars, and we sat down. Asche is sympathetic as far as my writing goes; he understands I'm not intellectual and my book isn't a general survey of the Vietnam war or anything like that. Incidentally many people assume I'm doing either a Bernard Fall kind of book (you know the type—with chapter headings like 'Indo-China and the West' and 'Montagnards and Vietnamese Society') or a series of humorous anecdotes about GI Joe. I never have the nerve to admit it's about my Selfe. Asche caught on right away, though. In the hotel room he told the two Vietnamese what I was doing, and then unexpectedly asked me to tell them my plan to visit the other side. The idea was that they might be able to help me.

I told them about it, briefly, and showed them the card I wrote you about (*Greetings! I am a civilian. I came to Vietnam to write a book about the war* . . . etc.)

They reacted strongly, to say the least. Mr. Hoang nearly fell over backward, literally—he brought his legs up so violently he almost overturned himself. Major En just stared aghast.

They were against it.

We discussed it at length. I'm not going to reproduce the conversation because I'm too embarrassed. After Hoang got through with me I felt like a fool. He wiped the floor with me. At one point he snatched my little card and read the salutation aloud.

'People are killing each other and he says *Greetings!*'

I laughed too, because suddenly the whole thing struck me as absurdly naïve.

Major En was courteous but just as scornful of the idea as Hoang. They said my chances of surviving were slim.

I crawled out of there with my tail between my legs, and yet exhilarated because it was dawning on me that I wasn't going to have to do it after all. It was all over! My stomach was my own again; for weeks it had belonged to my throat. I allowed myself to think seriously for the first time about going home.

I wandered around the stinking Saigon streets in a high daze. I saw the Pan-Am office and decided to go in and ask a few tantalizing questions, like *How often do planes leave for New York?* and so on; but it was shuttered down for the noon-to-three siesta. I went into a bar and had a couple of drinks. It was the first time I ever wanted a drink to celebrate something. I only wished Jack Moseley had been there, or any familiar friendly face.

After lunch I went to the Vietnamese press office to take care of my visa, and guess who I ran into—the dreaded Mr. Hoang! He was polite, although he spoke to me as one would to a retarded child. He didn't suspect I was liking him madly for being the instrument of my happiness. Of course I was drunk when I saw him, so drunk I could hardly find my mouth with my cigar, and I don't imagine this improved his opinion of me.

Later that afternoon, having nothing better to do, I went to the JUSPAO building for the daily news briefing, sometimes referred to as the Five O'Clock Follies. The main piece of news turned out to be a sort of punctuation to what I had undergone in Asche's room. There had been a Viet Cong ambush near Dalat. Some of the victims were American civilians, employees of Page Communications Engineers, Inc. Others killed were a Canadian, a Filipino, a Vietnamese and four Koreans, all civilians.

I don't have much to say about the Delta visit.

I went out on two 12-hour patrols on the Bassac River. On the first we got into a fire-fight. One of the other boats was fired on from shore and we sped to the rescue, firing streams of tracers and M-79 rounds. There were extra weapons at hand—a Garand rifle and an Armalite—and I had an urge to grab one and blaze away like John Wayne; but that would've been unseemly, I decided.

The patrol captain, Lt. Fred B. Franklin of San Diego, called me a good luck charm afterward—not because his crew escaped unhurt but because they made contact. There hadn't been any in weeks.

All I did for the next two days was moon around in a daze, dreaming of going home. I asked nobody anything, didn't even bother to get the details of the fight. The swabbies kept glancing at me—I suppose wondering when I was going to interview them or do something, anything. I did nothing except trail my hand in the water for two days.

December 14th, press center

. . . I have a new friend named Frank Womack, a free-lance illustrator and artist. Right now he's working for the Navy, doing pictures of Marines in action. Womack is forty-five, has a short white beard and nut-brown skin. He holds a black belt in judo, but his manner is mild. He lives with his young wife on a houseboat in Miami. She teaches grade school in Coral Gables.

He has told me some secrets, since we are somewhat on the same wave-length. But not entirely. He loves Marines as I do (he's a former Marine himself) but tends to glorify them, seeing the bravery and the camaraderie and the patriotism, but never the dark side. To him a Marine's death is a glorious noble event. His outlook is a 1943 outlook, when Marines were dying in the surf off Tarawa, back in the days when war was simple and a soldier's duty was clear.

I accused him of being a sucker for Marine bullshit. He laughed and admitted it. He'd do anything for a Marine. He's always inviting them to visit him on the houseboat. He told me proudly that no less than forty-three showed up last summer. Two of them stayed three weeks. I asked him if he liked that.

'No,' he said, 'but after all I invited them. They be-haved themselves—never brought dames, did their own housekeeping.'

There's something appealing about him; maybe it's simply that he likes people. His eyes are droopy and melancholy and at the same time filled with affection for his fellow man. He's a good listener too; before I knew it I was telling him about my Congland plan and how it all turned out.

'I think that's wonderful,' he said in his quiet voice.

The thing is, we get drunk together every night. When I come back from the movie, half gone already, I find him sitting on his bunk reading (MacArthur's memoirs) by a solitary bedside lamp, and there's a bottle of Johnnie Walker on the table.

We start talking and drinking. As he gets drunker his voice gets softer, his eyes droopier, and he tells secrets. Afterward he stares at me aghast and asks: 'Now why did I tell you that?'

One of his secrets was that he got shot in ambush last year and his jaw is out of whack (that's why he wears the beard).

As the night wears on he repeats himself and forgets he's already shown me the pictures he carries of his wife. Hanging from the wall above his bunk is a Christmas greeting she sent him: a paper tree with family photos hanging from the branches and on top, representing the star, a shot of Womack's mournful puss with cotton pasted on for the Santa beard, and a jingle-bells cap. Hanging from the bottom is a scroll with a message ad-dressed to *Mister Womack*, signed by the kids in his wife's class.

He admits he likes 'playing Marine' as he calls it—going out on patrols and so on, which he's done a lot of. This is his fourth visit to Vietnam and, if he survives it, probably won't be his last. I give him hell for this. One night I told him how I felt when I saw all the ripped-up corpses and the beetle and the tumbling sow. I think I was trying to convey to him what a dangerous, death-stinking place this is, and that he should get out before it's too late. But it turns out he's seen worse than I, and more of it. He told me about some of the Marines he's seen, big tears rolling down his cheeks.

('Now why did I tell you that?')

When he starts speaking to me in Spanish I know he's about had it. After I turn out the light he always says *Buenas noches, amigo.*

Our third roommate is, or rather was, an unhappy fellow named Major Wade Ostermeyer, an Air Force transportation officer. Everyone called him The Minor. He was amiable and harmless and fat. He was the press center's 'character.'

Last night was his final night in Vietnam. The staff threw a party for him in the bar. There was a sign saying *Bon Voyage, Minor.* When the party broke up around midnight, in comes the Minor, making a terrific racket with the double-doors, banging and scraping them until Womack and I yelled at him to cut it out. This somehow inspired him to turn around and stumble outside for a whole new entrance, louder and more boorish than before. He finally hove to at the end of Womack's bunk and made a drunken speech. It was long and rambling and repetitious, but what he said was essentially that he thought himself a born fool and that he'd just spent the past year trying to do a job he was incapable of and that he was exhausted now. Womack listened, beard in hand, and when it was over and Ostermeyer was standing there swaying and red-faced with embarrassment, said: 'Wade, I've never liked you as much as I do now.' And the Minor went waddling outside and treated us to a final cacophonous grand-entrance. We were all sick with laughter.

Next morning our Vietnamese maid came in, saw the empty luggage rack, pointed to the bunk and said: 'Monsieur finis?'

'Finis,' said Womack.

(Cablegram)

December 26th, press center

. . . Here's how it happened.

Last week I decided to spend a day riding a Medevac helicopter. It was too late in the afternoon, though, and we only made one trip—ferrying a German shepherd and its Marine master from one place to another, just outside Danang. When we got back to the base (the Marble Mountain Air Facility) I ran into Frank Womack, in full combat get-up. He was waiting for a lift out to one of the infantry regiments, where he was to go on patrol. We sat outside the pilots' ready-room, the setting sun in our faces, and talked. I told him, not for the first time, that he was a sucker for the military and ought to go home before he gets himself fucked up. He nodded solemnly and said it wouldn't be long now ('I'll be folding up my sketchbook soon') but I didn't believe him. He enjoys playing Marine too much. He's still under the influence of the brainwashing he received at Parris Island (where they break you down into nothing and remake you, and no matter what happens in later life, some part of you will always belong to the Corps). Womack was a happy man when he was in, and now it seems he's trying to recapture the days of yore when he was young and free and immortal.

His helicopter showed up and he left, and I hitch-hiked back to the press center.

Next morning, December 18th, I caught a ride back to Marble Mountain and hadn't been there more than ten minutes when the 'Medevac chopper' clattered down for refueling and I climbed aboard.

Our first pick-up was a boy of eight with a broken leg, and his father. The boy lay on a stretcher; his father sat on the floor by the open hatch. It was probably the man's first helicopter ride and yet he gazed out with a blank face. Magnificent cloud banks sailed before his eyes, rich green paddies below and dark mountains beyond, but he sat there, his bare feet like hooves, his black pajamas flapping in the wind, playing Inscrutable Oriental. We dropped him and his son at the Vietnamese hospital in Danang.

We flew back to Marble Mountain for refueling, and took off again. We had been summoned to pick up two wounded Marines—and the fire-fight was still going on. I could see the corpsman, the crew chief and the gunner were excited.

We spent ten or fifteen minutes cruising around, waiting for the battle to die down, before we began our descent. The crew chief and gunner hunched tensely behind their machine guns, scanning the dikes and tree-lines, ready to spray the area. I got a little nervous thinking about how vividly we were outlined against the sky, a perfect target for any Viet Cong in the area. But I wasn't scared. I mention it only because this was the last minute I believed in my own immortality. I guess that's corny, but in the next minute my whole attitude changed.

We landed at the edge of a hamlet in the middle of a vast paddy complex, with a mountain range to the west. Stretcher-bearing Marines lugged two wounded men up to the hatch and loaded them aboard. Both were conscious. One was hit in the legs, the other somewhere in the upper body. Looking through the portside window I could see part of the Marine perimeter, about thirty yards away. The men were crouched behind a raised dike, weapons pointing outward, ready to return fire.

We lifted off, rotors hammering, motor straining to claw its way into the sky. At times like this you realize a helicopter is all engine, with cabin attached. Anyway I was talking to you in my mind, as I do when I'm tense, giving you a running narration of what was passing before my eyes: '. . . and now we're about thirty feet above the ground, picking up speed, and I see our racing shadow below. Now we're passing over the edge of the perimeter and starting to climb—'

Blam!

an explosion inside the cabin and something hit me on the inside of my upper right arm, as if I'd been spanked by a board. The noise of the explosion had whanged me in the right ear and was still ringing. Naturally I thought my arm was hanging by a thread, and I didn't dare look at it. I glanced around. The crew chief was feeling himself all over. The gunner was clutching his leg and looking shocked. The two men on the stretchers had raised their heads and were peering down along their bodies and feeling themselves. For a second I thought this was a slaughterhouse situation like I saw in Korea when seven Marines were hit by a single 82 mm. mortar shell. I still didn't know what had hit us. I thought it might have been an anti-aircraft shell, the noise and shock were so great.

The craft seemed stable enough—we weren't plummeting or anything. Only two or three seconds had passed, maybe less.

Corpsman Darryl Stuckey (Phenix City, Alabama) yelled at me to pass him his bag. I did so, and learned that my arm was still attached and everything was okay, although it still stung. I noticed a thin rivulet of blood poking slowly out from under the sleeve. I rolled it up all the way and found three tiny holes, blood running from one. The only other man hit was the gunner; he had a gash in his thigh. When Stuckey was through with him he turned to me. By now I was exhilarated. Wounded in Vietnam! It makes the whole lousy trip worthwhile!

Meanwhile Stuckey slapped on three junior Band-Aids, and that sort of deflated my balloon.

We headed for the medical compound near Danang called Charlie Med. Stuckey, the crew chief and I spent the time looking for holes in the skin of the craft. We found nine, all very small. What had hit us, I was surprised to learn, was a single sniper's bullet. Apparently it had shattered on impact, some of the fragments hitting the gunner and me.

When we landed at Charlie Med, eight corpsmen in tee-shirts came running out to fetch the two Marines on stretchers. The gunner got out and limped after them. I got out too and ran after him to ask how he felt. 'It hurts,' he said. Then I went back and joined the pilot and co-pilot, who were walking around the craft looking at the holes. Everybody had a sort of glazed look.

We flew back to Marble Mountain for refueling. I sat in the ready-room for a few minutes. When the pilot, Major Davis, came in, I asked him to show me on the wall-map where the incident had taken place. I learned that the unit that summoned us was none other than 1st Battalion, First Marines, which I was with in Korea when I got wounded (May Day, 1953)—which makes a neat little package.

While we were at the map a bell rang three times—the Medevac signal—and Davis turned and ran outside. I looked around frantically for a flak jacket. There happened to be one under the dispatcher's counter and he threw it at me.

Our first pick-up was in the mountains, at an Arvin outpost. It was a wounded Viet Cong prisoner. The replacement gunner, a hard-looking guy with a black mustache, drew his pistol and kept it on him throughout the flight. The prisoner lay motionless on the stretcher, wrists tied together in front of him. Once he brought his hands slowly up to his head, but the nervous gunner waved the pistol threateningly and kicked them down. He got tired of holding the big .45 and handed it to Stuckey, who looked at it distastefully and rested it on his knee in a sort of peaceable way. The gunner immediately snatched it back, glaring irritably at him.

Our next pick-up was in Tam Ky, in Quang Tin province. As we descended I recognized the shop where Bizelle, Suggins, Trung and I had our *pho so* 1 that day. The helicopter settled down on the same pad where I saw the women looking at the faces of the dead. A crowd of soldiers and civilians came running toward us. I thought I was going to be bumped off the flight. (I had been warned it might happen if things got too crowded, and for that reason brought along some food and a poncho.) But it turned out there was plenty of room, even after three kids and two women climbed aboard. The three kids were on one stretcher. I didn't know what was wrong with them, but there was a lot of bloody cloth. As we were lifting off, one of the women stared out the hatch for a few moments, then turned away in fright to wrap her scrawny arms around the gunner's legs and press her bunned old head against his knee. He ignored her, yet let her cling all the way to Danang. It was another of those natural photographs. As for the kids, I doubt if they'd ever been this close to Americans. Their faces were stony. Stuckey tried to make contact with a series of funny faces. The eldest, a boy of six, reached blank-faced into his shirt and pulled out a big yellow cookie, took a gromf at it and put it back.

The next summons was again from 1st Battalion, First Marines. The battle had broken out again and there were more wounded men. The crew chief and Stuckey got taut-faced when word came. I decided we couldn't possibly get hit twice in the same morning in the same place. But as we started to descend I realized how dumb that was. The odds were in favor of it happening again.

Now I got scared, the way a man is supposed to.

I found myself folding the flak jacket around me, as you'd do with a coat in a cold wind. I was sitting in the same spot as before, the forward left corner of the cabin, which I figured was the best spot—because lightning really doesn't strike twice in the same place. So there was I expecting the shot to come, not at me but at the helicopter, and when it did—exploding in my left ear—I was flabbergasted.

Blam!

This time he got me for sure, I thought. All I knew was that something had hit me on the back of my left shoulder and jarred me wholly. There was a sharp pain for a moment. I turned my back to Stuckey, who was staring at me (confirming my fear I was badly hurt), and took off the flak jacket. He jumped at me and went to work. I couldn't see or even feel what it was he was doing, but I had the idea he was trying to save my life. Somewhere in the back of my mind was the notion that you can be seriously hurt and yet feel fine for the first few moments. I sat there waiting for the pain to start.

But there was no pain. I whipped out my notepad and scribbled a question.

What kind of wound?

When he finished doing whatever it was he was doing he took the pad and pen and wrote:

Just a flesh wound.

Which was a bit of a letdown. All that shock and violence and nothing to show for it but a flesh wound. But I felt good anyhow. Wounded twice in two hours! Sensa-tional!

We still didn't know what had hit me. We searched the inside of the cabin and found it finally—the entry point of the bullet. It was interesting to see where it cut through the panel so neatly, leaving a round hole. I bent down and peered through and saw two others lined up with it. The bullet had entered the craft near the bottom of its nose, and continued up through the engine into the cabin and out through the ceiling. If Id've been sitting six inches inboard it would've gone through my heart.

Doc Stuckey was staring at me, shaking his head. I sat there grinning inanely. The crew chief examined the flak jacket and found a hole in it, just back of the left arm-hole.

We landed at Charlie Med. I got out and shook hands with everyone and walked across the bridge into the screened hut where I had seen the wounded Marines car-ried earlier. The first person I saw was Doc Blaylock, leaning against the door. He was the corpsman on the County Fair who was willing to let the cadre die rather than waste supplies on him, the one who sprinted in his bare feet out to the pagoda, exposed to enemy fire.

He and another corpsman started poking and rubbing me all over to make sure I hadn't been hit anywhere else. The hut we were in was fifteen yards long and seven wide, open at both ends. The only thing in it was a series of metal uprights designed to support stretchers. Along the wall was emergency gear like plasma bottles and sterilizing pans and rubber tubes. I found out later this place is called *triage* (tree-ahzh) which is French for sorting. A wounded man is brought here first, and if emergency treatment is needed here's where it's done; otherwise he's shunted to Surgery or Orthopedics or Minor Surgery. If he's dying and there are others needing immediate attention he's taken outside to a screened-in porch. There are stretcher-supports out there, a jug of water and a plastic cup.

That's triage.

I was taken outside and up the covered ramp to Minor Surgery, where I was made to lie facedown on a stretcher. A young doctor (Lt. Jay Woodward of Detroit, Michigan) sat down beside me and debrided the wound. That's pronounced dee-breed and it means cutting away the dead tissue and any live tissue in danger of becoming infected. When he was through, the wound was long and elliptical (he handed me a mirror so I could see it). It was superficial but looked satisfactorily gory. Dr. Woodward said he was going to leave it open a few days, so that in case of infection he could tend to it readily, then he'd sew it up. He said I'd have to stay in the hospital a few days.

Major Davis came stomping in in his flight suit, his

crash helmet dangling from one hand. He looked oddly guilty. It turned out he was still sort of shocked. The crew chief had yelled *They hit the correspondent* and, as Davis remarked to me then: 'I thought we had correspondent smeared all over the inside of the cabin.' He told me the gunner from the earlier incident had already been evacuated to Cam Ranh Bay, where there's a big Army hospital. Davis shook my hand, still looking guilty, and left. In a few moments I heard the helicopter lift off.

Dr. Woodward took a stiff brush and some antiseptic soap and proceeded to scrub the three holes in my arm. One of the corpsmen gave me a tetanus shot. I was taken over to a quonset-hut ward and signed in. The corpsman there issued me a pair of blue pajamas and a terry-cloth bathrobe and assigned me a bunk. There were ten bunks altogether, six of them occupied. The ward was dense with Christmas decorations—little trees and tinsel and cotton snow everywhere. The whole scene was like in a children's hospital.

I think this was a ward for oddballs. There was one boy who had constant headaches. We had a long conversation after supper. I think he was thrilled to have a sympathetic listener, especially one who'd had trouble with headaches himself. It was sort of a technical discussion, all about *sansert* and *cafergot* and *darvon*. Unfortunately none of these drugs had helped him.

Another boy didn't know what was wrong with him. The following day I watched from across the aisle as two doctors talked to him. One was probably a psychiatrist. I got the impression there'd been other interviews of this kind. The boy sat on the edge of the bunk in his blue pajamas and slippers, his hands folded politely in his lap, and answered their questions so softly they had to lean

forward to hear. He seemed cooperative enough—
although he answered in monosyllables—but I don't think
the doctors got any closer to the answer than before. He
seemed innocent and childlike, but you got the impression
of inner inexpressible pain. I saw him as a formerly care-
free lad who made the mistake of joining the Marines and
now found himself with a headful of dark clouds, and too
tongue-tied to tell anyone about it. Poor little old grunt.

That afternoon I stood in one corner of triage for an
hour and watched the traffic there.

A helicopter is about the noisiest thing going; the rotor
blades beat the air so fiercely you hear one coming a long
way off. At Charlie Med the corpsmen are waiting, and
when the helicopter lands they rush across the bridge and
grab the loaded stretchers and help the walking wounded
into triage. I saw some terrible things that afternoon.

The thing that impressed me most were the holes. Everybody that came in had them, and they were visually
fascinating.

The first batch of Marines were brought in on stretchers and set down on the raised stands, and the corpsmen
and doctors began cutting away their jungle fatigues.
You could smell the paddies and mud and salty sweat they
brought in from some remote hell-hole. The fatigues were
all slathered with green mud and some of it was on their
faces and arms. Pretty soon all three men were entirely
naked, and that's when the scene began to bother me a
little. It was all too reminiscent of a series of paintings I
saw as a child of patients being operated on most gorily
by 19th Century doctors, students leering from amphi-
theaters above. There was also the helplessly displayed
genitals, wizened cringing sausages in thickets of hair, the

doctors and corpsmen poking about with ghastly debriding instruments. I stood there like a stork, one leg crossed over the other.

I was too bug-eyed to notice what was wrong with two of these men—I only saw the amazing holes. They were jagged and of various sizes and shapes, and none that I saw were bleeding, which surprised me. The holes were bright red and vivid against white skin, and in one case against black skin—which was like some kind of pop art exhibit. I found out later that these men belonged to Echo Company, 2nd Battalion, First Marines, and that their patrol had been ambushed: two men killed at once and a third shot in the side but still going. One man had stepped in a punji-stake pit as he was running for cover. The survivors set up a perimeter around them and took incoming mortar rounds until a reactionary force showed up to drive the enemy away. The man who'd stepped in the pit was hit by mortar fragments and so were three others. Two of these were now in Minor Surgery having their holes debrided.

You wouldn't believe the holes I saw.

A lot of strange feelings were flowing in and out of my head. I could only identify one, a feeling of shame for thinking of myself as truly 'wounded.' Here I was walking around comfortably, while over there was a kid with a bullet inside him who was maybe going to die, another who might lose a foot, a third with so many raw red holes in his black body I didn't see how he'd ever pull through.

But all this was shallow emotion. There was deeper stuff bubbling below but it didn't come up till later.

The kid who'd stepped on the stake was conscious and cheerful. He was high on morphine and aware he had a classic million-dollar wound. The doctor had already told

him he was going home. The stake was about twelve inches
long and made of iron. It had a barb at one end. It was
sticking up out of the top of his foot, the skin all puffed
and purple around it. The base of the nail was set into a
thick board about a foot long. The boy's name was Pfc.
Stephen W. Styles (Columbus, Ohio) and his mom
would've been proud of him, I think: he was as brave as
they come.

The corpsmen picked up the handles of the stretcher
and lugged him outside and set him down on the ground.
There was a spigot and hose there. They turned it on and
sprayed him, sluicing the green mud away. He started
shivering and the corpsmen razzed him.

'What're you shivering for on a hot day like this?'

'I'm cold, man.'

'Cold? He says he's cold.'

Dr. Wheeler, the head of Charlie Med, said I could
watch the extraction. I followed along as they carried him
down the ramp into one of the quonset-hut Surgery
rooms.

The surgeon showed up in shorts & tee-shirt carrying a
fearsome pair of wire-cutters in one hand, a flash-bulb
camera in the other. He turned out to be something of an
eccentric. He had short bristling blond hair and looked
like a football player. I think the reason he got the assignment was because he was the strongest surgeon. He
grinned and flexed his muscles and did a couple of deep-
knee bends to show he was in shape for the job. Before he
got started, he took a picture of the foot in question (the
corpsmen had cut away the boot). Then he applied the
jaws of the cutter until they bit into the iron and held. He
stepped back and took another picture. If I'd been Styles
Id've bopped the silly freak right there—and got away

with it too, pleading morphine delirium. Anyway he finally took ahold of the handles and applied all his strength, turning purple in the face, and the jaws cut through cleanly and the barbed end fell to the ground. Time for another picture. Styles grinned giddily through all this, his foot anesthetized. (People are completely submissive before a camera, it seems. A guy armed with a camera could practically conquer the world. Don't get me started.) At last the surgeon grabbed Styles' foot and slowly extracted the long nail.

I watched another operation too. This one was the champ; I can't imagine a more violent operation. It was performed on the Marine who'd been shot in the side. The bullet was still in him, and they (two surgeons) had to open him up to find it. Here's how it went.

First they shaved his chest and stomach with a straight razor. Then one of the surgeons took a glinting scalpel and lowered it toward the patient's chest—and I decided to look away, because I didn't want to faint. I learned in the next few minutes that nothing could make me faint, but at the time I didn't know that. When I looked back, a few seconds later, the patient was slit from his breastbone all the way down to where the pubic hair begins. The surgeon had cut a little detour around the belly-button, leaving a semi-circular flap jutting out over the maw. The patient's guts lay open to my viewing pleasure, like a long vat of sausages. Blood had not poured out all over the floor as I expected—there was no outflow at all. The lips of the long incision had separated and spread apart easily and under the edges, where the shiny wet red lining of the chest cavity met the mess of sausages, were little pools of blood.

And of course we had to have sound effects. As the surgeons in their rubber gloves lifted the skin and under-skin away from the sausages and reached down into the red depths, there was all sorts of juicy succulent farting. Next the maniacal overcompensatory surgeons (I already saw them as creatures from another world) began taking bundles of sausage in their hands and flopping them over the side until much of the patient's guts were hanging in yellow coils from both sides of his body. (Stay away from Charlie Med if you've got any kind of a hole in you, because they'll only make it bigger!) Then the drooling bug-eyed surgeons inspected every inch of the slithering limp mile-long tube and found that the bullet had frag-mented. Whenever they came upon one of the fragments or holes they cut the tube in two places, one on each side of the find, snip snip snip, and lifted the piece out and dropped it in a can under the table. Then working to-gether, their fingers amazingly dexterous, they clamped and sewed the ends together, thereby allowing food and various regurgitational fluids to flow freely through the intestinal fortitudes—and somewhere along in here I de-cided not to become a doctor but stick with undertaking instead.

One of the fiendish body-rapers turned to me and said: 'If you have any questions, ask away.'

At that moment a thin stream of watery blood spurted straight up in the air and he turned back to apply a clamp while the other surgeon sank a vacuum hose among the remaining sausages and sucked up a pool swilling there, and I croaked a reply:

'Later maybe.'

I was standing beside the patient's head, the corps-man-anesthetist on the other side. The patient's arms were

stretched out on little side-tables and his wristwatch
ticked away just below me. There was a high-school ring
on his other hand. His mouth was taped up and a brown
hose ran from the corner of his mouth, under the tape. His
eyes were not entirely closed and you could see a jelly-like
film on the eyeballs. The skin of his face was a ghastly
yellow, the color of his guts.

The only question that came to mind was *How soon is
he going to die?*

And then, because I was really quite shook, my mind
began filling up with all sorts of asinine questions, statements and outcries such as *My God, you're killing him!* or
(in a calm voice) *Are you sure you washed your hands
thoroughly, gentlemen?* or falling on my knees and blaring out a horrible prayer of some kind. In short, I felt like
I was going crazy. Instead I stood there and watched
them sew the patient up, right to the bitter end. The
operation lasted three hours.

I went back to the ward and ate a graham cracker.

That afternoon Dr. Woodward told me that since
Charlie Med wasn't a recuperation-type hospital I'd have
the choice of being evacuated to the Navy hospital near
Marble Mountain or the Army one at Cam Ranh Bay. I
chose the former and he said an ambulance'd take me
there at noon the next day.

I spent the evening in the officers' club, celebrating my
being alive and well, and that I hadn't ended up like the
others.

Later I saw lights burning in Minor Surgery and went
in. Dr. Woodward had his rubber-gloved finger inside
some poor Marine's elbow, the latter grinding his teeth in
silence. Several corpsmen stood around talking casually

while others read in corners. It was a peaceful scene. One man had a guitar and was strumming blues chords. Someone asked him to sing a certain song for me and he did, without a trace of self-consciousness. It was a slow, mountain-type song about the life of a corpsman in Vietnam, with long pauses between phrases to give you time to think it over. The chorus went: *The corpsman wears the green of a cold-hearted Marine. He fights with his hands, not a gun.*

In the middle of the night I got up and went outside briefly. I saw the deserted helicopter pad with blue lights glowing. I began to think how close I had come to death a few hours earlier and for the first time the whole experience got to me. All I know is, I cried—but I think it was in humble gratitude for being alive and able to go home soon. I understood it wasn't a thing I was necessarily entitled to.

The following morning I went back to triage. It had been such a disturbing place the day before, so hard on the emotions—even though I hadn't been able to identify them—that I wanted to try and pin the labels while I had the chance.

Around nine o'clock a helicopter came booming down and four stretcher-cases were carried in. A minute later another helicopter brought three walking-wounded, from the same action. The patient I'm going to tell about was one of the first four. He and the other three were set down on the uprights, with most of the doctors and corpsmen crowding around him—because it was obvious he was the only one in hand-to-hand combat with the reaper. They worked with a frantic breathlessness I found shocking, because it so starkly dramatized the all-or-nothing of it. The other three were given emergency treatment and carried out, and now there was only this one boy lying in the middle of the room while doctors and corpsmen attacked him with knives and scissors and plasma and gauze, and it seemed at times they were trying to torture him to death.

These Marines had been on patrol and their point man had stepped on a mine. He was killed. The boy on the stretcher had been behind him, and his legs were in sorry shape. All there was from hips to ankles was red hamburger. The bones were intact, or seemed to be. You could see them—the femur and shinbone—on his left leg. His buddies had carried him to the landing zone in a poncho and the poncho, slimy with blood, was still crumpled under him. You could smell the blood and sweat and the muck of the paddy. When the corpsmen had cut away all his clothing you could see red holes in his arms, but these were ignored for the moment. The legs were the thing right now.

Most of the time the doctors and corpsmen hid him from view, except his feet and head which had escaped the flying shrapnel entirely. They were the color of death-is-approaching, a mixture of yellow and grey. As the minutes passed they became less yellow and more grey. He had been moaning unconsciously ever since they brought him in, and every so often he'd break out in a long scream that didn't seem to bother anyone but me. He spoke fuzzily several times. Mostly he asked for water. Once he said, very distinctly: 'Mom! I cut my leg!'

At one point I spoke briefly with Dr. Wheeler, another onlooker. 'He might live,' he said. 'If he's lasted this long he might go all the way.' I asked if he'd lose both legs. 'The left one for sure,' he said. 'We might be able to keep the other for him.'

A few minutes later I noticed a wonderful thing: the color of his right foot had changed—it was yellow now and had a tinge of pink in it.

Come on, lad, come on!

Inside I felt some strange emotion coming to a boil. It wasn't until I saw the chaplain's face on the other side of the crowd that I knew what it was. His name was Father Pfaff, from Kentucky; a powerfully built man of fifty, known for his jolly banter. There wasn't much jolliness now. He stood there with a stunned, grieving, bitter expression on his face. He looked as if he were going to spit. Somehow seeing his face like that clicked the last click into place and I knew what it was frothing up inside me, up to my very throat. It was outrage.

After awhile the screaming stopped and the boy spoke one last sentence: 'Mom! I'm dead!'

The Naval Hospital (NSA) was a jumble of quonset huts and covered walks amid white sandhills. Compared to the rough & ready Charlie Med it seemed luxurious.

As I was about to check in, two helicopters dropped down and disgorged several wounded men—so I had to wait outside. A young Marine in full combat get-up sat down on the bench with me. He was waiting to go into Minor Surgery and have his dressings changed. (He told me this after introducing himself.) I was in a non-talking mood but that didn't stop him. He nearly drowned me in words, and I got grumpier and grumpier. He related in the most melodramatic terms his experiences in combat, the general idea being that it's worse than Iwo Jima out there. The first thing he asked me was 'What outfit you with?' and it came out unavoidably I was a civilian and a writer. Well, this set him off and he sort of granted me an interview in depth.

'Hey, I guess you're wondering what I think about being over here and all. Well, I'll tell you. First off, let me say this: I believe in democracy. I really do. It is the greatest. Second, I believe we gotta stamp out Communism.'

He went on and on like this, and it was plain I was supposed to be furiously scribbling on my notepad, getting it all down for *The New York Times*. After awhile he noticed I was ignoring him and slowed down to an embarrassed halt. After a long silence I started asking him questions, but he was a first-class blowhard and every time he started up I let my face curdle and he came down again. His name was Pvt. Bernard Reid, from Chicago. His dream of glory was to become a famous singer. His hero was Dean Martin. He was hit in three places by mortar fragments during a patrol near Khe Sanh. When I thought about that my attitude changed, and I saw him as another poor little grunt caught up in something that shouldn't happen to a dog.

I was called into Minor Surgery. There were Christmas decorations and a tape-machine playing continuous carols, while the doctors and corpsmen snipped and swabbed and snipped some more. There were four Marines stretched out on stainless steel tables, alert and naked and sporting the usual red holes. A corpsman or doctor sat beside each, snipping at the ragged edges with scissors and knife. In the middle of the room a doctor was standing behind a combat-dressed lieutenant on a stool, debriding a small wound in the back of his head. They were gabbing about Oregon. I listened hard but they didn't mention any towns, and I didn't feel like breaking in. (I found out later the doctor is from Portland, but the lieutenant went back to his outfit so I never got a chance with him.)

One of the Marines on the tables was feeling a lot of

pain but only grimaced, keeping tight-lipped silence and shivering mightily as a jolly fat corpsman cut strips of bacon off his legs and cracked jokes:

'Some guys'll do anything to get out of work.'

The Marine kept shivering and trying to put his mind elsewhere.

'We still on the same side?' asked the corpsman.

The Marine nodded absently and that encouraged the corpsman to make another joke:

'Okay if I autograph this?'

Across the aisle another Marine, whose holes were smaller and fewer than any except the lieutenant's, broke out into a bloodcurdling scream that shivered my timbers pretty good. Finally one of the doctors told him to shut up and he did for awhile but then started up again. I couldn't help thinking about women giving birth, how they say some yell more from fear than pain. I must say, I'd ten times rather hear a woman yell than a man.

When my turn came they put me on a table and went to work. One of the doctors re-debrided my crease. He decided not to sew it closed ('The lips are too far apart') but let it heal under a big scab. The head doctor came in and took a look at me. His name was Dr. Hopper; a pug-nosed man of fifty-five with a wooden leg. He noticed the three holes in my arm and told the young doctor to debride them too. So they shaved the hair off there and the doctor made elliptical incisions around the original pin-pricks, incidentally removing a fleck of metal from each, thereby changing the holes into respectable-looking slashes which I can roll up my sleeve and exhibit nicely.

Afterward the doctor took me to a ward and turned me over to a corpsman in dark glasses. Mother, as everyone called him, showed me to an empty bunk and tossed me a pair of blue pajamas. I made the stupid error of asking where my bathrobe was, and he turned aghast to all the wounded Marines: 'Hey you guys—this guy says he wants a *bathrobe*.' It was almost like being in the service again. Fortunately nobody paid any attention to us.

The ward was very long, two hundred yards or so; you could barely see the beds at the far end. Somehow it was a cheerful place, even though everyone had holes in him. There was music going all the time and decorations everywhere, and Mother with his service humor.

There were several Red Cross girls in the ward when I arrived. By the time they got to me I had my pajamas on, was under the covers, and had a thermometer in my mouth so I couldn't talk, even if I had wanted to. One of the girls said: 'I see you can't talk, so I'll just wish you a Merry Christmas' and handed me a card with a picture of Claus and his reindeer. On the back was written in ink: *Seasons greetings. We hope you recover quickly and return home to your family soon* and it was signed *from the 4th Grade, Campbellsville Elementary School, Campbellsville, Kentucky.*

On my right lay Pfc. Daniel Shanahan of Harwood Heights, Illinois, who had been shot through the shoulder, a second bullet creasing his head. He was lucky. On my left was Cpl. Jonnie Kanuha of Hilo, Hawaii. This is the brave young man who didn't cry out when the corpsman was cutting bacon off him. (He told me he and the others were hit by the same mine; it had killed two men.) Pfc. Shanahan was well enough to get up and walk around a bit, but Cpl. Kanuha had to stay put—had to use a bedpan and so on.

These two were fine young men. You'd have loved them.

* * *

Sometime that afternoon the big helicopter honcho, Colonel Kline, showed up, accompanied by Major Davis. The colonel read me a goofy citation, recounting the events of the morning before and awarding me the Purple Shaft—a pipe nailed to a lacquered board. He apologized that civilians weren't eligible for the Purple Heart. Both officers shook my hand and left, and I carted this big crazy-looking board with the purple pipe on it back into the ward and stuck it under the bed. That's how the guys in the ward found out I was a civilian. I couldn't play Marine after that.

I was happy at NSA. The food was sensational—so good I ate six meals a day. Here's how I did it. Every mealtime they'd roll steam-tables up and down the aisle and pass out trays to bed-ridden patients. I always managed to be bed-ridden at steam-table time, and then an hour later I'd show up at the messhall for a big sit-down. (I asked Dr. Hopper how come the food was so good at NSA and so lousy at Charlie Med. 'They eat Marine food over there,' he said. 'Marines like to be miserable.')

The following morning several doctors and corpsmen came into the ward, moving slowly from patient to patient, reading the charts and having big consultations and so on. When they got to me Dr. Hopper looked bleak and said to the doctor beside him: 'You want to tell him?'

The other doctor turned to me and asked: 'Are you on an expense account over here?'

I said no. The doctor gulped and turned to Dr. Hopper and said: 'I wish you'd tell him, since you're bigger than me.'

Dr. Hopper explained that civilians have to pay for their treatment and care and food and so on.

I said that was fair enough and asked how much they charged.

'Forty dollars a day.'

I asked him if this was some sort of Naval joke.

'Afraid not,' he said. 'Do you happen to know Joe Brill?'

He's a reporter for Scripps-Howard; I'd seen him at the press center. He broke his ankle a few weeks ago and got it taken care of at NSA.

'Well,' said the doctor, 'Mister Brill took a turn for the better when I told him that.'

I said I didn't wonder, and reached for my jungle fatigues under the bed. As I got dressed there was a consultation between Dr. Hopper and two others as to whether they'd release me or not. They didn't know I was leaving no matter what they decided. Finally they said that I could leave as long as I agreed to check in every day and have my holes looked at. They were amused by the speed with which I was dressing. The young doctor told me to relax: 'Check-out time isn't till noon.'

I was back at the press center within two hours. The little maid touched me sympathetically. I dunno how she found out.

Next day I went over to Charlie Med with a truckload of newsmen who wanted to photograph and interview a Marine who'd been hit in the neck by an M-79 round which had stuck in his throat without exploding. Dr. Jude Weil had risked his life removing it surgically. After I got my dressings changed I went over and joined the milling noisy crowd of newsmen in the Post-Surgery Ward. I was offended by their tactless, aggressive behavior, particularly the ABC television crew who set up glaring hot

lights to illuminate this miserable Spanish kid lying there
helplessly with bleary eyes and an obscenely swollen neck.
Maybe he was having the time of his life. I've always
wondered why disaster victims are so ready to pose and
gush for anyone who thrusts a camera or mike at them.
Anyway there were four other patients in the ward, all
seriously ill. One of them was the Marine I'd seen operated
on two days before. He was conscious and I got his name:
Pfc. Thomas Ted Harper of Oxnard, California. He's
going to be all right. One of the other patients was a tiny
Vietnamese girl recovering from heart surgery. It seemed
almost criminal to allow such noise and bustle in a place
like that. I was angered at the way the newsmen were
ordering Dr. Weil to pose beside the patient, and I left to
cool off on the grass outside. As I walked out, they were
demanding that the patient write a message on a slate
they'd thrust in his hands, while ABC filmed it for seven
o'clock America. All through this the boy's syrup-like
drool was rolling down his chin into a pan.

I guess one of the reasons I'm contemptuous of newsmen is because their commodity is mainly crap. I'm not
talking about the television crews now but writers who
turn out one glorification of the fighting man after another, each wrapped in a neat package with a cheap ribbon around it. ('Pfc. Willis Bruno used to deliver papers
in his hometown of Milwaukee. Now he is in Vietnam, and
he delivers hand grenades.') As far as newsmen in general
are concerned, they seem eerily alike—bored, jaded, sophisticated young men, too glib and shallow to have a
point of view.

(Cablegram)

   . . . TRANSFER 650 DOLLARS TO SAIGON BRANCH
CHASE MANHATTAN. CABLE ME WHEN DONE. . . .

(no date)

I was sitting on my bunk yesterday when in comes
Frank Womack, just in from some patrols with the First
Marines. He looked wonderful, his beard silvery against
his brown face. When he saw me he dropped his pack on
the floor and called me all sorts of names. That evening we
resumed the old routine. I wanted to talk to somebody
about the red holes, and since Womack digs me I told him.
But I had to restrain my sick humor somewhat, because he
has conventional feelings about wounded Marines.
Around midnight I made my speech on what a sucker he is
for the military and how he ought to pack up and run.
This time I was sort of impassioned, and had my bandages
to back me up. I told him the sheer statistics should scare
him home: he's already been hit once and, as I told you,
this is his fourth trip to Vietnam. As I droned on and on,
his eyes got a hollow haunty look, and suddenly—around
one o'clock—he said I was right and he had all the
sketches and photographs he needed and he was going
home.

But I'm afraid it was only Johnnie Walker talking.

Womack went to bed then (*'Buenas noches, amigo'*)

but for me the night was young. I was still celebrating my survival, I think—I know I was celebrating something. There was a party going on next door and I went over. Memory is hazy from here on, but I recall seeing Leon Koontz sitting in a far corner behind his dark glasses, staring fixedly at the wall, probably brooding over not being able to sell any of his pieces. (He's broke. Let's not think about that.) I recall listening to a lot of intense speech-making by some newsmen, until the room began to whirl and, knowing tomorrow's hangover was going to be bad, I stumbled back to bed.

Next morning the living death. Selfe in bed like a statue, staring up at the slow-turning ceiling fan blowing cool air down on me. My skinny little pal, the maid, kept the doors closed and the windows shuttered and didn't try to make the bed with me in it, which she usually does to late-sleepers. (I'm sure she assumed my 'wounds' were bothering me.) As I lay there my whole life rolled before me as they say it does when you're drowning—but only the bad parts, the regrets and boats missed. In the midst of it came Frank Womack to say he really had decided to go home. And right then a sort of sunburst went off inside me. I decided to go home too. All I have to do (I told myself) is cable Lucy for plane fare. . . .

Phu Bai, December 27th

Writing this in the airport shed, waiting for a flight to Dong Ha; but the weather's so lousy they may ground everything.

You probably read in the papers about the 48-hour ceasefire over Christmas and the upcoming one over New Year's. I decided to go out on another Recon insert during the ceasefire because there'll be a lot of North Viets infiltrating across the DMZ then.

There were several newsmen on the flight up, and I learned of a battle going on a few miles northwest of Hue. Third Battalion, 26th Marines, had launched an operation two days earlier and yesterday were jumped on by a big Viet Cong unit. Attacks and counterattacks had been going on ever since. By the time our plane landed at Phu Bai (a stop on the way to Dong Ha) I had decided this'd probably be my last chance to witness a formal battle, so I got off with the newsguys.

We hitched a ride to the battle area, arriving at nightfall. I had a frantic time climbing about on the muddy slopes trying to learn where the next attack was most likely coming from, and trying to shake a big inanely-grinning newsman from Taiwan named Mr. Hsing who for some inscrutable and possibly perverse reason wanted to stick with me. I finally settled down—alone—with Mike Company, which was occupying the highest hill. The terrain, except for some small paddies, reminded me of southern Wyoming: low rolling country, open and brushless. It was a perfect spot for a battle.

As soon as it got dark we began seeing lights in the gullies and bare ridges to the north. The company commander called in artillery on them, white-phosphorus rounds that exploded in a silent shower of sparks. An hour later there were flares in the sky a mile to the northwest. The company commander said they were enemy flares but didn't know what they signified.

'Better get in your hole,' he said. 'It might mean incoming.'

The gunny sergeant had already shown me to a muddy pit I was to share with a private. This private turned out to be the bullshit artist of the world and I groaned inwardly when he began talking.

'See that slope down there? It's littered with dead gooks from last night's attack. They were suicide troops, see— trained special in Hanoi to die. I wouldn't kid ya! Tomorrow we'll have to go down and search the bodies. But you gotta be careful: these gooks're real tricky, you know— they dig spider holes and crawl inside and when you go by, *whammo!* you're dead. Each VC gets a five-thousand-p reward from Ho himself for every Marine he kills. Not only that, but he gets *ten* thousand for every one he captures alive. No gook's gonna get me alive, though. See this here? This here's my special *Death Or Dishonor* grenade. All I gotta do is pull the pin and hold it up like this, see? Blow my head clean off!'

He was almost inhuman. I couldn't get through to him at all; he was hidden in the blizzard of his own snow-job.

The first round came whistling down just after midnight, abrupt and startling because I hadn't heard the rounds leaving the tubes. They were 82 mm. mostly, with three 120's. None landed anywhere near Mike Company. There was no infantry attack. When the barrage ended I fell asleep and had a dream in which the corpses of two white horses were lying in a deep puddle in the road, and as I watched they changed into two Marines in combat gear who rose up like zombies—but turned out to be alive and well.

Dong Ha, December 28th

More about the Phu Bai side-trip. I never did see any infantry action, but there are a couple of things I want to report. The following morning I had a choice of going along on a combat patrol or accompanying one of the body-searching teams. It turned out that the slope really was littered with bodies. The teams were supposed to count them and strip off any equipment. I decided to go on the patrol.

It was a dull experience. I'm afraid patrolling has lost its excitement for me. We slogged around for five hours in a driving rain, fording three streams and making no contact. I used to think a patrol was the most exciting thing in the world.

When we got back inside our lines I peeled off and headed toward battalion headquarters, where I'd left my pack. The rain was still coming down hard, the road all mucky, and I wasn't watching where I was going. I nearly tripped over a corpse and, looking up, saw what turned out to be fifteen more. They were stacked up beside the road. Five were wearing pajamas—probably civilian porters. The rest wore khaki shirts and grey or brown pants of a light dishrag material. Two wore blue raincapes, tied around their neck. They were all barefoot. Their equipment had been stripped away. They lay stiff in the rain, many with their eyes open, all with the usual red holes in their hide. They were all scrawny, their cheeks hollow, their eyes sunken.

There seemed a certain terrible majesty to that pile. They had left home & family behind to live like hunted deer, exposed to rain, heat, hunger, malaria and sudden death. One had to salute them.

The average life expectancy in this wretched country is thirty-seven; so these little fellows only missed out on a few years—it wasn't as if they'd had their whole life ahead of them.

Ten minutes later, from under a tentflap at headquarters, I watched a jeeplike vehicle called a Mite come up the gully pulling a wheeled cart filled with bodies, the arms & legs sticking out ludicrously. It stopped beside the stack, and four mud-slathered Marines began yanking the bodies onto the ground, making a new pile. I climbed up to where they were working. The new corpses, five in all, still had some of their equipment—cartridge belts and various pouches. Two had felt hats jammed down on their heads and I noticed one of the Marines had a third stuffed halfway in his pocket. I asked him what was going on.

'You're a reporter, aren't you?' He told me I'd have to take my questions to the major or the colonel.

The reason for all the mystery, I soon found out, was that the corpses (more than a hundred in all) were being taken to a nearby village suspected of providing aid & comfort to the enemy, and dumped unceremoniously in the marketplace.

'The only thing these people understand,' explained the major, 'is force.'

I hung around one more day waiting for an infantry attack that never came, eating C rations and sleeping under a muddy poncho. I used to like C's, now they disgust me. That night I had another dream: I'm running along a gulch (seemed like it was Korea days) with a sniper firing at me from a distant overlook. The gulch leads to an opening in the side of a hill, like a mineshaft entrance, and I go skidding inside. I find myself in a big echoing vault with tiers of wooden shelves, and each has a corpse on it wrapped in a white sheet.

I finally got so bored out there in the rain and muck I gave up and hitched a ride back to Phu Bai. That night I got sick: headache, stomach-ache, diarrhea, and spells of shivering alternating with a fever that made my clothes stink. Naturally I thought I had malaria. I lay awake all night, waiting for the next diarrhea attack, and when it came I was almost too weak to get up. The nearest outhouse was over on the other side of the parade field. On one of these trips I had a little adventure. Halfway across I felt too weak to take another step so I stopped and hunkered down awhile. The cold rain pattered off my poncho. Red beacon-lights blinked from a nearby radar station. I crouched there, not paying attention to anything, then realized I was being stalked by two white-helmeted sentries. The nearest snapped on his flashlight, only fifteen yards away. He had been yelling the password, he said, and my not answering and being crouched as if trying to hide, well— 'You're lucky I didn't blast you,' he said, and the thought came to me that the statistics were against me too.

Next day I crawled to sickbay and they ran some tests. By noon I knew it wasn't malaria. I spent the next two days drinking kaopectate, swallowing pills and listening to the monotonous lashing of the rain. The worst thing about it was what went on in my mind. For seventy-six hours straight (it seemed) I had visions of truck convoys, sentry posts, C ration dumps, barbed-wire fences, muddy ponchos, radar towers, messhalls—all the dreary paraphernalia of war, all the dun-colored junk that is a visual blight on this green and beautiful landscape.

January 6th, Grand Hotel des Nations, Saigon

Here are the lyrics to a song I've just written:

I'm coming home. I'm coming home.
I'm coming home. I'm coming home.
I'm coming home. I'm coming home.

(It's called *I'm Coming Home*.)

* * *

Pan-American flight 842—Saigon to San Francisco—departs at 10:05 next Wednesday morning. If I sound calm it's only because I won't believe it till the plane is airborne.

Tomorrow I'm heading back to Danang, because Saigon is no place to kill time in. It's the world's most expensive city, and I'm almost broke now. My plan is to spend the next four days getting something for nothing (room & board) by visiting the carrier *Enterprise*. I'll stoke up on that good Navy food, catch a few movies, and finish my last Spillane.

But I've done my last 'work.'

To continue where I left off.

From Phu Bai I dragged my carcass up to Dong Ha for three inserts with 3rd Recon Battalion. The weather was terrible. Marine helicopter pilots require a ceiling of not less than 1500 feet plus two-mile visibility before they'll insert or extract a Recon team. We had to wait around several days for those conditions. Every morning we'd get up long before dawn, eat breakfast, saddle up and go to the helipad and sit inside a tent if it was raining, fool around outside if it wasn't.

The memories of Vietnam that'll haunt me—if any do—will be of waiting at various helipads and airstrips. The crowded little building at Tan Son Nhut called 8th Aerial Passenger Port. The echoing shed at Danang called Marine Air Freight. The helipad at Dong Ha. And I may be haunted too by the breakfasts they served us in the Recon messhall, the same messhall where I watched *Batman* so long ago. The food was unusually poor, I dunno why. (One unit has access to the same rations as the next.) Anyway we'd stand in line in that cold damp galley

every morning, watching hung-over Cpl. Angel Cumba
frying eggs on a grimy field stove. He'd stand there with
his gung-ho cap pulled down over his eyes, a cigaret dangling from his lips, and the only part of him that moved
was the hand with the spatula. You told him how many
eggs you wanted and he'd plop them onto your greasy
plate. Nobody ever asked for less than six.

One night several helicopters landed on the nearby
Medevac pad and, since I had nothing better to do, I
pulled on my poncho and went outside for a look. It
turned out there'd been a mortar attack on an outpost
held by 3rd Battalion, Third Marines, and there were
something like twenty wounded and six dead. I followed
the stretcher-bearers down the muddy road to Able Med
and slipped into triage behind them. A doctor challenged
me and I had to leave.

Outside two men came along carrying something big
zipped up in a green rubber bag with handles, and naturally they had to put it down beside me. A doctor (or
maybe he was a chaplain) came outside to verify death or
something. He bent down and unzipped the bag partway,
looking, I imagine, for the face. But he had opened the
foot end. He zipped it up and came round to the head.
When he had finally unzipped the right zip he peered
inside and then scoffed, or rather snorted sardonically, as
if to say *He's dead all right!* A few minutes later the
Graves Registration people showed up and lugged the
bag downroad to where their tent is, beside a grey refrig-
eration truck. I wanted to follow along and watch the
embalming routine, or whatever it is they do, but something held me back—and it wasn't propriety. Maybe I
was afraid of being taken for a ghoul.

I stood in the rain outside Able Med, glancing every now and then at the tent down the road. Light streamed from one end where they neglected to close the flap tightly, and this was inviting. Finally I got up the nerve. My boots made a big sucking noise every step I took. I was all set to run, if anyone came out of the tent and challenged me.

No one did. The interior was brilliantly illuminated. The men were standing around the body, cutting away muddy clothing. Their heads were cut off by the angle of my peephole view. The axis of the corpse was aimed at me, and the first thing I saw was the vivid red pudding of the man's neck, or what was left of it. The head was gone, and I understood why the doctor had snorted. The men had already cut away the jacket and you could see he'd been wounded earlier because the torso was all wrapped with muddy blood-soaked bandages.

I didn't feel anything in the way of emotion. I guess I need some sort of face to get worked up; but this was just a side of beef.

January 7th, Danang press center

I made three inserts in all, but so little happened on the first two I'm going to skip them. I decided to keep going out on inserts until I saw some action, and this would end my relationship with the United States Marines.

So this is an account of my last patrol forever.

The weather stayed bad. On the day of the insert it was so bad the helicopters were grounded. Major Pierce decided to truck us in as far as possible and let us walk the rest of the way. There are only two paved roads in Quang Tri province: Route 1, which runs north-south along the coast, and Route 9, running from the South China Sea inland thirty miles to the Laotian border. The latter runs more or less parallel to the Demilitarized Zone, roughly five miles south of it. Generally speaking, the area between the road and the DMZ was 3rd Recon Battalion's area of operations.

The team leader was Lt. Harley Russell of Yazoo City, Mississippi, a former enlisted man. In the late fifties he was a drill instructor at Parris Island, and more recently a member of the embassy guard in Tokyo. (One night over a beer he pulled out his wallet and showed me a letter of commendation from Ambassador Reischauer.) Russell chews Day's Work tobacco and surveys the world through inscrutably-squinted eyes. He wears a floppy felt hat with a very wide brim, making him look like an old-time mountain man. His voice is soft, his manner courtly, and he looks dangerous. Somehow he seems straight out of a Faulkner novel—a man of honor, a Confederate cavalryman, a coon hunter, a man who would calmly kill a field hand for winking at his wife. The only incongruous note about him is that he owns a record player and sits for hours in the old French barracks listening to Herb Alpert and the Tijuana Brass.

The others were: Cpl. Al Alongi of Simi, California; Pfc. Robert Murphy of Bemis, West Virginia; Pfc. Edward L. McKone of Austin, Texas; Pfc. Alonzo Gibbons of Bowling Green, Kentucky; and Pfc. Harry Zimmerman, Jr., of North Tonawanda, N.Y.

We all wore camouflage paint on our faces and every time we passed civilians on the road the kids'd gawk, the more lively ones going into big spasms of mock terror. (Vietnamese kids are the most vivacious in the world, I'll bet.)

Before I forget: I got fairly friendly with Lt. Russell

and told him about the lanterns I saw on the DeLucas insert. He wasn't surprised. 'Sure, Vietnamese are a-scared of snakes. They carry lanterns so they can see where they're putting their feet.' That's what he said. I dunno.

Our truck traveled parallel to the river I forded so often last July. It looked cold and bleak now. We drove through the village of Cam Lo and I saw the graveyard where —— Company had been. Back in July it was green and yellow in the sun; now it was all grey and bleak, and I'd never have recognized it if I hadn't been on the lookout.

We drove on, passing squat grey milestones telling how many kilometers to Lao Bao and Tchepone and Savannakhet, towns in Laos. Then we were swallowed up in the low hills, and finally came to the place where the mountains begin. The truck stopped and we got out, formed a column and headed toward the river. The driver turned his truck around and disappeared. We were left alone in silence.

The bridge had been blown out, and we had to wade across. The current was powerful, the river waist-deep and cold. There was a bombed-out building on the opposite bank, probably a schoolhouse; it was the only sign of civilization, except for the road and the bridge.

To the west was the isolated miniature mountain called The Rockpile and behind it a long ridge called Razorback. Fierce battles were fought there during Operation Prairie, and we could see scars on its south end. The big Laotian mountains rise up a few miles to the west, but at that moment were shrouded in mist. In front of us was another miniature mountain, dark and rocky but not as lofty as Rockpile. A mile to the north there were hills covered with high tawny grass. Two of these were occupied by 3rd Battalion, Third Marines. In the background was a particularly sinister skyline called Mutter's Ridge, with a few blackened skeletal trees.

The whole area gave off a smell of disaster, past and impending. Many sightings had been reported in the last few days by the 3/3 Marines. Two days earlier one of their patrols had been ambushed. Five days earlier the outpost itself was mortared (the headless corpse was a casualty of this action). And there were all sorts of ghosts and phantoms gliding about from Prairie and Hastings.

So we were nervous and watchful.

Our reconnaissance zone lay north-northwest of Razorback. We had to walk out to the spot where we'd ordinarily have been inserted by helicopter, and in order to avoid being seen hugged the soaring face of Razorback where the jungle, though narrow, is thick. It was slow, monotonous, hypnotic work. As we crept along we kept seeing faces staring up from the ground, faces of Vietnamese men. They were on propaganda leaflets that had been dropped during Prairie, each showing a just-captured soldier and a message in his own handwriting, telling how well he was being treated and so on.

We left the jungle strip and started across the open hills—open in that they're treeless, although the yellow grass is high. Razorback towered malevolently above us, a sheer wall pitted with hawk caves. We kept glancing back over our shoulders at it.

The sky was overcast, the light grey and gloomy—a perfect setting for a nightmare.

Images of home began going round in my head, like a circular film with sound, and I kept hearing the announcement over the loudspeaker at Tan Son Nhut: *Pan-*

*American World Airways announces the departure of
Flight 842 to San Francisco. All aboard, please.* But
mostly what I saw was a sort of impressionistic travelogue
of America the Beautiful. I kept getting a lump in my
throat.

And I was aware, as we picked our way through the
swaying grass, that my thoughts were those of a 'mur-
deree.' In every war movie there's a character you know is
doomed. Either he's going out on his last patrol or his wife
in Wichita is about to have her first baby, or both.

I kept pushing these things out of my mind to concen-
trate on being alert, but they kept sliding back, and I
could hear the announcement echoing in the terminal:
*Pan-American World Airways announces the departure
of Flight 842 to San Francisco. All aboard, please.* I
pictured myself high over the Pacific, a cigar in one hand,
a drink in the other.

We descended a long hill, the wind blowing the grass in
billowing waves like wheat in Kansas, and halfway to the
bottom someone shouted and two shots rang out.

I saw McKone and Russell and Gibbons scatter and
disappear. The shout and the shots had come from the
jungle below. I took a couple of steps to my right and
dropped into an old shell crater.

There was silence for about thirty seconds and then a
dull *pop* and I poked my head over the rim to see what was
going on. At the bottom, only a few yards from where
Gibbons lay, an indeterminate something was taking
shape at the edge of the jungle. It took me a few seconds
to figure out what it was—smoke from a purple-smoke
grenade, a dense blob that slowly engulfed the vegetation
around it, wind catching the top of it in a long tapering
smear.

I heard another shout, more like a muffled bark, coming from the jungle. Lt. Russell rose up in the grass and, followed by McKone and Gibbons, headed back up the slope. They didn't run, though; just a good steady climb, sideways like crabs, their weapons trained on the jungle below. They seemed calm.

Gibbons spoke to me as he climbed past the crater. 'Must be *twenty* of 'em down there.'

I was the fourth man in column, so I got up and followed him. Al Alongi followed me, with Zimmerman bringing up the rear. Our hill was overshadowed by a higher hill, the two connected by a saddle.

'The fuckers're trying to flank us,' said Alongi in a loud and not very calm voice.

Lt. Russell stopped and looked back over his shoulder.

Alongi pointed off to the right and downhill. 'They're coming up on the other side.'

'Come on,' said Russell and we ran like hell, maintaining the column, cutting across the saddle, trying to reach the summit before they did.

I hadn't seen anything.

The top of the hill was windblown and bare of vegetation, with fist-sized rocks all around. The Marines began using them to make fortlike shields. I noticed they all had the same expression on their faces, an expression of faint amusement, with a touch of embarrassment. The old American dislike of being 'dramatic,' I guess.

Lt. Russell sat alone in a crater behind our half-moon line of defense. He had taken Gibbons' radio and it lay beside him as he jotted down coordinates from a map. Nothing was happening in the way of an attack, so I crawled back and joined him and watched him relay the range & azimuth directions to the 3/3 mortarmen, a couple of miles to our rear.

Russell was almost phlegmatic; he could've been ordering groceries on the phone at home. I was dull too—aware that I was in no sense turned on. I even felt bored. I tried to rouse myself, tried to get interested in Russell's radio lingo, even going so far as to take notes on what he was saying.

As I sat there writing, loud frantic shooting broke out close by, and that turned me on pretty good.

When, seconds later, there was a pause, I scrambled back to the fort Zimmerman and I had thrown up, calling *Hello* inanely so he wouldn't whirl round and blast me for a creeping Cong.

Far down the slope I saw a blur of movement just inside the jungle. I said nothing. A few seconds later Alongi and McKone opened up simultaneously, Alongi with his automatic rifle, McKone his M-79. You could clearly see the gold-tipped projectile floating lazily into the jungle, exploding with a sharp crack that crashed off the wall of Razorback and echoed all the way to Mutter's Ridge.

When it was over Gibbons said 'Must be *ten* of 'em down there.'

'I think I got one,' said Alongi.

'I heard groaning,' said Murphy. 'You guys hear it?'

Just then Russell called us to follow him. He was already descending the hill, heading northeast. I had time to ask Alongi what kind of uniform they were wearing. He said he thought khaki but couldn't be sure.

We wandered around that area for two days without running into anyone else. Around midnight that night Russell learned in a long whispered conversation with our relay station that the smoke grenade had been thrown by a patrol from 3/3. That is, our team had blundered head-on into a Marine patrol, neither group having been forewarned of the other's presence. Alongi and Ed McKone insisted the men they saw later, from the hilltop, were Vietnamese. Russell indicated his doubt by winking at me surreptitiously. I don't know what to think. It seems unlikely that two Marine patrols and a North Viet unit could run into each other inadvertently at the same time, but war is full of craziness like that.

The extraction was, for me, an epic thing. It was also, in a strange way, a sentimental thing because I knew it was closing out my ambivalent relationship with the U.S. Marines, and because it was the beginning of the end as far as these letters & journals go. But more than that I was spooked and longed to get back to the safety of the press center.

At 9:20 a.m. we heard the distant beating of the helicopters. We searched the sky—filled with low ponderous clouds, grey and black, unfolding majestically. At last the helicopters came into view. From the angle of their bearing it looked as if they were going to pass us by; but then they banked and swooped, and one landed while the gunships circled. Lt. Russell motioned me aboard first. I stumbled on the step and the crew chief hauled me in, the rest of the team jumping in behind me. We lifted off. I was tight inside, expecting a sniper shot, but we climbed safely. I watched the green jungle drop away. It seemed so empty and harmless from up there, so unlike what it was on the ground. I couldn't imagine anyone living down there. But many do, and they don't have helicopters to carry them home.

Goodbye, jungle.

(Cablegram)

ARRIVE THURSDAY FOR BREAKFAST. . . .

January 11th, Tan Son Nhut

I'm sitting beside the Pan Am gate with an hour to kill before boarding. The big jet is highly visible from here, gleaming brilliantly in the sun.

There are many angelic-looking soldiers and airmen gathered here beside the gate. They've survived their twelve months of tedium and terror and're headed back where every man belongs. It's a great moment for everyone.

Yesterday I strolled around Saigon digging the sights. There were so many giant Americans abroad the Vietnamese seemed like interlopers. I just moseyed around, fascinated with everything—now that I was seeing it for the last time. I looked at the bird-sellers and the lottery-ticket vendors and the portable kitchens and the kids selling fresh pineapple on bamboo sticks. Later I looked at the sunset from the ninth-floor overlook in my hotel. Saigon is a beautiful city from the ninth floor.

I'm on the plane, all strapped in. Passengers arc still coming aboard.

* * *

We're rolling now, very slowly, out to the main runway, passing the 8th Aerial Passenger Port, where I spent many hours waiting for a flight to Danang. How wonderful never to have to see it, or Danang, any more.

We're vibrating at the end of the runway, poised like an arrow.

We're airborne, Saigon out of sight, rivers and dragon-shaped tributaries below. We climbed steeply after take-off and then banked, and it occurred to me (a sudden tingling on the soles of the feet) this was to avoid sniper fire.

We're out over the sea now. Vietnam is just off portside, dropping behind. A layer of clouds blankets the interior, but the beaches glow in the sun.

The stewardesses, American girls, are already taking orders for drinks. Fantastic!

One last look back. Vietnam, you're on your own.

We soar serenely in glacial blue savannas. Almost everyone has a drink before him. I've finished mine, which is why I'm calling the sky glacial blue savannas.

Pan Am, I love you and all you stand for. I love your sleekness, your gloss, your speed.

I'm working on a second Scotch—not for stimulation (who needs it flying homeward five miles above the sea?) but for purposes of ecstasy.

The sea is like lake-ice now. Below us there's a massive sculptured cloud, like an MGM version of heaven, touched by the lowering sun, gold-sheened on the side facing Asia.

In a few hours, Hawaii, and then the jeweled cities of the mainland winter night.

Going home, to study war no more.